HOME STYLE:
HOUSE MEMBERS IN THEIR DISTRICTS

LONGMAN CLASSICS *in* POLITICAL SCIENCE

HOME STYLE:
HOUSE MEMBERS IN THEIR DISTRICTS

Richard F. Fenno, Jr.
University of Rochester

With new foreword by John R. Hibbing
University of Nebraska-Lincoln

New York   San Francisco   Boston
London   Toronto   Sydney   Tokyo   Singapore   Madrid
Mexico City   Munich   Paris   Cape Town   Hong Kong   Montreal

Vice President and Publisher: Priscilla McGeehon
Executive Editor: Eric Stano
Senior Marketing Manager: Megan Galvin-Fak
Production Coordinator: Shafiena Ghani
Cover Designer/Manager: Wendy Fredericks
Cover Illustration: ©Frank McMahon/CORBIS
Technical Desktop Manager: Heather A. Peres
Junior Manufacturing Buyer: Kara Frye
Printer and Binder: RR Donnelley & Sons, Inc.--Crawfordsville
Cover Printer: Coral Graphics Services, Inc.

Please visit our website at http://www.ablongman.com

ISBN 0-321-12183-X

5 6 7 8 9 10—DOC—09 08 07

Foreword

I began studying Congress when I started graduate school at the University of Iowa in early 1977. For me, the timing could not have been more fortuitous because David Mayhew's *Congress: The Electoral Connection* had been published just a couple of years earlier (1974), Morris P. Fiorina's *Congress: Keystone of the Washington Establishment* came out shortly thereafter (1977), and Richard F. Fenno, Jr.'s *Home Style: House Members in Their Districts* made its eagerly awaited public appearance the next year (1978). Of course, at the time, I had no sense of perspective and thus had no idea how unusual this brief period was. I suppose I assumed clusters of subfield-altering books were the norm. I thought the sense of excitement present then would continue. A quarter of a century on, the remarkable nature of that short stretch during the mid to late 1970s is readily apparent to me—and to all other students of Congress. I now realize that those were the salad days—and that they could not continue forever.

What made these books so special? How did they combine to reinvent the study of Congress specifically and legislatures generally? To oversimplify, these books brought the subfield out of an unhealthy fixation on roll call votes. Certainly, one of the more important tasks undertaken by legislators is voting for or against the many legislative proposals that pass through their chamber. These votes create public policies, so scholars were not wrong to try to understand why legislators voted as they did. The job of a legislator, however, involves much more than casting roll call votes. In fact, given the public's tepid policy knowledge and casual interest in most of the votes cast by members, it is quite likely that roll call voting is far from their most publicly salient or politically relevant act.

But in the dimness of the pre-Mayhew-Fiorina-Fenno cave, congressional scholars often had difficulty making out anything other than roll call activities. There were exceptions, of course, including one of my favorite books, Donald Matthews' magisterial *U.S. Senators and their World*

(1960), but legislative votes make for such a seductive data set that it was difficult for scholars to resist. Legislative roll call votes contain a sufficiently large but still manageable number of cases and limited, clearly defined, objective coding categories. Measurement is relatively clear and importance indisputable. Moreover, unlike people responding to a survey item when legislators cast a roll call vote, it constitutes a real behavior—just what a discipline in the midst of a "behavioral revolution" needed.

So, beginning in the late 1950s scholars used roll call votes to make comparisons across time, across issues, across members, across parties, across chambers, across genders, across stages of the electoral cycle, and across levels of electoral security. Not only were the data readily available but advances in computer technology also made it possible for scholars everywhere to crank those data through various statistical packages. Votes could be scaled, factored, regressed, and interacted—and they were. I have no intention of demeaning roll call analyses. Indeed, this would be blatantly hypocritical as I have done my share of them. But it is possible for certain types of studies to become unhealthily ascendant in a subfield and this was probably true of roll call analyses in the 1960s and early 1970s. Sometimes legislative scholars were so eager to mine roll call data that they did not ground their work in appropriate theory.

But all this was about to be changed by the appearance of *The Electoral Connection*, *Keystone*, and *Home Style*. First came Mayhew's assertion that members of Congress worry more about taking positions, claiming credit, and advertising themselves than they do about casting votes. This is not a message Congress scholars—or many ordinary citizens— much like to hear, but it is true. The key is often the packaging of a vote (or other decision), not the vote inside the package; the key is often the spin not what is being spun.[1] Next came Fiorina's demonstration of the importance of constituency service activities. It may be possible, he said, for legislators to endear themselves to constituents by handling the idiosyncratic problems citizens encounter as they interact with increasing numbers of governmental programs. Unlike many other countries, the United States has no federal ombudsperson, largely because members of Congress are eager to play this role themselves: finding lost social security checks, securing waivers from one regulation or another, providing information to interested parties back home. Individually, these acts may not

---

[1]This part of the message is consistent with that found in what is best seen as a transitional work between roll call studies and investigations with broader concerns. John Kingdon pointed out the importance of "explanations" of roll call votes (1973). He noted that more than casting a vote that is right or wrong, members need to be able to explain their votes to constituents.

sound like much but Fiorina's work suggested that many constituents may be more interested in knowing they have someone to go to when they are in trouble than someone who votes a certain way on a welter of confusing and only marginally relevant issues.

As important as they were and are, the studies by Mayhew and Fiorina in many respects set the stage for the third act: Fenno's *Home Style*. It takes nothing away from Mayhew's and Fiorina's provocative, creative, and remarkably influential works to note that while *The Electoral Connection* and *Keystone* are essays, *Home Style* is a book; that while (outside of a couple of brief case studies), *The Electoral Connection* and *Keystone* do not present original research, *Home Style* reports on more than 8 years of painstaking personal participant observation; and that while *The Electoral Connection* and *Keystone* begin to push us away from a policy issue dominant view of representation, *Home Style* provides a full-blown alternative vision of what it means to serve as the representative of other people.

THE MANY CONTRIBUTIONS OF *HOME STYLE*: REPRESENTATION PROPERLY UNDERSTOOD, CONCENTRIC CIRCLES, AND CAREERS IN THE CONSTITUENCY

Home Style's most important contribution, by my reading, is its demonstration that representation involves not just the act of casting roll call votes, but also being the kind of person the represented want representing them. Of course constituents are likely to be more comfortable with a representative who consistently casts votes that are perceived to be consistent with district interests, but Fenno stresses the vital stylistic components of representation that extend well beyond decisions on policy details. He points out that members of Congress spend a good deal of their time back in the districts, presenting themselves for inspection. He shows how seriously members take this part of the job by documenting the number of trips home they take as well as the number of staffers they assign to home offices.

More important, on the basis of extended personal observation ("soaking and poking," as he so famously described his research strategy) of 18 members of Congress during the 1970s, he weaves a revealing and entertaining account of the efforts members make to present the particular image or style the people prefer. This is not to say they give labor groups one line and business groups another—Fenno found remarkably little of this kind of thing. But it *is* to say members will act differently around labor groups than they do around business groups. Their dress, comportment, demeanor, humor, diction, dietary preferences, small talk, and tastes are all likely to change in ways that are sometimes subtle and other times painfully obvious. More than that, members endeavor to capture the overall style of the district and will seize opportunities to underscore how they (the representative and the constituents) are different from people elsewhere in the country, especially those in Washington, DC. Differentiation from an out-group is an important part of bonding and Fenno presents the first-ever detailed insider account of representatives bonding with the represented by paying attention, sometimes consciously, sometimes not, to matters of style.

Fenno centers his idea of home style around Erving Goffman's notion of "presentation of self" (54). As Fenno puts it, "members of Congress go home to present themselves as a person" (55). They hope to win accolades such as "he is a good man," "she is one of us," "he will go to bat for people like us," and "she will express our concerns back in Washington." How do they do this? By saying in a speech to a farm group, "it's pretty strange up there [in Washington] for a country boy like me. . . . I went to the White House for breakfast one time. Imagine me from over here on Duck Lake eating at the White House with the President" (58). Or by saying to a collection of blue-collar bingo players, "I managed to grow up thirty-five miles down highway 80 in Montrose. So I know this country. My father worked for twenty-six years in this county for U.S. Steel as a member of Local 121. So I know something about you and your problems" (60).

Of course, the "down-home" card is better played in some districts than others. Fenno describes this wide variation in appropriate styles in the space of three chapters (3, 4, and 5), first with six arresting and detailed case studies of the activities of Congressmen "A," "B," "C," "D," "E," and "F" in their districts and then with special attention to the manner in which the members he observed explained their Washington actions to their constituents. These chapters are the core of the book and provide a marvelous account of the life of a member of Congress and especially the manner in which members strive to connect with their constituents. Interactions with staffers, spouses, powerful interests, election opponents, journalists, other members, and most of all the constituents themselves are all part of the mix. The political figures introduced in these pages are as intriguing as the problems they face.

But Chapters 1 and 6 are also worthy of special note here. In Chapter 1, Fenno introduces the different constituencies members see when they look at their district. The different constituencies Fenno saw as he peered over the shoulders of representatives do not go by labels such as suburbanites, farmers, and workers at the plant but rather geographic, reelection, primary, and personal constituencies. Fenno distinguished these constituencies by asking readers to imagine four concentric circles. The largest circle includes everyone living in the geographic district, some of whom voted for the member and some of whom did not. But they are all constituents after a fashion and as such may demand and deserve part of the representative.

The next circle as we move inward is the reelection constituency, composed of those people the member believes gave their electoral support in the last election. Members have a definite sense of those parts of the district "on board" and those that are not. Those parts that are in the reelection constituency are likely to receive different treatment since no member wants to lose a part of the previously supportive coalition, particularly since by definition that coalition was sufficient to win the last election. Those within the smaller third circle, the primary constituency, are not just electoral supporters but supporters. They do not merely vote for the member, they work for the member. This is the base that every successful politician needs. It may be organized labor, it may be an ethnic group, it may be Christian fundamentalists, but it is almost always the group that was with the member during the very first effort to be elected. Finally, the very smallest circle consists only of those people "whose relationship with the member is so personal and so intimate that their relevance cannot be captured by any description" (24). These are the people who help the member to relax, to obtain emotional support, to strategize, to blow off steam, and to stay grounded. It is the one group whose trust the member can take for granted.

I suppose it would be possible to add or delete circles but that is not really the point. The point is that observers of Congress have found Fenno's notion of concentric constituencies to be an extremely useful analytical tool. It is the clearest indication, perhaps, of Fenno's success in describing the district as it appears to a member of Congress in that it draws attention to the fact that from the perspective of the member of Congress, there are constituencies and then there are constituencies.

The innovation Fenno introduces in Chapter 6 is to look at home district activities across careers. His research design—at least the part that was completed when *Home Style* was written—did not permit Fenno to follow certain members over extended portions of their congressional careers, but he did have in his sample of 18 members representatives of several different stages of the congressional career. This feature allowed Fenno to discuss careers in the constituency. Most important, Fenno observed that members tended to be in an "expansionist" mode early in a career before settling into a "protectionist" mode later. In other words, as the years and electoral victories roll up, members usually feel less need to try to bring additional parts of the geographic constituency into the reelection or even primary constituencies. Converting opponents into supporters is much more difficult than reinforcing those already supportive, although Fenno also provides plenty of evidence that members can never take existing voters/supporters for granted. Everyone, again perhaps except for the personal constituency, demands continued attention from the member. The last thing a member needs is for word to go out that she or he has "gone Washington" and forgotten about the people back in the district. Few congressional careers can survive when that image has taken root.

A REMARKABLY UNINFLUENTIAL BOOK?

In one sense, *Home Style* has been a terrible disappointment. Although the vision of representation Fenno expresses in it has been internalized by large numbers of students and scholars, although phrases like "soaking and poking," "concentric constituencies," and "constituency careers" have become standard components of the lexicon, and although the book more generally has greatly affected thinking about Congress, *Home Style* did virtually nothing to affect the manner in which research on Congress (and all legislatures) is conducted. The questions being asked in research projects changed after *Home Style* but, for the most part, the methods employed to answer those questions did not. Few scholars adopted the research techniques Fenno so meticulously described.

One of the more amazing and oft-cited portions of *Home Style* is the 50-page appendix on the method of participant observation that Fenno employed. Observing members of Congress is not an easy thing to do. Recognizing this, Fenno wisely provides advice based on the wealth of experience he developed in writing the book. As he notes, compared to the "Capitol Hill" style of research undertaken by most analysts, participant observation of members of Congress interacting with ordinary people back in their home districts is "qualitatively different" (250). It is not a technique that can be taught in a tightly contained graduate seminar and much of it probably has to come with experience. But Fenno undertakes to help us realize what participant observers are in for and how they can avoid serious mistakes.

He describes how to make initial contact with a member, how to allay politicians' innate suspicion of academics, how to schedule meetings, how to establish rapport, how to avoid the Heisenberg principle (in which the act of observing alters that which is being observed), how to collect and record participant observation data, and how to interpret the results. More generally, he describes how those who want to learn more about politics can survive in the world of politics. As much as anyone since Weber, Fenno has a feel for the different talents involved in analyzing politics and practicing politics.

Reading the appendix of *Home Style* will not magically give everyone this feel, but it will help them to understand how analysts can move among practitioners productively.

Why have so few heeded Fenno's call to engage in participant observation? Some of the reasons are obvious and intractable. It is immensely time-consuming and difficult. To use Fenno's words, "it requires. . . . physical stamina and psychological adaptability" (253). It is almost impossible to work extended participant observation even into the somewhat flexible schedules of academics. And to be done really well it requires great personal skills. Rereading *Home Style* only deepened my long-held belief that Dick Fenno is amazingly good with people. He has an uncanny ability to read them and the situations they are in, to know when to talk and when to be quiet, to know when to be patient and when to make his move, to know when to be supportive and when to be distant. These are skills that cannot be learned from a 50-page appendix, no matter how insightful it may be.

But other reasons people avoid this kind of research are inaccurate or at least fixable. One misconception of the research method Fenno promotes is that at its core is interviewing politicians. As survey researchers know all too well, people often answer questions in a fashion designed to put themselves in a favorable light in the eyes of the questioner. Although to do so is only human nature, it means true answers may not have been elicited. The problem is even worse when politicians are subjects since they generally have years or even decades of experience at parrying difficult questions and offering guarded responses to others. Being concerned for so long about the potential public reaction to their every statement probably makes it difficult for politicians to reflect on their real, personal sentiments.[2] Most scholars therefore conclude that real data on behavior are superior to the trumped up images of themselves that politicians are so skilled at presenting.

I confess to being sympathetic to this point of view, but it is largely irrelevant to the topic at hand since interviewing members of Congress is not at all an accurate description of the type of research Fenno did and wants us to do. He did not spend 110 days on 36 separate trips with 18 different House members peppering them with survey items. Rather, he

---

[2] I once asked retired members of Congress if they had quit because they feared they might not be reelected if they ran again. This was not a popular question and was usually met with an indignant recitation of how many elections the member had won and how unreservedly the people of the district loved him or her. But when I looked at the hard data, retiring members were indeed more likely than their counterparts to have had a recent close race or to have an unfavorable pattern in recent electoral results. I do not think they were being duplicitous; I just think they were not in the best position to see the whole picture on a matter so important to them.

observed the members, often when their focus was on something other than the person doing the observing. Of course he asked occasional questions and later jotted down quotes, but never did he have any desire to conduct systematic interviews. He wanted to get a feel for the members' relationships with their constituents, not force them to respond to preset, closed-ended questions with socially acceptable answers. In a large portion of the quotes in *Home Style*, the members were talking to someone other than Fenno. The style of research Fenno describes in the appendix does not involve interviewing members of Congress. It is much more informative than that—and sadly, it is also much more difficult.

Perhaps the biggest reason more of the Fenno style of research is not done is that reporting on the "feel" one has obtained for a topic—in this case relationships between the represented and the representative—is not very scientific. We cannot precisely replicate Fenno's procedures and determine where he was right and where he may be wrong. I have little doubt his observations are on target, but that is not the same thing as saying he has provided firm scientific evidence of those observations. There is too much artistry in what he did.

Let me be clear. I believe in the scientific approach to studying the social world and in this sense I would not want all social scientists to adopt Richard Fenno's techniques for open-ended participant observation—and neither would Fenno. We would lose much if this were done. But we also lose much when we abide by disciplinary norms that discourage scholars from sticking a toe in the water of qualitative participant observation of the Fenno variety. At the least, this type of research is a rich source of insights and hypotheses that can then be tested in more traditional scientific fashion. This is precisely what Fenno has in mind when he repeatedly refers to his work as exploratory. Alas, junior scholars are not much rewarded for deriving hypotheses but rather for testing them. Perhaps this is as it should be, but if it is, then we need to encourage senior scholars, those with established reputations or at least tenure, to follow in Fenno's footsteps. Exploration generally is followed by colonization or at least by more explorers. In this case, the colonizers and secondary explorers have not come. Among academic political scientists, participant observation of legislators is no more popular now than it was before Fenno told us all how to do it—and our understanding of legislators specifically and representative governance generally is no doubt the worse for it.

Scholarly access to members of Congress is difficult. They are busy people with other priorities. When access *is* granted it is necessary to treat it in the manner it deserves so future scholars will not be spurned out of hand. For his part, Fenno treated this trust with incredible respect. This is apparent in the relevant passages from the methodological appendix (261–3) on how to treat members and also on the basis of a personal experience I had. In the very early 1980s I undertook to understand better why so many members of Congress had been retiring voluntarily from elective politics, some well before retirement age. I interviewed two dozen recently retired members at their post–Congress residences or places of employ. Before I had asked my first question to one member, he blurted out, with all the pride of a new father, "I am Fenno's Congressman A." He went on to make it clear that he had a most favorable view of political scientists thanks to his encounters a few years previously with his "friend, Dick Fenno." Not surprisingly, my interview with this member was by far the best. Not only was he open and loquacious but he was also entertaining. The "interview" grew to include several hours of reflection on life as a member of Congress, stops at the houses of many members of his erstwhile "personal constituency" for drinks, grilled salmon in his backyard, and an overnight stay in his guesthouse. So when Fenno writes that he conducted himself so as to "maintain access for all congressional scholars" (262), he should be taken seriously.

CONCLUSION

One of the great features of *Home Style* is that it can be read at many levels. The combination of rich, sometimes fascinating, raw material, minimal and accessible quantitative passages, and deft writing make it a book that everyone can enjoy. We like to read about people, how they react under pressure, how they view relationships, and how they treat their friends and enemies—and there is plenty of this in *Home Style*. An important part of the book's appeal is that it is fun to read, a rarity for political science. I do hope, however, that the enjoyable nature of the prose does not give readers an excuse for missing the numerous important messages they contain. I hope, for example, that on reading the book people have a better appreciation for the fact that elected officials, though as flawed as all humans, are generally working hard to do what the people want them to do. And most of all I hope that they take from the book an expanded view of representation, which bring us back to the point I made at the beginning of this essay.

What Fenno wrote in 1978 is still largely true: the dominant view tends to hold up "policy congruence as the only legitimate basis of representation, and to denigrate extrapolicy bases of representation as "symbolic"

(242). He continues, "the extrapolicy aspects of representational relationships have tended to be dismissed as. . . . somehow less substantial than the relationship embodied in a roll call vote in Washington" (243). Fenno points out two reasons for the bias against "extrapolicy" matters. First, these factors are not typically studied. "For lack of observation, political scientists have tended to downgrade home activity as mere errand running or fence mending, as activity that takes the representative away from the important things" (243). And second, extrapolicy matters are frequently viewed by scholars "as a calculated effort to avoid policy congruence," as nothing more than "image selling, and as evidence that members spend too little of their time 'on the job'—that is, in Washington, making policy" (242–3).

Fenno, of course, hopes that readers will take a different view from *Home Style*, a view that "values both Washington and home activity" and that recognizes district and Washington activities are often "mutually supportive" (244). My own recent research has focused on public attitudes toward Congress and democratic government and based on this analysis, I have gained a new appreciation for Fenno's message. In fact, I have come to the conclusion that he did not go far enough. People do not crave policy accountability the way most political scientists assume. At best, people have an issue or two they care about, meaning that most of the roll call votes tendered by members of Congress are going to be of little concern to the people. The reason people sometimes feel unrepresented is not the belief that members voted yea when they should have voted nay but the belief that members live in a world that is different than the people's world and therefore cannot understand the needs and concerns of ordinary people. They want to feel that people like them—or at least people who understand them—are in power.

As such, I am convinced that members pay substantial attention to their home style not just because it gives them leeway on policy votes or helps them to understand how constituents want them to vote but because, setting aside the small percentage who care deeply about issues and who have had a disproportionate effect on how representation is perceived, most people merely want their representative to be able to understand, to like, and to empathize with the people they represent. They want their member to come home to the district not because they need to in order to get reelected but because they authentically enjoy being there. As Fenno so rightly observed, if the people sense that the member is not "at home" among them—and they will sense this immediately as they are very good at sniffing out fakes—it spells trouble. Narrow policy congruence of the sort usually studied by political scientists is not nearly as important to ordinary people as is typically assumed. Home style is important not because people are being manipulated by self-serving politicians and substance averse media outlets but because it is what people most want out of their representative.

So, my appreciation of *Home Style*'s central message has only deepened over the years. As research continues to indicate that people are more concerned with the overall motive, orientation, and style of their representatives than with the specific issue votes of those representatives, Fenno's account of representatives working hard to match their home style to what the people want it to be takes on additional relevance. In this sense, the republication of *Home Style*, approximately 25 years after it initially appeared, is propitious. I wish for it the widest possible dissemination and am delighted that a new generation will now be likely to take note of the value to legislative scholars of participant observation and the value to ordinary people of representatives conveying the proper home style.

RECOMMENDED READINGS

Davidson, Roger H., and Walter J. Oleszek. 2000. *Congress and Its Members.* Washington, DC: CQ Press. The leading textbook on Congress and the book that probably is more faithful than any to Fenno's contrast between members in Washington and at home.

Fenno, Richard F., Jr. 1996. *Senators on the Campaign Trail: The Politics of Representation.* Norman: University of Oklahoma Press. As close as we get to a discussion of home styles in the very different world of the United States Senate.

Fiorina, Morris P. 1977. *Congress: Keystone of the Washington Establishment.* New Haven: Yale University Press. Bigger government means more opportunities for members of Congress to service their constituents and "serviced" constituents are usually supportive constituents.

Kingdon, John W. 1973. *Congressmen's Voting Decisions.* New York: Harper & Row. Inventive use of interviews to determine why members of Congress tend to vote the way they do on roll call matters.

Matthews, Donald R. 1960. *U.S. Senators and Their World.* Chapel Hill, NC: University of North Carolina Press. Classic analysis of the Senate, bringing together all kinds of data to understand, not just policy votes, but the "folkways" of the body.

Mayhew, David. 1974. *Congress: The Electoral Connection.* New Haven: Yale University Press. How much of congressional behavior can be accounted for solely by the desire of members to get reelected? Quite a lot, but not everything, it turns out.

STUDY QUESTIONS

1. If you were assigned to understand members of Congress, would you observe them in Washington, DC, or in their home districts? Why? What would be the strengths and weaknesses of each location?

2. What are the dangers of using participant observation as a method of studying members of Congress? What are the dangers of not using it?

3. How would you like representatives to behave? What could they do to make you feel more represented?

4. In what ways would you expect a new member of Congress to interact with constituents differently compared to a member who has been serving for, say, two decades? How does Fenno's research suggest these interactions change over the course of a congressional career?

5. Should members of Congress be as sensitive to all the people in their geographical constituency as they are to those individuals in their personal constituency? Is it possible for members to do so? Defend your answers.

BIOGRAPHICAL SKETCH OF RICHARD F. FENNO, JR.

Richard F. Fenno, Jr., is the Distinguished University Professor and William R. Kenan Professor of Political Science at the University of Rochester. He has been a New Englander and long-suffering Red Sox fan most of his life, earning his Ph.D. from Harvard and later settling in upstate New York. His early scholarship focused on the Executive Branch and in 1959 he published *The President's Cabinet*, then the definitive treatment of that topic. An interest in budgetary politics, however, forced him to pay more attention to the legislative branch, a shift that was first evident in his widely acclaimed *The Power of the Purse* (1966), which naturally gave substantial attention to the House Appropriations Committee. This topic led to a more general interest in congressional committees and the result was *Congressmen in Committees* (1973), in which he encouraged scholars to see members as pursuing three goals: reelection, power, and policy, not necessarily in that order. Like his other books, it has become the standard reference for other scholars' subsequent investigation of the topic.

Congressmen in Committees was followed in 1978 by initial publication of the book that is now being honored with republication, *Home Style: House Members in Their Districts*. Since the publication of *Home Style*, however, Professor Fenno has not stopped writing pathbreaking books. His findings on House members in their constituencies led him to wonder whether senators acted differently in their constituencies, that is states. Initially, Fenno resisted the urge to combine results of his Senate observations into a single book as he had done so effectively for his House observations in *Home Style*. Thus, there followed a series of highly readable and eminently useful short books on the home activities and related matters of individual senators. Freed from the need to hide the identity of these politicians (which would have been impossible with senators, anyway), Fenno published his observations of the following senators: John Glenn, Dan Quayle, Pete Domenici, Mark Andrews, and Arlen Specter. In 1996, he pulled together observations of these senators and others in a book called *U.S. Senators in Senators on the Campaign Trail: The Politics of Representation*. And finally, in 2000, he returned to the House of Representatives with yet an additional twist. One of the 18 members of the House Fenno featured (anonymously) in *Home Style* was Jack Flynt who had represented a formerly rural Georgia district that was being swallowed by the growth of suburban Atlanta. Fenno decided to use the baseline understanding of the district he had obtained during his earlier travels with Flynt to assay the sizable changes in southern politics that had occurred since the mid-1970s. Fenno spent time with one of Flynt's successor, Mac Collins (between Flynt and Collins the district had been represented by Newt Gingrich) and was therefore able to produce an intriguing portrait of representational change in the South.

Richard Fenno has received too many honors and awards to mention. He is the premier scholar of the U.S. Congress, one of the few political scientists to have been inducted into the National Academy of Sciences, a former President of the American Political Science Association, one of the most widely known students of American politics, and a wonderfully warm human being.

JOHN R. HIBBING
University of Nebraska-Lincoln

Contents

Acknowledgments

In the pages that follow, my primary indebtedness to eighteen members of the House of Representatives, their staffs, and their families will become, I hope, amply evident. They know who they are. But, since they are anonymous in the book, they must accept my grateful thanks in anonymity. Among my friends in academia, I wish to acknowledge a special indebtedness to Theodore Anagnoson, John Bibby, John Kingdon, Viktor Hofstetter, and Herbert McClosky. In diverse ways, their help was indispensable in bringing the book to its present condition. Many other colleagues commented constructively on written material at one stage or another of the project. I thank for their help: David W. Brady, Joseph Cooper, Morris Fiorina, Charles Jones, John Kessel, John Manley, Donald Matthews, David Mayhew, Bruce Oppenheimer, Norman Ornstein, Nelson Polsby, Kenneth Prewitt, H. Douglas Price, Austin Ranney, Randall Ripley, David Rohde, Edward Schneier, Kenneth Shepsle, Richard Smith, Sidney Waldman, Aaron Wildavsky, and Raymond Wolfinger. For their assistance I also thank David Bantleon, Joel Beckman, Sandra Bloch, Joanne Doroshow, Larry Fishkin, Nancy Hapeman, Arthur Kreeger, John Levi, Joel Pelcyger, Bruce Pollock, Joyce Rubin, Kenneth Sankin, Fred Schwartz, Susan Weiner and Jacob Weinstein. My thanks, too, to Paul Montebello and Neil Wintfeld for enlisting their talents. For their financial support, I am indebted to the University of Rochester, The Russell Sage Foundation, The Helen Dwight Reid Foundation, and the John Simon Guggenheim Memorial Foundation. From the transcription of my field notes to the typing of the final manuscript, I have relied heavily on the cheerful competence of Janice Brown. My lasting debt is to Nancy, for managing the most difficult constituency with the nicest home style.

Introduction

As it is essential to liberty that the government in general should have a common interest with the people, so it is particularly essential that the branch of it under consideration [the House of Representatives] *should have an immediate dependence on and an intimate sympathy with, the people.*
— JAMES MADISON: *The Federalist*

The requisites in actual representation are that the Representatives should sympathize with their constituents; should think as they think and feel as they feel; and that for these purposes should even be residents among them.
— GEORGE MASON: Remarks at the Constitutional Convention

This book is an exploration. It is an exploration of the relationship between members of the House of Representatives and their constituents about which the Founding Fathers philosophized. It is also an exploration of the place where that relationship was thought to originate and to thrive — the constituency. Explorations of such a relationship and such a place are not especially newsworthy or glamorous; nor have they been especially popular among political scientists. It is not hard to see why.

I recall an occasion in one congressional district when a representative's district aide and I were eating dinner, waiting for the representative to fly in from Washington for an evening of election campaigning. When he arrived, he was keyed up and visibly elated:

> I spent fifteen minutes on the telephone with the president this afternoon. He had a plaintive tone in his voice and he

pleaded with me. I suppose he figured he would win if he broke me away from the others. But I knew more about it than he did — more than anyone. I've lived with this problem for years. We won. We ended up with a stronger bill than we had three days ago; and now he knows we will override another veto.

The House member regaled us with the intimate details of the fascinating and exciting legislative struggle as he ordered and gulped his dinner. Then the three of us got up and went out to the aide's car, the back of which was piled from floor to roof with campaign ammunition — hundreds of shopping bags, all with the representative's name and picture on them. As he sat down beside the driver, he turned around to look at me, wedged among the shopping bags. He sighed, smiled, and said, "Back to this again." He had moved from one political world to another. It is the first of these two worlds that normally attracts our interest. This book, however, is not about the world of telephone conversations with the president of the United States nor the world of legislative battle. It is a book about the world of the shopping bags.

Political scientists have produced a voluminous amount of literature on the general subject of representative-constituency relations. We have literature on party government that argues that constituency pressures explain why representatives so often fail to vote their party.[1] We have survey research that measures the congruence between constituency attitudes on public policy and the roll call votes of their representatives.[2] We have decision-making literature that assesses the relative influence of constituency factors in the voting calculations of the representative.[3] We have literature on role orientations that differentiates between types of representative-constituency relationships — between the "trustees" who vote their independent judgment and the "delegates" who vote their constituents' wishes.[4] We also have literature on recruitment that traces legislative styles of representatives to the recruitment patterns in their constituencies.[5] We have communications literature, which emphasizes the two-way, interactive, interdependent character of the representative-constituency relationship.[6] And we have reformist literature that protests that representatives spend too much of their time on constituent service — too much the errand-boy; too little the lawmaker.[7]

Despite this outpouring, one question central to the representative-constituency relationship remains underdeveloped. It is: *What does an elected representative see when he or she sees a constituency?* And, as a natural follow-up, *What consequences do these perceptions have for his or her behavior?* The key problem is perception. And the key assumption is that the constituency a representative reacts to is the constituency he or she sees. The corollary assumption is that the rest of us cannot understand the representative-constituency relationship until we can see the constituency through the eyes of the representative. These ideas are not new. They were first articulated for students of the United States Congress by Lewis Dexter.[8] Their importance has been widely acknowledged and frequently repeated ever since. But despite the acceptance and reiteration of Dexter's insights, we still have not developed much coherent knowledge about the perceptions members of Congress have of their constituencies.

A major reason for this neglect is that most political science research on the representative-constituency linkage is conducted at one end of the linkage — in the world of legislative combat and not in the world of the shopping bags. Typically, our interest in the constituency relations of senators and House members has been a derivative interest, pursued for the light it sheds on some behavior — like roll call voting — in Washington, D.C. When we talk with our national legislators about their constituencies, we typically talk to them *in Washington* and, perforce, in the Washington context. But that is a context far removed from the one in which their constituency relationships are created, nurtured, and changed. And it is a context equally far removed from the one in which we might expect their perceptions of their constituencies to be shaped, sharpened, or altered. Asking constituency-related questions on Capitol Hill, when the House member is far from the constituency itself, could well produce a distortion of perspective. Researchers might tend to conceive of a separation between the representative "here in Washington" and his or her constituency "back home," whereas the representative may picture himself or herself as a part of the constituency — me-*in*-the-constituency, rather than me-*and*-the-constituency. As a research strategy, therefore, it makes sense to study our representatives' perceptions of their constituencies while they are actually in thir constituencies — at the constituency end of the linkage.[9]

From the fall of 1970 until the spring of 1977, I traveled intermittently with some members of the House of Representatives while they were in their districts, to see if I could figure out — by looking over their shoulders — what it was they saw there. These expeditions were totally open-ended and exploratory. I tried to observe and inquire into anything and everything these members did. I worried about whatever they worried about. Rather than assume that I already knew what was interesting, I remained prepared to find interesting questions emerging in the course of the experience. The same with data. The research method was largely one of soaking and poking — or just hanging around.

During nearly eight years of research, I accompanied eighteen individuals in their districts: fifteen sitting representatives, two representatives-to-be, and one representative-elect. I made 36 separate visits and spent 110 working (not traveling) days in the eighteen districts. In fourteen cases, I visited the district more than once; in four cases, I made only one trip. Because I was a stranger to each local context and to the constellation of people surrounding each representative, my confidence in what I saw and heard increased markedly when I could observe at more than one time. The least amount of time I spent with any individual was one three-day visit; the most was three visits totaling eleven days. Nearly two-thirds of the visits occurred during the fall election period.[10] In eleven cases, I supplemented the district visit with a lengthy interview in Washington. In the district, I reconstructed my record from memory and from brief jottings, as soon after the event as was feasible. In Washington, I took mostly verbatim notes during the interview and committed them to tape immediately thereafter. Wherever necessary, I have given the representatives pseudonyms in the text, in order to preserve their anonymity.

I have tried to find a variety of types of representatives and districts, but I make no pretense at having a group that can be called representative, much less a sample. The eighteen include ten Democrats and eight Republicans. Three come from two eastern states; six come from five midwestern states; one comes from a border state; three come from three southern states; and five come from three far western states. Since I began, one has retired, one has been defeated, and one has run for the Senate. There is some variation among them in terms of ideology, seniority, ethnicity, race, age, and sex,[11] and in terms of safeness and diversity of district. No claim is made, however, that the group is ideally balanced in any of these respects — only that the group is diverse enough for the exploratory purposes to which it has been put. These and other matters of method have been elaborated in a lengthy Appendix.

A final word about what this book does not do. First of all, it does not compare the attitudes of constituents with the attitudes or behavior of the representative; it is written entirely from over the representative's shoulder. It does not investigate constituent attitudes, and cannot compare them, therefore, with anything. Nor, second, does this book compare representatives' perceptions of their constituencies with some "objective" or "real" or "true" version of those constituencies. The perceived constituency is the only one we know anything about. In the third place, this book is not a study of "constituencies" that may lie outside a representative's congressional district. Some House members attract financial contributions and other forms of support from people across the state or nation. Though I have run across traces of these — in examining the appointment schedules of members, for instance — I have excluded them from this study on the grounds that ordinary constituency relationships are complicated enough.

Fourth, I do not delve into the personalities of the representatives being studied. Here again, I have stumbled across intriguing hints that these things may be important. For instance, a long-time friend of one member of Congress told me, gratuitously, that I could never understand that congressman's ambition unless I understood the relationship between him and his mother — "a tough old woman" who wanted her son to be "perfect." "He could never please her. Nothing he could do would please her." I have let all such matters lie untouched, because it is beyond my competence to do anything else with them.

Finally, this book is about the early to mid-1970s only. These years were characterized by the steady decline of strong national party attachments and strong local party organizations. They were characterized, also, by considerable public cynicism and distrust toward our national political institutions, including Congress. Had these conditions been different, House members might have behaved differently in their constituencies. Even with these several caveats, it will be task enough to figure out the perceptions that a few members of Congress have of their constituencies and to examine some possible political consequences.

NOTES

1. For example, Edward Schneier and Julius Turner, *Party and Constituency: Pressures on Congress*, rev. ed. (Baltimore: Johns Hopkins Press, 1970).
2. For example, Warren Miller and Donald Stokes, "Constituency Influence in Congress," *American Political Science Review* 57 (March 1963): 45–56.
3. For example, John Kingdon, *Congressmen's Voting Decisions* (New York: Harper and Row, 1973).
4. For example, Roger Davidson, *The Role of the Congressman* (New York: Pegasus, 1969).
5. For example, Leo Snowiss, "Congressional Recruitment and Representation," *American Political Science Review* 60 (September 1966): 629–39.
6. For example, R. Bauer, I. Pool, and L. Dexter, *American Business and Public Policy* (New York: Atherton, 1963).
7. For example, M. Green, J. Fallows, and D. Zwick, *Who Runs Congress* (New York: Bantam, 1972).
8. Dexter's seminal article was "The Representative and His District," *Human Organization* 16 (Spring 1957): 2–14. It will be found, revised and reprinted, along with other of Dexter's works carrying the same perspective in: Lewis Dexter, *The Sociology and Politics of Congress* (Chicago: Rand McNally, 1969). Another early example of the perceptual emphasis in constituency studies is Charles O. Jones, "Representation in Congress: The Case of the House Agriculture Committee," *American Political Science Review* 55 (June 1961): 358–67.
9. Political science studies conducted in congressional constituencies have been few and far between. The most helpful to me have been: *On Capitol Hill*, ed. John Bibby and Roger Davidson (New York: Holt, Rinehart and Winston, 1967); *On Capitol Hill*, ed. John Bibby and Roger Davidson (Chicago: Dryden, 1972); John Donovan, *Congressional Campaign: Maine Elects a Democrat* (New York: Holt, Rinehart and Winston, 1957); Charles Jones, "The Role of the Campaign in Congressional Politics" in *The Electoral Process*, ed. Harmon Zeigler and Kent Jennings (New York: Prentice-Hall, 1966); John Kingdon, *Candidates for Office: Beliefs and Strategies* (New York: Random House, 1966); David Leuthold, *Electioneering in a Democracy* (New York: Wiley, 1968). And no one interested in this subject should miss Richard Harris's superb "How's It Look?" *New Yorker*, April 8, 1967, pp. 48ff. The most recent study, conducted simultaneously with this one, is: *The Making of Congressmen*, ed. Alan Clem, (North Scituate, Mass.: Duxbury, 1976).
10. A full listing of the district visits will be found in Table A, Appendix.
11. The group contains seventeen men and one woman. In this Introduction, I have deliberately employed the generic terms "House member," "member of Congress," "representative," and "his or her" to make it clear that I am talking about men and women. And I have tried to use the same language wherever the plural form appears in the book. That is, I have tried to stop using the word "congressmen." However, I shall often and deliberately use "congressman" and "his" as generic terms. Stylistically, I find this a less clumsy form of the third person singular than "congressperson," followed always by "his or her." This usage has the additional special benefit, here, of camouflaging the one woman in the group.

HOME STYLE:
HOUSE MEMBERS IN THEIR DISTRICTS

CHAPTER ONE

Perceptions of the Constituency

What does a House member see when looking at his or her constituency? Kaleidoscopic variety, no doubt. That is why there can be no one "correct" way of slicing up and classifying member perceptions — only "helpful" ways. Most helpful to me has been the member's view of a constituency as a nest of concentric circles. In one form or another, in one expression or another, in one degree or another, this bullseye perception is shared by all House members. It is helpful to us for the same reason it is common to them. It is a perception constructed out of the necessities of political life.

THE GEOGRAPHICAL CONSTITUENCY: THE DISTRICT

The largest of the concentric circles represents the House member's most encompassing view of his or her constituency. It is "the district," the entity to which, from which, and within which the member travels. It is the entity whose boundaries have been fixed by state legislative enactment or by court decision. It includes the entire population within those boundaries. Because it is a legal entity, we could refer to it as the legal constituency. We capture more of what the member has in mind when conjuring up "my district," however, if we think of it as the *geographical constituency*. We then retain the idea that the district is a legally bounded space, and emphasize that it is located in a particular place.

The Washington community is often described as a group of people all of whom come from somewhere else. The House of Representatives, by design, epitomizes this characteristic; and its members function with a heightened sense of their ties to another place. There

1

are, of course, constant reminders. The member's district is, after all, "the Tenth District of *California*." Inside the chamber, he is "the gentleman from *California*." In the media, he is "Representative Smith (D. *California*)." So it is not surprising that when you ask a member, "What kind of district do you have?" the answer often begins with, and nearly always includes, a geographical, space-and-place perception. Thus, the district is seen as "the largest in the state, twenty-eight counties in the southeastern corner," or "three layers of suburbs to the west of the city, a square with the northwest corner cut out," or "a core district, the core of the city." If the boundaries have been changed by a recent redistricting, the geography of "the new district" will be compared to that of "the old district": "I picked up five northern counties and lost two on the eastern edge. The new district is a lot more spread out."

If one essential aspect of "the geographical constituency" is seen as its location and boundaries, another is its internal makeup. And House members describe their districts' internal makeup using political science's most familiar demographic and political variables: socioeconomic structure, ideology, ethnicity, residential patterns, religion, partisanship, stability, diversity, etc. Every congressman, in his mind's eye, sees his geographical constituency in terms of some special configuration of such variables.

> The basic industry is agriculture; but it's a diverse district. The city makes up one-third of the population. It is dominated by state government and education. It's an independent-minded constituency, with a strong attachment to the work ethic. A good percentage is composed of people whose families emigrated from Germany, Scandinavia and Czechoslovakia. I don't exactly know the figures, but over one-half the district is German. And this goes back to the work ethic. They are a hard-working, independent people. They have a strong thought of "keep the government off my back, we'll do all right here."

> It is a middle America district. It is poorer than most, older than most, more rural than most. It is basically progressive. It's not a conservative district; it's a moderate district. It is a heavily Democratic district — the third most, or second most, Democratic district in the state. It is very concerned with bread and butter issues. It is environmentally conscious as far as rural districts go. . . . It is a basic working-class district with pockets of professional leadership.

Some internal configurations are more complex than others. But no congressman sees, within his district's boundaries, an undifferentiated glob.[1] And the rest of us should not talk about his relations with his "constituency" as if he did.

All of the demographic characteristics of the geographical constituency carry political implications. But as most representatives make their first perceptual cut into "the district," political implications are left implicit (as in the first comment) or mentioned after the demography (as in the second). Only one of the eighteen put politics first: "My description always has political connotations. . . . I always describe it as a mainstream Democratic district, in the sense that Scammon and Wattenberg used it." For all the other members, it was as if they wished first to sketch a prepolitical background against which they could then paint in the political refinements. Students of American politics know, for most of the demographic variables, what some of the political refinements are likely to be. They would guess, correctly, that the first district just described is more Republican than Democratic. And they would have guessed that the second district is more Democratic than Republican, had not the member mentioned it himself. There is no point to dwelling on the possible political relevance of each particular variable. Students of American politics have mined that vein extensively.

It should be noted, however, that not all members of Congress are expert political demographers. A member whose district is filled with people of German, Scandinavian, Polish, and French ancestry said, "You have to understand the kind of person you're talking to. I don't know any of the percentages of nationality groups. I don't even know which one is the largest." An urban congressman deputized a local politician to drive me around his district, because the congressman was not familiar with the location or characteristics of its various wards and neighborhoods. Another district staff aide described how she worked with the neighboring congressman in redistricting her member's district:

> Dave Sullivan and I redrew the lines of our two districts. I remember once we were down on our hands and knees on the floor of Henry's Washington office with the map in front of us dividing the districts block by block, bargaining and compromising. Dave would say "I don't want that son of a bitch in my district, you take that block." Or I'd say, "We won by 70 percent in that block, no way you're going to get

that one." Henry just sat in his chair and laughed at us. Things like that bore him. He thinks it's an aberration that Dave and I should be interested in such things as census tracts and demographic reports of all sorts.

When House members contemplate their districts, some of them may not see the same demography that political scientists see. And herein lies an early warning that more uncertainty may attend a congressman's perceptions of his constituency than students armed with census data and standing at a distance might have expected.

However a congressman comes to his view of the district, it is important that we try to see it as he does. In the one case when I observed two successive House members in the same geographical constituency, their perceptions of "the district" differed considerably. One member stressed its diversity:

> It's a microcosm. It has rural poverty, urban poverty, big business, unions, wealthy farms, and poor farmlands. It's a microcosm of the United States.

The other member saw the district as much more distinctive:

> It is more or less rural and dominated by one metropolitan area. It is far-flung and culturally rural — not blue collar like Dayton or Akron or Gary. It has very few blacks. . . . [It is] homogeneous. That relates back to its cultural homogeneity. It's an older area that has not had a lot of move-ins and move-outs.

There is no way that a political scientist could infer these perceptual differences from census data. If, then, behavior is related to such differences, we cannot understand behavior without gathering perceptual data.

Of all the internal characteristics of the district, the one that best illuminates subsequent member perceptions and behavior is district homogeneity or heterogeneity. As the following answers to the question "What kind of district do you have?" suggest, representatives do think in terms of the relative homogeneity or heterogeneity of their districts:

> It's geographically compact. It's all suburbia — no big city in the accepted sense of the word and no rural area. It's all

white. There are very few blacks, maybe 2 percent. Spanish surnamed make up about 10 percent. Traditionally, it's been a district with a high percentage of home ownership. . . . Economically, it's above the national average in employment. . . . The people of the district are employed. It's not that it's very high income. Oh, I suppose there are a few places of some wealth, but nothing very wealthy. And no great pockets of poverty either. And it's not dominated by any one industry. The Greene County segment has a lot of small, clean, technical industries. I consider it very homogeneous. By almost any standard it's homogeneous.

I tell people it's a wonderfully heterogeneous district and then explain the word if they don't know what I mean. We have every kind of Jew. We have every kind of Catholic from the most parochial Italians to the most highly sophisticated Irish. Eighteen percent of the district and 25 percent of the vote is black. They didn't used to have leadership; now they are getting some. Next to them live the blue-collar Italians, who feel neglected; and they have been. They have been the whipping boy too long. It's a district as much affected by agriculture as any other. . . . In income we have everything from a silk stocking area to a flat ghetto.

Not all members spontaneously characterized their districts using the language of homogeneity ("uniform," "solid," "all pretty much the same") or heterogeneity ("microcosm," "diverse," "a cross section of everything"). But only one, when queried, was uncomfortable with the distinction. Because it is a summary variable and because it seems to have perceptual meaning and political consequences, it has proven especially useful. We shall return to it often throughout the book.

As a summary variable, however, the perceived homogeneity-heterogeneity characteristic is admittedly hard to pin down and to measure; and I propose no metric. Both the number and the compatibility of significant interests within the district would seem to be involved. The greater the number of significant interests the more likely it is that the district will be seen as heterogeneous. But, if the several significant interests were viewed as having a lowest common denominator and, therefore, as being quite compatible, the district might still be viewed as homogeneous. One indicator, therefore, might be the ease with which the congressman finds a lowest com-

mon denominator of interests for some large proportion of his geographical constituency. The basis for the denominator could be
any of the prepolitical, demographic variables. But we do *not* think
of it as a political characteristic — as the equivalent, for instance,
of party registration or political safeness.[2] The proportion of people
in the district who would have to be included in the denominator
to indicate homogeneity remains a matter of arbitrary judgment.
Perhaps somewhere between two-thirds and three-quarters is about
right.[3] All we can say, for sure, is that the less conflict a congressman
perceives among district interests, the more likely he is to see his
district as homogeneous, and the more conflict he perceives among
district interests the more likely he is to see his district as heterogeneous.

Whether by design or by accident, the most homogeneous districts are likely to have boundaries which incorporate pre-existing
communities of interest. Among the most heterogeneous districts, on
the other hand, are those with boundaries determined by partisan
interests or mathematical design. An urban congressman described
his recently redistricted territory as "a residual district," "the result
of everyone else's political machinations." As we drove around, we
were constantly reminded of its artificiality.

> I'll bet there isn't another district as hard to get around in
> as this one. It's so cut up that I can't deal with any single
> community as a whole.

> Let me pull over to the curb and look at the map. I can't tell
> whether this area is in the district or not. It could be, but I'm
> not sure. That must have been some redistricting when the
> congressman who represents the district can't even tell
> whether he's in it or not. What a mess.

His district had not always been so "cut up" or messy. The redistricting had removed the largest and most dominant community from
his district, a community which had been a homogenizing influence.

> Until the last redistricting, L was a classic representative of the
> district. Then I lost Castle Heights, a constituency where I
> was on the same wave length. . . . Castle Heights was the
> cream of my district — psychologically, sociologically, educa-
> tionally, politically — any way you want to measure it.

His new geographical constituency was altogether more artificial, less reflective of any natural community of interest and, hence, more heterogeneous than the old.[4]

Still another kind of heterogeneous district contains groups that, while potentially in conflict, have little actual interest in or contact with one another's problems. Were they not so insulated, these elements would very likely be at odds with one another. Most such districts cover a good deal of territory, and distance acts as a barrier to contact and to interest. We have called them *segmented* districts. It is characteristic of homogeneous districts that new controversies are highly contagious. Soon after they break out, these controversies affect and engage almost everyone in the district. It is characteristic of segmented districts, however, that new controversy remains localized: "My district is so spread out that I can have a lot of fires without any spreading." A member who sees his rural small town district as having "very diverse interests," said:

> Here we are driving through the hills, 50 miles from one town to the other. In the southern part of the district we drive 50 miles from one town to the other across the flattest land you ever saw. There's no communication between north and south, and they don't understand each other's problems. I'm their only link. The same thing is true within the north and the south. Medford doesn't care much about Downsville, and Benton doesn't care about Norris. Each town is interested only in its own problems.

In heterogeneous geographical constituencies of this sort, lowest common denominators are especially hard to come by.

In talking about their geographical constituencies, as said earlier, members of Congress focus on prepolitical description. That is, they do not leap to descriptions of partisanship or safeness. Neither does this broadest perception have much emphasis on specific issues. Interests, yes; ideology, yes; but issues, not much. Only one of the previous descriptions of "my district" mentioned either partisanship or issues. That proportion — one in four or five — is about right. The only other member who mentioned issues when characterizing "the district," said:

> It's a fairly diverse district. But it is held together by a common interest in lumber and wood products and in fishing.

Those are the two economic interests that dominate the district. The great issues are environmental issues, where you have deeply entrenched interests and polarized points of view — nuclear power, clearcutting, wilderness. These are no-win issues politically unless you want to come down totally on one side or the other. So, the natural wonders of the district create natural conflicts.

Of course, issues lie implicit and potential in all discussions of the geographical constituency. But they rarely surface or are made explicit at this, the outermost perceptual circle.

THE REELECTION CONSTITUENCY: THE SUPPORTERS

Each congressman does perceive an explicitly political constituency nested within his geographical constituency. It is composed of those people in the district who he thinks vote for him. We shall call it his *reelection constituency*. The idea is the same as John Kingdon's "supporting coalition." But, because all members do not perceive their support in coalitional terms and because all members do see support in reelection terms, we shall use the more universal language.[5] As they move about "the district," House members continually draw the distinction between those people who vote for them and those who do not: "I do well here"; "I run poorly here"; "This group supports me"; "This group does not." By distinguishing supporters from nonsupporters, they articulate their fundamental political perception.

House members use two reference points — one cross-sectional, the other longitudinal — in shaping this perception. First, by a process of inclusion and exclusion, they come to a rough approximation of the upper and lower ranges of the reelection constituency. That is to say, there are some votes a member believes he nearly always gets. There are other votes he believes he almost never gets. Among those he thinks he usually gets, the perceived partisan component of the electorate is always a basic element. Every member begins with a perception of his partisan support — estimated by registration figures or poll data, and by political demography.

It's a good Democratic district now — 59 percent registered Democrats. And for the first time I feel safe. . . . I used to brag that my old district was the wealthiest, best-educated district in the country represented by a Democrat. But I wasn't a bit sad to give up the wealthy part of the district and pick up all those poor, ill-educated good Democrats in the new part of the district.

When the partisan composition of the district is clearly insufficient for reelection, members express ideas about the nature of their cross-party supporters.

> My district registers only 37 percent Republican. And they have no place else to go. My problem is, how can I get enough Democratic votes to win the general election. . . . Civil servants, bank clerks, insurance salesmen, bricklayers, carpenters, the craft unions; these have been the mainstream of my Democratic support – middle class and working class. . . . The hard hats are the people most likely to vote for me. That's my lucrative territory – not the liberal, intellectual wing [of the Democratic party].

Every member has some idea of the people most likely to join his reelection constituency, his "lucrative territory." During a campaign, these people will often be "targeted" and subjected to special recruiting or activating efforts.

A congressman's sense of the people least likely to join his reelection constituency is usually as well developed as his sense for his "lucrative territory." Comments like "I'll never carry this town"; "This part of the district is hopeless"; "I've never been able to crack these space industry guys"; "I'd love to get the pickup truck vote, but I never do" punctuate his travels in the district. If a member chooses to attack "the special interests" in his district, it is from these perceived never-supporters that the objects of his attacks will come. One member summed up his reelection constituency:

> My supporters are Democrats, farmers, labor – a DFL operation – with some academic types. . . . If you take it by community, I'll get the majority of farmers and city votes. I won't do well in the small villages – towns of 400, 600, 800, 1000. That's the rock-ribbed Republican constituency. . . . The opposition tends to be the main street hardware dealer. I look at that kind of guy in a stable town where the newspaper runs the community – the typical school board

member in the rural part of the district — that's the kind
of guy I'll never get. At the opposite end of the scale is the
country club set. I'll sure as hell never get them, either.

Starting, then, with people he sees, very generally, as his supporters
and leaving aside other people he sees, equally generally, as his nonsupporters, each congressman fashions a view of the people who give
him his victories at the polls.

In thinking about his reelection constituency, he is helped by a
second, more time-related perception — of who voted for him "last
time" and of how well he did overall "last time." Starting with that
calculation, he adds or subtracts incrementally on the basis of
changes that will have taken place, or could be made to take place,
between "last time" and "this time" or "next time." The results of
previous elections give every member a baseline against which to
estimate future results. "Last time we lost the northern area by 5000
votes. This time we should at least break even." "I'll be a much
stronger candidate than I was last time. 1970 was an exceptionally
good year for Democrats in the Midwest. And incumbency counts
for something." Earlier elections are particularly useful in giving
members a basis for estimating the achievable size of their reelection
constituencies.

> I got 64.2 percent in 1972, but that was because of McGovern
> who was thought to be a bad candidate. Last time I got 60
> percent and I think that's all there is for me in this district.
> The extra 4.2 percent was a phony figure. When I got 60
> percent, I ran ten miles ahead of every other Republican
> candidate. If things are right I should get 60 percent next
> time, too — maybe less.

Working back and forth incrementally from "last time" to "this
time" or to "next time" helps the congressman to delineate his reelection constituency. It helps because election results provide him
with one of the few certainties he operates with. He knows that he
won "last time" and by how much. Sometimes, that is all he knows.

Members of Congress campaigning at home want to get reelected.
But the process by which their desire for reelection is translated into
their perception of a reelection constituency is fraught with *uncertainty*. At least that is my strong impression. House members see

electoral uncertainty where outsiders would fail to unearth a single objective indicator of it. Because political scientists rely so heavily on the statistics of safeness and marginality, it seems worthwhile to elaborate here on some of the sources and manifestations of House member reelection uncertainty.

Member perceptions of their supporters and nonsupporters are quite diffuse. Their perceptions, we have seen, often involve very general demographic groupings. Furthermore, we recall, not all members of Congress earn passing grades as political demographers. Among those who can, some find reason to worry about who is really out there.

> Inevitably, you tend to spend most of your time with the people you are most compatible with, the people you identify with. That colors your perception of your district. These people, though, are only a part of your district. So it's a very imperfect mechanism.

Even when members feel fairly sure about the makeup of their current supporters, they may perceive population shifts that threaten their established calculations.

> Some changes are going on. A lot of apartments are being built. The district originally was all private homes. I think the condominiums that are being built are replacements for homes. But the apartments — I don't know for sure what people you are getting in there.

> What worries me is not that I will neglect my district and lose it. That's just not in my schedule. What worries me is that the district will change. How long that will take, I don't know.

Uncertainty about demography is particularly acute in the mobile suburbs and in the changing urban centers.

In the years of my travels, the prospect of redistricting meant added demographic uncertainty. Because boundary changes cause massive relocations of voters, the subject may be a fateful one for members affected. And they react accordingly: "The 1971 redistricting was the best thing that ever happened to me." "Only one thing would make me feel worse than this last redistricting — to have my testicles laid on a stump and hit with a mallet." One member retired from Congress as the result of "an outrageous redistricting" that removed nearly half the voters from his district. House members, then, worry about boundary changes. Charles Bullock's finding — that most of the defeats of House "careerists" in the 1960s came about in redistricted districts — indicates that member concern is, in the long run at least, justified.[6] It is this electoral uncertainty implanted in the minds of our politicians in the House of Representatives — more than policy change — that constitutes the real "reapportionment revolution" nationally.

Thinking about "last time's" electoral margin, if it was an apparently safe one, should assuage a good deal of a representative's uncertainty about his reelection constituency. And it does. But it does not produce certainty. Far from it. Most House members will have experienced, at some point in their careers, "the fight of my life" — a testing election they felt especially hard pressed to win. When members recall their testing elections they dwell on the immense organizational and personal efforts required to win. Frequently, the severest test is the first. One member recalled the last TV appearance of his first campaign:

> While the other candidates were speaking, I just sat there with my head hanging down. When it came my turn, I could not remember my name. The next day they were to have a TV show in the city. I said I was too tired to go. I was completely exhausted.

"After the [first] election," said another, "I was so tired I just took a bottle and sacked out for two days." And a third recalled that his first campaign left him "dead": "There was very little human being left in me after the campaign." Remembering how painful it was for them to get to Congress in the first place (five of the eighteen had to run twice before making it), heightens their worry about staying there. They worry in proportion to their investment. And their initial investment may be enormous.

Of course, members may face testing elections at any time in their careers. Thirteen of my eighteen members have had at least one election margin below 55 percent, even though eleven of the thirteen have also had election margins over 60 percent. One easy election does not guarantee another one. Indeed, the reverse can happen. Members worry that, in the absence of competition, their organizations will atrophy and may no longer be available when a testing election comes.

> I remember when Charlie came up to me on the House floor in 1970 I had just gotten 72 percent in the election. He said, "It looks like you've got that district sewed up." I said, "It's the worst thing that could have happened to me. Everyone will think I'm safe and get complacent as hell. Then some son of a bitch will come along and defeat me." That's just what happened. I went from 72 percent in 1970 to 53 percent in 1972 — a drop of 20 points.

Once having gone through a testing election, early or late, a member will entertain the possibility of its recurrence forever. Even when he is being spared, it will be happening to someone he knows. And he will take it as a warning signal to himself. These frequent warning signals also remind the member that his security is not proportionate to the rise and fall of national electoral tides. He will be more affected, for better or worse, by his efforts to help himself.

Representatives worry about vote drop-offs much smaller than 20 points. They believe that there is always a good bit of latent opposition in the district that will surface if it appears they are losing their electoral grip.

> People can be mad at you, but if they don't see a chance of beating you, they will keep it inside. If I looked vulnerable, the right-to-life people would be on me like a hen on a junie bug. And the gun control people, too.

Similarly, there are potential opponents out there waiting for signs of slippage.

> It's important for me to show strength to keep the young state representatives and city councilmen away. If they have the feeling that I'm invincible, they won't try. That reputation is very intangible. [But] your vote margin is part of it.

"Last time's" election margin, therefore, must be maintained — however lopsided or statistically "safe" it may be — to discourage potential adversaries. Big reelection constituencies may be far more worrisome to a member than an outsider, ignorant of political dynamics, would have imagined.

If it seems patently ludicrous to worry about the general election, there is always the possibility of a primary. "Even though I have a safe district and never have any trouble in the general election, I always have to keep my eye out for a primary contest. . . . I have to keep my flanks protected at all times." Indeed, it is precisely when reelection margins are greatest that the threat of a primary is most serious.[7] The congressman who was quoted earlier as saying "for the first time I feel safe," frets nonetheless about a particular primary opponent:

> If he ever runs against me, he'll give me fits. I'll need
> $100,000 and three months of campaigning. The first free
> ride he has is in 1980 and he may try then. The only thing
> that will stop him will be his feeling that his talents are
> better suited to a different position.

Renomination is as much a part of the electoral process as reelection. And it is the most nagging electoral imponderable for many members.

No matter how secure their electoral circumstances may seem, therefore, members of Congress can always find reasons to feel insecure. And not without some foundation. None of them wants to leave the Congress by way of electoral defeat. Yet Robert Erikson has shown that between 1961 and 1964, 41 percent of all members leaving the House did so involuntarily, by defeat at the polls — 11 percent in the primary election, 30 percent in the general. From 1965 to 1972, 35 percent of the members left involuntarily — 24 percent in the primary election and 11 percent in the general.[8] Though "last time's" reelection constituency will have been ample, electoral trouble may be only a couple of elections away. In sum, knowing or sensing or fearing these several unhappy electoral possibilities, House members will continue to be a lot more uncertain than the statistics of their last election would warrant.

Of all the sources of uncertainty, the most constant involves the electoral challenger. It is the challenger who holds the greatest potential for altering the makeup and size of the congressman's reelection constituency. Members apply their own discount rate to

prior election results depending on their estimates of the challenger.
"Fifty-three percent was a Republican vote, 5 percent was for the
incumbent, and 5 percent was because I had a dumb opponent. This
year I don't know how to figure it." "It was an unbalanced election
last year. They ran a complete unknown against me and he was
incompetent. I won by 65 percent and spent $30,000. Normally I
spend $60,000 and win by 55 percent." "I got some support from
business last time, not because they liked me but because they
thought my opponent was a clown." Weak opponents add weak
supporters to the reelection constituency, supporters who were there
last time but may not be there this time.

> I pulled a lot of Republican votes last time that I'll lose this
> time — everywhere — and it will be worse in the few coun-
> ties I mentioned. My opponent has a strong identification
> with the Republican party, having been state chairman all
> those years. My last opponent never had that identification.
> He was a minister. . . . He was duck soup.

This time's challenger may have very different sources of political
strength from last time's challenger. And if he does, the House
member's support patterns will be altered too. Often, therefore, a
major off-year uncertainty is whether or not last time's challenger
will try again. And an enormous amount of nervous energy is ex-
pended between elections trying to find out what the last opponent
is up to.

Although it is true that members of Congress campaign all the
time, "the campaign" can be said to start only when the challenger
is known. At that point, a redefinition of the reelection constituency
— actual and potential — may have to take place. If the challenger is
chosen by primary, for example, the congressman may inherit support from the loser.[9] A conservative Republican, waiting for the
Democratic primary to determine whether his challenger would be
a liberal black or a liberal white, speculated about the possible configurations of his reelection constituency, i.e., who would vote for
him in the general election:

> It depends on my opponent. Last time, my opponent [a white
> moderate] and I split many groups. Many business people
> who might have supported me, split up. If I have a liberal
> opponent, all the business community will support me. . . .

> If the black man is my opponent, I should get more Demo-
> cratic votes than I got before. He can't do any better there
> than the man I beat before. Except for a smattering of
> liberals and radicals around the colleges, I will do better
> than last time with the whites. . . . The black vote is 25
> percent and they vote right down the line Democratic. . . .
> [But] against a white liberal, I would get some of the black
> vote.

So long as the challenger is unknown, the shaping of perceptions
proceeds under considerable uncertainty.

Even in the face of a reputedly weak challenger, members find
reasons to worry about their electoral support patterns. After all, if
the challenger is an unknown quantity, prudence may foster some
fear of that unknown. As one member expressed it, "I don't know
where his support is. And that's what bothers me. Every time he
makes a statement, I think the campaign is lost." And another said:

> He's out campaigning ten hours a day, seven days a week.
> He's well informed and articulate. It makes me nervous
> knowing there's a guy out there beating the bushes like that.
> You don't know whether he's making any sales, but he's
> sure making the calls.

One October midnight, walking down a deserted city street, a member shouted into the empty darkness at his unseen opponent, whose
campaign had been largely invisible, "Donald Fox! Why aren't you
campaigning? Donald Fox! Where the f_____ are you?" None of
these members expected defeat at the polls. (Their electoral totals
turned out to be 65 percent, 80 percent, and 70 percent respectively.)
Still, none would express certainty about the makeup of his reelection constituency.

Just as a new challenger may alter the reelection constituency, so
can a new issue. Often, of course, new challengers mean new issues.
Members of Congress face this uncertain prospect, too. "You never
can tell what's going to get people excited. You worry about this
vote and that vote, but something you hadn't expected comes right
out of the blue." Most issues are predictable. But it is the possibility
of the unexpected event that worries members. None of the four
Republicans with whom I traveled in the fall of 1972 could have
predicted that before the next election he would face the issue of

the impeachment or resignation of his party's president. Yet one of the four was defeated because of it. So too were other Republicans. For some Democrats, the recent flaring of the busing issue has had similar consequences. Such examples of their fallen comrades are imbibed by the House members who survive, adding issue uncertainty to their store of electoral worries.

If, of course, members of Congress knew for sure which of their campaign efforts succeed in holding or attracting which kinds of supporters, they might be more sure of just who supports them and who does not, or who might be persuaded to do so. The fact is, however, that although representatives campaign furiously — and sometimes quite systematically — against their challengers, there remains a sizable residue of uncertainty as to which campaign activity is related to which element of their support. "I'm skeptical of just about everything we do in a campaign. I don't know whether anything we do does any good." "You never know in this business. I spent $75,000; but you piss it away and you never know whether it did you any good." "I've never been able to figure out any correlation between the amount of handshaking I do and the number of votes I get." "Seventy-five percent of all the money we spend in a campaign is wasted. But we don't know which 75 percent." [10] They worry about reelection support because they don't know for sure how to go about getting reelected. They know how they campaigned last time. And they know that they won. But they do not know, in the manner of a statistical analysis, how much of what kind of campaigning contributed how much to their victory. They often decide, therefore, to campaign "just the way we did last time." But the nagging uncertainty they feel about the effectiveness of "the campaign" only adds to whatever other uncertainties they may feel as they contemplate their reelection constituencies.

Members of Congress do have an idea of who votes for them and who does not. And their perceptions are probably more accurate more often than are the perceptions of anyone else in their districts, though we have no way of checking. Our assumption is that because their jobs depend on it, the members will work harder than others to achieve a reasonable level of perceptual accuracy. So we should not leave this section with the notion that our representatives have no idea who their supporters are. They have a pretty good idea. Our point is only that when members think about their electoral support, they do so with a good deal less certainty in their minds than we might previously have guessed. They worry a lot. They exhibit great caution in making perceptual judgments. Their favorite electoral exercise is "worst case analysis." They rarely allow themselves the luxury of feeling "safe" electorally. They do not take their reelection constituency for granted. Political scientists cannot know these things by reading election statistics. When we generalize about their electoral situations, we must supplement our statistical perspective with a perceptual one.

THE PRIMARY CONSTITUENCY:
THE STRONGEST SUPPORTERS

In thinking about their political condition, House members make distinctions *within* their reelection constituency, thus giving us a third, still smaller perceptual circle. Having distinguished between their nonsupporters and their supporters, they further distinguish between their weak supporters and their strong supporters. Weak supporters come in both the routine and the temporary varieties. Routine supporters do no more than vote for the member, often simply following party identification. Temporary supporters back the member as the best available alternative "this time," as "the lesser of two evils." Strong supporters display an intensity capable of producing additional political activity, and they tender their support "through thick and thin," regardless of who the challenger may be. Within each reelection constituency, then, nests a smaller constituency perceived as "my strongest supporters," "my loyalists," "my true believers," "my political base," "my hard core," "my nucleus," "my tough nut," "my bread basket." We shall think of these people as the ones each congressman believes would provide his last line of electoral defense in a primary contest, and label them the *primary constituency*.[11] We do not mean this label to include all the people who vote for him in a primary, only those from whom he expects a special solidity of support in a primary election.

A protected congressional seat is one protected as much from primary defeat as from general election defeat. And a primary constituency is something every congressman must have one of.

> Everybody needs some group which is strongly for him — especially in a primary. You can win a primary with 25,000 zealots. . . . The most exquisite case I can give you was in the very early war years. I had very strong support from the

> antiwar people. They were my strongest supporters and they made up about 5 percent of the district.
>
> To be honest with you, I couldn't have a difficult primary. No, I grew up with the party people and have kept up with them through the years. I've been in and out of the party machinery since I was in college. . . . I've been in the home of every person active in the Republican party in my district. I've stayed in many of their homes overnight. Before we had many motels out in the rural areas, it was tradition that you stay with the party people overnight. I have an ideal relationship with the party people. Nobody could touch me in a primary.

In these cases, "the antiwar people" and "the party people" are the primary constituency. For each member, this inner constituency will probably include his earliest supporters — those who recruited him and those who tendered identifiably strong support in his first campaign.[12] From its ranks will most likely come the bulk of his financial help and most of his volunteer workers. From its ranks will least likely come his electoral challenger.

The primary constituency, we would guess, draws a special measure of a congressman's attention:

> When I look around to see who I owe my career to, to see those people who were with me in 1970 when I really needed them and when most people thought I couldn't win — these are the people I think I owe.

And it should, therefore, draw a special measure of ours. But it is not easy to delineate — for us or for them. Asked to describe his "very strongest supporters," one member replied, "That's the hardest question anyone has to answer." The primary constituency is more subtly shaded than the reelection constituency, where voting (or polling) results can provide an objective membership test. In the primary constituency, the test for inclusion and exclusion goes beyond a vote, to the intensity and the durability of one's support. And political loyalty is not the most fathomable of human qualities. Also, members resist drawing invidious distinctions among their supporters, as if it were only borrowing trouble to begin classifying people according to their fidelity. Despite the difficulty, most members will, because they must, make some such distinctions.

Members who have recently fought a primary election or who are actively contemplating one may be the most able and willing to identify their hard-core support. Thus, the member quoted earlier as saying "for the first time in my life I feel safe," but who worries nonetheless about a prospective primary, was asked who would support him in such a primary. He replied without hesitation,

> Organized labor. I can't imagine that organized labor would abandon me for him. There will be a few disgruntled ones who may support him. But organized labor will be my base of support.

A member whose testing election had been a primary two years before has a fairly elaborate perception of his current primary constituency:

> My hard-core support are the people who were with me in the primary, many of whom have gone on to make political careers of their own. . . . I'd say there are about 25 of these core supporters throughout the district. . . . They will come if we need them and stay till the bitter end. Then there is another ring that we could get almost immediately — Sarah could get 300, Mary Lou 100 — I'd say that number would be about 400 or maybe 500 or 600. Then we have a support list of about . . . 4000 people . . . whom we would call upon and with whom we have a personal relationship.

This comment suggests that within a primary constituency there may exist further gradations of special support — a subset of concentric circles. Because most members do not readily elaborate these gradations, we shall think of the primary constituency mostly by distinguishing it from the less supportive reelection constituency. For now, that task is challenge enough.

Answers to the question, "Who are your very strongest supporters?" provide a starting point. A Democrat and a Republican replied:

> My strongest supporters are the working class, the blacks, and labor, organized labor. And the people who were in my state legislative district, of course. The fifth ward is low income, working class and is my base of support. I grew up there; I have my law office there; and I still live there. The

> white businessmen who are supporting me now are late converts — very late. They support me as the lesser of two evils. They are not a strong base of support. They know it and I know it.

> I have a circle of strong labor supporters and another circle of strong business supporters. . . . They will "fight, bleed, and die" for me, but in different ways. Labor gives you the manpower and the workers up front. You need them just as much as you need the guy with the three-acre yard to hold a lawn party to raise money.

Each answer reveals the working politician's penchant for inclusive thinking. Each tells us something about a primary constituency, but each leaves plenty of room for added refinements.

We have tried to make such refinements by observing, as well as by talking with, the congressman as he comes in contact with various constituents. For both he and they act' and talk in ways that help us delineate the "very strongest supporters." Like other observers of American politics, I have found the touchstone of "at homeness" a useful one in helping me to sort the relationship between politicians and their varied constituents.[13] Does the congressman seem to be "at home" or comfortable in the presence of this group or these people? The assumption is that he will be most at home with his strongest supporters and least at home among his most determined nonsupporters.

Members make it pretty clear when they are not at home in a situation. Climbing out of the car at a small-town country club, one member said,

> This is the hardest thing for me to do, talk to these small-town businessmen. Nothing mean happens, but it's very uncomfortable for me. They won't support me anyway and they'll find more reasons for it after they've heard me.

Riding through the black neighborhoods of a city, a white congressman who says, "I concede the black vote," exchanged observations with his district staffer:

> *Staffer:* I wouldn't want to be out there walking on the sidewalk.
> *Congressman:* It's like some Caribbean country.
> *Staffer:* It sure is a different country here.

For these two representatives, "small-town businessmen" and "the black vote" lie outside their respective reelection constituencies. Gradations of at homeness will be, of course, less stark within the reelection constituency itself.

House members do, however, make such gradations in talking about their reelection constituencies — more easily in heterogeneous than in homogeneous districts. A Republican representative who had been redistricted from a wholly urban into a partly suburban district said, "My old district was easier to run in. I've never felt representative of Madison County strangely enough — because it is more Republican than the city. I don't feel comfortable in surburbia." Moving about the district stimulates these kinds of distinctions.

> I was born on the flat plains, and I feel a lot better in the plains area than in the mountain country. I don't know why it is. As much as I like Al [a county party chairman whom we had just lunched with in a mountain town], I'm still not completely comfortable with him; I'm no cowboy. But when I'm out there on that flat land with those ranchers and wheat farmers, standing around trading insults and jibes and telling stories, I feel better. That's the place where I click.

It is also the place where he wins elections — his primary constituency. "That's my strong area. I won by a big margin there (last time) and offset my losses. If I win next time, that's where I'll win it — on the plains." Obviously, there is no one-to-one relationship between the groups with whom a congressman acts and feels most at home and his primary constituency. But it does provide an observer with a pretty good unobtrusive clue.

I found myself, therefore, fashioning a highly subjective *at-homeness index* to rank each congressman's rapport with and support from the various people he meets.[14] In my earliest travels, I watched a man whose district is predominantly Jewish participating in an afternoon installation of officers ceremony at a Young Men's Hebrew Association attended by about forty civic leaders from the local community. He drank some spiked punch, began the festivities by saying, "I'm probably the first tipsy installation officer you ever had," told an emotional story about his personal dependence on the YMHA, and traded banter with his friends in the audience throughout the ceremony.

> *Congressman:* . . . and so I decided to name my son "Morris
> Irving Berman," after the man who was the founder and
> greatest benefactor of my boyhood Young Men's Hebrew
> Association.
> *Friend calling from audience:* Well, it's a good thing you
> didn't name him "44th Street Y!"

That evening, as we prepared to meet with yet another and much
larger (Democratic party) group, I asked where we were going. He
said, "We're going to a shitty restaurant to have a shitty meal with
a shitty organization and have a shitty time." And he did; he went
from high to midway on the at-homeness index. On the way home,
after the meal, he talked about the group:

> Ethnically, most of them are with me. But I don't always
> support the party candidate, and they can't stand that. . . .
> This group and half the other party groups in the district
> are against me. But they don't want to be against me too
> strongly for fear I might go into a primary and beat them.
> So self-preservation wins out. . . . They know they can't beat
> me.

Both groups are Jewish. The evening group was part of his reelection constituency, but not his primary constituency. The afternoon
group was part of both.

In delineating the primary constituency, observation of the congressman in action often provided a necessary corrective to his own
statements. For example, watching the congressman quoted earlier
as saying that he had equal sized circles of labor and business supporters indicated strongly that the labor group was larger than the
business group. Having recently defeated an incumbent, he drew a
standing ovation at his city's Labor Temple when he was introduced
with, "Isn't it nice for the ordinary working man to have a congressman again?" During his talk, he spoke personally to supporters in
the audience: "Kenny, you get a lot of complaints in your job.
When you get them, I hope you'll let me know." "Ralph, it's good
to see you here. You helped in the election. I hope you'll continue
to help me." Afterward, he stayed for an hour and a half to drink
beer, eat salami, and mingle. The next day, he attended the annual
Christmas luncheon of his city's businessmen. He received neither
an introduction nor applause when the main speaker acknowledged

his presence, saying, "I see our congressman is here; and I use the term 'our' loosely." He was not asked to speak or even to stand up; and we left early. He seemed vastly more at home in the union hall than at the businessmen's luncheon. And though there are doubtless some businessmen who support him strongly, I came to discount their putative equality within his primary constituency.

Because of their uncertainty, perhaps, House members have a tendency to talk more inclusively than they act. There are nuances revealed in action that do not appear in words. In elucidating their perception of a given constituency, therefore, observation of their behavior in context can give a sharper contour to their comments. This is especially true and especially helpful with the primary constituency.

THE PERSONAL CONSTITUENCY: THE INTIMATES

Within the primary constituency, House members perceive still a fourth, and final, concentric circle. These are the few individuals whose relationship with the member is so personal and so intimate that their relevance cannot be captured by any description of "very strongest supporters." Some of them are his closest political advisers and confidants. Others are people from whom he draws emotional sustenance for his political work. They are all people with whom the congressman has shared some crucial experience — usually early in his career, and often the "testing election." Times of relaxation are thick with reminiscence. Fellow feeling is heavily "we few, we happy few, we band of brothers." Sometimes a staff assistant is among these intimates; sometimes not. Sometimes the member's spouse is involved, but not always. These are the people, if any, to whom he has entrusted his political career. He can meet with all of them in one place, face to face, as he cannot with any of his other constituencies. He knows them by name, as individuals. He thinks of them as his friends. "A guy is lucky in politics," said one congressman. "He's carried here by his friends and he is kept here by his friends. That gives you a nice feeling." We shall think of these politically and emotionally supportive friends as the member's *personal constituency*.

One Sunday afternoon, I sat in the living room of a congressman's chief district staff assistant ("He is my best friend. . . . I trust him more than anyone in the world"), watching an NFL football game with the congressman, the district aide, the state assemblyman from the congressman's home county, and the district attorney of the same county. The last three were among the five people with whom the congressman had held his first strategy meeting four years earlier, at the time he decided to run for Congress. Between plays and at halftime, over beer and cheese, the four friends discussed every aspect of the congressman's campaign, listened to and commented on his taped radio spots, analyzed several newspaper reports, discussed local and national personalities, relived old political campaigns and hijinks, and discussed their respective political ambitions. Ostensibly they were watching the football game. Actually, the congressman was exchanging political advice, information, and perspectives with three of his oldest and closest political associates.

Another congressman begins his weekends at home by having a Saturday morning 7:30 coffee and doughnut breakfast in a cafe on the main street of his home town with a small group of old friends from the Rotary Club. The morning I was there, the congressman, a retired banker, a hardware store owner, a high school science teacher, a retired judge, and a past president of the city council gossiped and joked about local matters — the county historian, the library, the board of education, the churches, and their lawns — for an hour. "I guess you can see what an institution this is," he said as we left.

> You have no idea how invaluable these meetings are for me. They keep me in touch with my home base. If you don't keep your home base, you don't have anything. I'm still considered a local community leader, and though I don't like to get into community affairs too deeply, I have to know what's going on.

The congressman took no advice from this "gossipy group of old men." ("There just isn't any group I go to for advice.") They are his "home base" because they keep him in contact with his community roots. When he moved to town as a young lawyer, these were the men who befriended him and launched his career.

> [They] propelled me into the Rotary Club over the dead bodies of several local attorneys who had been trying to get

in for years, and over the dead bodies of the two attorneys
who already were members. It was a key move for me, because it put me in contact with the business community in
town – all 120 of them.

In the company of these "dear friends of mine," his oldest and
least selfish friends, he relaxes, reminds himself of his political
origins, and recharges his emotional batteries.

The personal constituency of a third congressman is focused more
purposefully on his election campaign. They are his "volunteer committee," a group of nine or ten men and women who run his campaign each year and whom he thinks of as his "core group" of
supporters or, simply "the group."

> We're a group of people who have the same philosophy of
> government – we are philosophical soul mates. We all be-
> lieve that people should be involved in their government.
> We've all been in politics and all came to the group through
> the Republican party. And then there is an emotional grab.
> We all like each other.

Like the other two sets of intimates, the volunteer committee has
nothing whatever to do with his activity in Washington. "I never
call them together to ask how I should vote." They tend his career
at home. On the one occasion when a personal problem put that
career in jeopardy, the congressman assembled "the group" for
advice:

> I had to decide whether I should kill myself, resign from
> office, not run again next time or stay and fight it out or
> what. So I called the core group together, and we discussed it.
> That was a classic example of consultation – at a turning
> point in my career.

I spent a long February evening listening to the volunteer committee plus the congressman and his daughter lay out the themes,
organization, and budget allocations for the fall campaign. More
overtly political than either of the other two occasions described, it
nonetheless had a heavy dosage of "remembering when," reminding
them of what they had already been through together, coupled
with a display of good humored affection for the man who is so
reliant upon them.

Those three examples indicate how idiosyncratic the personal constituency probably is. Not all representatives will open it up to the outside observer. Nine of the eighteen did, however; and in doing so, each usually revealed a side of his personality not seen by the rest of his constituencies. "I'm really very reserved, and I don't feel at home with most groups — only with five or six friends," said the congressman after the football game. So generalizations are hard to come by. The relationship probably has both political and emotional dimensions. If there is a generalization to be made beyond that, the presence of the personal constituency reminds us of a crucial decision made by every member of Congress — indeed, by every person in political life. The question is: Whom shall I *trust?* The various circles of friends I have observed in action represent answers to that question. They are, of course, "home" answers, not Washington answers. But decisions on whom to trust at home may be as important to the success of his political career as any others a representative makes. Unless we identify these trusted intimates, we shall fall short of understanding the total milieu in which the congressman lives when he is in his "constituency."

CONCLUSION

Each member of Congress perceives four concentric constituencies: geographic, reelection, primary, and personal. This is not the only way a member sees his or her "constituency"; but it is one way. It is a set of perceptions that emphasizes the context in which, and the strategies by which, the House member seeks electoral support. It is a complicated context, one featuring varying scopes of support and varying intensities of support. The strategies developed for getting and keeping electoral support involve the manipulation of these scopes and intensities. We have taken each member's perceptions as we found them, and have not asked how he or she came by them in the first place. Later chapters, however, may shed light on the matter.

A perceptual analysis of congressional constituencies both complicates and clarifies efforts of political science to understand the relationship between congressman and constituency. It complicates matters both conceptually and statistically. For example, political scientists have a heavy investment in role conceptions that distinguish between the "trustee" who follows his independent judgment and the "delegate" who follows the wishes of his constituency.

But we now must ask, which constituency? And we cannot be content with a conceptual scheme that provides only two answers to this question: "the district" and "the nation." [15] More frequent, we think, than this kind of choice is one in which the congressman must choose among constituencies *within* the district. Also, when studies of party voting conclude that a member of Congress can vote independently because he or she "knows the constituency isn't looking," [16] we need to ask again, which constituency? One of the several constituencies may very well be looking.

Similarly, the variables we have used as surrogates for "the constituency" in our statistical analyses (for instance, in relating roll calls to constituency characteristics) have described only the geographical constituency — typically derived from census data. Rarely have we used variables capable of differentiating the other three constituencies, individually or collectively. A perceptual analysis warns us of the hazards of these oversimplified conceptualizations and representations of "the constituency." The most useful "first difference" to incorporate into our studies is that between the geographical constituency and the other three *supportive constituencies*. That is a distinction and a terminology we shall try to retain throughout, making added refinements where possible.

A perceptual analysis clarifies most by including the tremendous amount of uncertainty surrounding the House member's view of his or her electoral situation. Political scientists using the idea of electoral marginality to explain behavior, for example, will underestimate the effect of this uncertainty so long as they rely wholly on numerical indicators of electoral safety. Similarly, although political scientists may ask, in the manner of a regression analysis, which campaign activity contributed how much to the election results, a view from over the member's shoulder may reveal that he or she does not think in terms of the weights of variables. We might help ourselves by seeing the electoral situation the way the members see it, to ask ourselves the questions they ask: How much did I win by? Who supported me? Who worked especially hard for me? What net effect did the changes from last time have on the outcome this time? If members of Congress are more uncertain than we think they are and if they calculate more configuratively than we think they do, we might find these altered perspectives worth assimilating into our knowledge. Later, when we find House members acting conservatively, unwilling to take risks, preoccupied with self-preservation and relying on their homegrown rules of thumb, we shall at least be aware of the perceptions underlying such postures.

NOTES

1. Not surprisingly, the point was made eloquently ten years ago in an essay by Ralph K. Huitt, "Congress, The Durable Partner" in *Lawmakers in a Changing World*, ed. Elke Frank (Englewood Cliffs: Prentice-Hall, 1966). For some recently collected evidence, see Donald R. Matthews and James A. Stimson, *Yeas and Nays: Normal Decision Making in the U.S. House of Representatives* (New York: Wiley, 1975), pp. 28–31.
2. Marginal districts probably tend to be heterogeneous. But safe districts probably are both heterogeneous and homogeneous. On the relationship of electoral conditions to homogeneity and heterogeneity, I owe a lot to my conversations with Morris Fiorina. See Morris Fiorina, *Representatives, Roll Calls and Constituencies* (Boston: Lexington, 1974).
3. For the eighteen House members studied, the objective measure that coincides most closely with their subjective judgment appears to be an urban-suburban-rural measure. If we used a classification scheme in which homogeneous districts are those which fall by 75 percent or more into one of those three categories and in which all districts not meeting that standard are called heterogeneous, that scheme would coincide with the subjective judgment of fourteen of the eighteen representatives in this study. No other immediately available measure "works" as well. But because the underlying logic has not been developed, the idea is put forward merely as "interesting."
4. On the usefulness of this distinction see Donald Stokes and Warren Miller, "Party Government and the Saliency of Congress," *Public Opinion Quarterly* 26 (Winter 1962): 531–546. In Michael Barone, Grant Ujifusa, and David Matthews, *Almanac of American Politics* (Boston: Gambit, 1974), the authors often describe congressional districts as artificial, containing no natural community of interest (e.g., pp. 86, 133, 146, 162, 376, 402, 419, 473, 616).
5. John Kingdon, *Candidates for Office: Beliefs and Strategies* (New York: Random House, 1966), chap. 3. In her study of congressional challengers in New York, Linda Fowler finds that some did not perceive or think in terms of an electoral "coalition." Linda Fowler, "The Cycle of Defeat: Recruitment of Congressional Challengers," unpublished manuscript, University of Rochester, 1977. When asked to describe his "supporters," one congressman in my group answered, "That's very hard to evaluate. I never thought in terms of groups. . . . I never thought of my support as coming from groups. The middle group, I guess, homeowners. It's very hard to say." The importance of the reelection constituency is well argued (though not subsequently employed) in Aage Clausen, *How Congressmen Decide: A Policy Focus* (New York: St. Martin's, 1973), p. 126.
6. Charles Bullock, "House Careerists: Changing Patterns of Longevity and Attrition," *American Political Science Review* 66 (December 1972): 1295–1300.
7. In the period from 1960 to 1972, 189 House members were defeated for renomination or reelection — 39 in primary elections and 150 in general elections. Considering marginal districts to be those in which the defeated incumbent had 55 percent or less of the two-party vote in the previous election, 72 percent (28) of the primary defeats came in safe districts. By

comparison, 42 percent (63) of the general election defeats came in safe districts.

8. Robert Erikson, "A Reappraisal of Competition for Congressional Office: How House Careers Begin and End," paper presented at Conference on Mathematical Models of Congress, Aspen, Colorado, 1974, table 5.

9. Donald B. Johnson and James R. Gibson, "The Divisive Primary Revisited: Party Activists in Iowa," *American Political Science Review* 68 (March 1974): 67–77.

10. Representatives trying to sell themselves to an audience in campaigns operate with the same uncertainties as advertising executives trying to sell products to a TV audience. As one Xerox executive said, "The questions that plague everyone are what good do the commercials do for Xerox and do they sell more machines. Who is that guy in Philadelphia who said years ago that half my advertising budget is wasted, but which half? You can't figure that out. Everybody's tried to measure it." *Rochester Democrat and Chronicle*, December 8, 1975.

11. The term is from Leo Snowiss, "Congressional Recruitment and Representation," *American Political Science Review* 60 (September 1966): 629–639.

12. In their study of the Iowa legislature, Patterson, Hedlund, and Boynton found that among the constituents legislators designated as people they might turn to for advice, there was a good deal of recruitment activity. Samuel C. Patterson, Ronald D. Hedlund, and G. Robert Boynton, *Representatives and Represented: Bases of Public Support for the American Legislatures* (New York: Wiley, 1975), pp. 86–94. Occasionally, electoral challengers do come from the very heart of a member's primary constituency — his own staff. Many Washington and district staffers run for the seat of their employer when he retires. Some cannot wait that long. One of my members was opposed (unsuccessfully) by a former Washington staff member. Staffers are tempted to believe that they could do a better job and that their own district contacts have given them a local base of support. One reason some members give for keeping their district staffs small and strictly clerical is to discourage the breeding of such temptations.

13. For example, Theodore H. White, *The Making of the President: 1960* (New York: Atheneum, 1961), pp. 276–78; Marshall Frady, *Wallace* (New York: New American Library, 1970), pp. 2–4, 38–39; Theodore H. White, *The Making of the President: 1972* (New York: Atheneum, 1973), pp. 147, 414–15, 456–57.

14. Near the end of my later travels, I began asking members to rank the events during my visit in terms of their comfortableness. They also ranked events in terms of their importance. For all of the more important events, members had no trouble ranking them for comfortableness. I used this as a check on my own observations, and found that my judgment was nearly always the same as theirs.

15. For example, see Roger Davidson, *The Role of the Congressman* (New York: Pegasus, 1973).

16. Stokes and Miller, "Party Government and the Saliency of Congress."

CHAPTER TWO

Home Style: Allocation of Resources

HOME STYLE

What do the House member perceptions in Chapter One have to do with House member actions? The question of behavior naturally follows the question of perception. But what kind of behavior? Where? And with respect to what? The conventional political science answer would be: Behavior in Congress. How, we would ask, do member constituency perceptions affect their committee work, their voting record, their influence, their allegiances, their accomplishments — on Capitol Hill? These are legitimate, fascinating, time-honored questions. But they focus on a context removed from the one in which members puzzle out their several constituencies. The concern that generates and disciplines the perceptions we have just described is neither first nor foremost a Washington-centered concern. It is a concern for political support at home. Representatives and prospective representatives think about their constituencies because they seek support in their constituencies. They want to be nominated and elected, then renominated and reelected. For most members of Congress most of the time, this electoral goal is primary. It is the prerequisite for a congressional career and, hence, for the pursuit of other member goals. And the electoral goal is achieved — first and last — not in Washington but at home.

Of course, House members do many things in Washington that affect their electoral support at home. Political scientists interpret much of their behavior in Washington, particularly their voting records, as a bid for the support of their constituents.[1] Equipped with the more complex view of "their constituents" elaborated in Chapter One, we could, if we wished, reexplore the electoral rationale behind voting patterns in Congress. It is hoped that some political scientists will do exactly that. But the experience of traveling with members in their districts turns one's attention in a different direction. For one sees House members working to maintain and enlarge their political support at home by going to the district and doing things *there*. What they do at home to win support is not, of course, unrelated to what they do in Washington to win support. And we shall have some thoughts on the linkages later. But the starting point of this research — *behavior at home* — is a departure from the more conventional starting point, behavior in Washington.

Those who do political science research on Congress have, because of their Washington focus, systematically underestimated the proportion of their working time that representatives spend in their districts. As a result, we have also underestimated its perceived importance to them. In all existing studies of congressional time allocation, for example, time spent outside of Washington is simply not counted. So, political scientists talk about "the average work week of a congressman" as if he never left Washington. We have tallied and compared the amount of time members spend in committee, on the House floor, doing research, helping constituents with their problems — but all of it in Washington.[2] Yet thirteen of my representatives — those whose appointment and travel records I have been able to check carefully for 1973, a nonelection year — averaged twenty-four trips to the district and spent an average of eighty-three days in their districts that year. That is, on the average, they went home every other week for about three and a half days. A survey conducted in 419 House offices indicated that the average number of trips home during 1973 (not counting recesses) was 35, and the average number of days spent in the district (counting recesses) was 138 days.[3] No fewer than 131, nearly one-third, of the 419 members went home to their districts every single weekend. Obviously, the direct personal cultivation of the House members' four constituencies takes a great deal of their time. They must think it helps them win and hold political support. If they think it is worthwhile to go home so much, it should be worthwhile for political scientists to take a commensurate degree of interest in what they do there and why.

As they cultivate their constituencies, members of Congress display what I shall call their *home style*. When they discuss the importance of what they are doing, they are discussing the importance of an individual's home style to the achievement of his electoral goal. The remainder of this book will be mostly about home style — its elements, its antecedents, its varieties, its transformations, its consequences, and its relation to each member's perceived constituencies. Succeeding chapters will be organized around three basic ingredients of home style. The first is the congressman's *allocation* of his personal resources and those of his office. The second is the congressman's *presentation* of self to others. The third is the congressman's *explanation* of his Washington activity to others. Every congressman allocates, presents, and explains. And a large part of this activity takes place in the district. Each member's amalgam of these three activities — as manifested in the district — constitutes his or her home style.

ALLOCATION OF RESOURCES: TIME AND STAFF

Every member of Congress makes a basic decision with regard to his or her home style: How much and what kinds of attention shall I pay to home? Or, to put it another way: Of all the resources available to me, which kinds and how much of each shall I allocate to activity at home? For now, "home" means the geographical constituency, "the district." And the allocative decisions we study are those concerning distribution of resources between the district and Washington. The job of a congressman requires that some things be done in Washington and others be done in the district. At the least, legislation is passed in one place and elections occur in the other. The allocative problem, therefore, comes with the job. And this built-in strain between the need to attend to Washington business and the need to attend to district business affects the work of each individual and the work product of the institution. The strain is both omnipresent and severe. Members give up the job because of it. Congressional reforms are advocated to alleviate it. The allocative decisions we shall examine represent, individually and collectively, House members' efforts to cope with it.

There are, of course, different resources to allocate between Washington and the district, and alternative ways to allocate those resources. Our concern is with resources allocated directly to the district. And the resources we shall examine are the House member's *time* and the House member's *staff*. How much time to spend physically in the district and how much staff to place physically in the district are among the most basic of a member's allocative decisions. Separately and together they help shape each member's home style.

Time is a House member's scarcest and most precious political resource. If there is an exemplary congressional complaint, surely "there isn't enough time" must be it. In deciding how to spend his time, in Washington, in the district and, for our purposes, between Washington and the district, a member confronts his most difficult allocative dilemma. When he is doing something at home, he must give up doing some things in Washington and vice versa. He must choose and trade off. Different representatives make different allocative choices and different allocative trades.

We shall focus, first, on the frequency with which various representatives returned to their districts in 1973. "This is a business, and like any business you have to make time and motion studies," said one member. "All we have is time and ourselves, so we have to calculate carefully to use our time productively." It is not true, of course, that "all" the congressman has is time and himself. The office carries with it a large number of ancillary resources — a staff, office space, office expense allowances, free mailing privileges, personal expense accounts — all of which occupy our attention when we detail the advantages of incumbency. Each congressman chooses how he will use these resources. The most significant of these choices involve the use of staff. If "Whom shall I appoint to my staff?" ranks first in importance, "How shall I distribute my staff between Washington and the district" ranks next. Therefore, our second focus will be on this distributive decision. We shall examine one indicator of it — the percentage of a member's total expenditure on staff salaries he allocates to the salaries of his district staff.[4]

The information on trips home and staff allocation was collected on Capitol Hill in June 1974. Six students, each of whom had just finished working for four months, full time, in a House member's office, conducted a survey by visiting every member's office and talking to his or her administrative assistant or personal secretary. The question about the frequency of member trips home usually produced an educated estimate (e.g., "every week," "once a month," "every other week"). The question about staff allocation yielded more precise answers. Each student presented the *Report of the Clerk of the House* for 1973, with its list of each representative's staff members and their salaries; and the person answering simply designated which staff members were located in the district. A briefer, follow-up survey was conducted by four students with similar "Hill experience" in May 1975. This survey added to the store of information on those 1973 members who were still in Congress. It produced a little information, too, on the first-termers of that year.[6] In 1973, it should be noted, each representative was reimbursed for thirty-six round trips to his or her district. Members were not, of course, required to use any of these allowances to the maximum.

PERSONAL ATTENTIVENESS: TRIPS HOME. In 1973, members of Congress showed a good deal of personal attentiveness to their districts; but they also showed a lot of variation in the degree of their attentiveness. Members averaged thirty-five trips home that year; and the median number was thirty. But the least attentive of them went home four times, whereas the most attentive went home 365 times.[5] Because some members are home so seldom and others so much, there is considerable variation in home styles. So the question arises: Which members go home most often and which less so — and why? In this book we can only begin to answer the question. We can group House members according to the frequency with which they visit their districts. And we can then cross-tabulate these groupings with a number of factors that we might reasonably expect to be related. For this purpose we have grouped House members into three categories by frequency of 1973 trips home: *low* (less than twenty-four trips), *medium* (twenty-four to forty-two trips), *high* (more than forty-two trips).[6]

One reasonable supposition would be that representatives in electoral jeopardy will decide to spend more of their time at home than will representatives whose seats are well protected. As a generalization, however, this supposition receives no confirmation — not when political science's conventional measures of electoral safeness are used.

As Table 2.1 shows, the frequency of trips home does not increase as electoral margins decrease, or vice versa. There is just not much of a relationship at all.[7] But there is so much inherent plausibility to the original supposition that it probably should not be cast aside permanently. It may just be that our conventional indicators of electoral marginality are inadequate. Despite their extensive use, they have not helped to produce stable generalizations anywhere in the congressional literature.[8] Perhaps objective measures that cap-

Table 2.1
Trips Home and Electoral Margin

	Frequency of Trips Home (1973)			
Election Margin (1972)	Low (0–23)	Medium (24–42)	High (43+)	Total
Less than 55%	21 (29%)	28 (38%)	24 (33%)	73 (100%)
55–60%	18 (32%)	18 (32%)	20 (36%)	56 (100%)
61–65%	22 (27%)	17 (20%)	44 (53%)	83 (100%)
More than 65%	68 (33%)	66 (32%)	73 (35%)	207 (100%)
Total	129	129	161	419

Note: Gamma = −.03

tured more electoral history, included primary election information, and took into account the member's career stage would prove superior. But my experience, described in Chapter 1, inclines me to believe that subjective assessments of electoral safety are more valid. Electoral statistics cannot capture the uncertainty members feel about their renomination and reelection. (Nor can they capture any existing sense of security among members in objectively marginal districts.) Certainly, we cannot understand that uncertainty until we first figure out the logic underlying a member's assessment of his electoral situation. For now we can only guess that subjective assessments of electoral safeness (however arrived at) might be more strongly correlated with the frequency of trips to the district. But we cannot know. After all, members of Congress have other reasons for going home or staying in Washington.

A related hunch would lead us to expect that members who have been in office longer will spend less time at home. Part of the argument here overlaps with our previous one: the longer in office, the more secure the seat, the less the felt need to return to the district. But the more important, distinctive part of the reasoning would be that with increased seniority comes increased influence and responsibility in the House and, hence, the need to spend more time in Washington. The newcomer feels no such Washington pull. As one first-termer noted, "A congressman lives in two worlds, the one back home and the one in Washington. A freshman congressman can do more good at home than he can in Washington." A third leg of the argument might be that length of service correlates with age and that older members would return home less often than younger members because it would be more burdensome physically to do so. Our basic hunch is supported by the data — but not as strongly or as consistently as we had imagined. A simple correlation between terms of service and number of trips home shows that as seniority increases, home visits decrease — as we would expect. But the correlation is exceedingly weak.[9] And age appears to have little effect independent of seniority.[10] When the seniority data are grouped, however, the nature and the strength of the relationship become clearer.

Table 2.2 illustrates the relationship between the three categories of personal attentiveness and three levels of seniority. The summary statistics continue to be unimpressive. But the reason is that for the middle levels of seniority, no allocative pattern is evident. If we look only at the low and high seniority levels, it is clear that the frequency of trips home is much greater for the low seniority groups than it is for the high seniority group. The relationship between length of service and trips home, we conclude, is not a consistent, linear relationship. But for those at the beginning of their House careers and for those farthest along in their House careers, congressional longevity is likely to be one determinant of their time allocation decisions. The most senior member of my group, a man with important legislative responsibilities, spent twenty-one working days

Table 2.2
Trips Home and Seniority

	Frequency of Trips Home			
Seniority	Low (0–23)	Medium (24–42)	High (43+)	Total
Low (1–3 terms)	34 (22%)	44 (28%)	78 (50%)	156 (100%)
Medium (4–7 terms)	43 (28%)	59 (38%)	52 (34%)	154 (100%)
High (8+ terms)	52 (48%)	26 (24%)	31 (28%)	189 (100%)
Total	129	129	161	419
	(Mean seniority = 7.0 terms)	(Mean seniority = 5.0 terms)	(Mean seniority = 4.7 terms)	

Note: Gamma = −.30

at home in 1973. "I come home when I have something to do. If Paul [his district representative] says it's absolutely necessary, I'll come. . . . I may be at a stage in my career where I'll have to call in all my chips at home so that I can devote full time to legislation." By contrast, the least senior member of the group spent sixty-one working days at home in 1975. He said, "Our class works their districts much harder than the older congressmen. We're back here all the time." Congressional newcomers appear to be more single-minded in pursuing the electoral goal than are the veterans of the institution.

A third reasonable hunch would be that the more time-consuming and expensive it is to get to his district, the less frequently a congressman will make the trip. Leaving money aside, because we have no information on the private wealth of House members,[11] but recalling that for 1973 to 1974, each member was provided with a "floor" of thirty-six trips, we would expect to find that as distance from Washington increases the number of trips home decreases. It is not easy to get a measure of distance that captures each representative's actual door-to-door travel time. We shall use region as a surrogate for distance, on the theory that if any relationship is present, it will show up in a regional breakdown. And it does. Table 2.3

Table 2.3
Trips Home and Region

Region	Frequency of Trips Home			
	Low (0–23)	Medium (24–42)	High (43+)	Total
East[a]	5 (5%)	20 (20%)	76 (75%)	101 (100%)
South[b]	36 (35%)	32 (30%)	36 (35%)	104 (100%)
Border[c]	9 (26%)	10 (29%)	16 (45%)	35 (100%)
Midwest[d]	29 (28%)	47 (44%)	30 (28%)	106 (100%)
Far West[e]	50 (69%)	20 (27%)	3 (4%)	73 (100%)
Total	129	129	161	419

[a] Conn., Maine, Mass., N.H., N.J., N.Y., Pa., R.I., Vt.
[b] Ala., Ark., Fla., Ga., La., Miss., N.C., S.C., Tenn., Tex., Va.
[c] Del., Ky., Md., Mo., Okla., W.Va.
[d] Ill., Ind., Iowa, Kans., Mich., Minn., Nebr., N.Dak., Ohio, S.Dak., Wis.
[e] Alaska, Ariz., Calif., Colo., Hawaii, Idaho, Mont., Nev., N.Mex., Oreg., Utah, Wash., Wyo.

indicates that the members nearest Washington, D.C. (East) spend a good deal more time at home than do the members who live farthest away from the Capitol (Far West). The less Washington time members have to sacrifice to get home, the more likely they are to go. At least this proposition holds at the extremes of distance. If distance is a factor for the other three regional groups, it does not show up here. Our guess is that distance is a more problematical factor in those intermediate ranges.

Every member of Congress divides his or her time between work and family. If a member's family remains at home in the district, we would expect that member to return to the district more often than if the family moves to Washington. Table 2.4 strongly supports this supposition.[14] Almost nine out of ten (88 percent) representatives whose families remain at home fall into the high trips home category. Less than two in ten (17 percent) representatives whose families move to Washington fall in the high trips home category. To put the finding somewhat differently, the average number of trips home for House members with families in Washington was twenty-seven, for House members with families in the district, it was fifty-two, and for unmarried members the average was forty-four trips.

We have no basis for deciding whether the family decision produces the home style or whether the home style produces the family decision. That is, do members come home because their families decided to stay there, or do their families decide to remain at home because the member has decided to come home a lot? Both pro-

Table 2.4
Trips Home and Family Residence

| Family Residence | Frequency of Trips | | | |
	Low (0–23)	Medium (24–42)	High (43+)	Total
Washington area	87 (41%)	89 (42%)	37 (17%)	213 (100%)
District	3 (4%)	6 (8%)	69 (88%)	78 (100%)
Unmarried	5 (14%)	12 (32%)	20 (54%)	37 (100%)
Total	95	107	126	328

cesses seem plausible; and both are supported by interview data. Two midwestern members, each of whom considers his district marginal, explained:

> The family decided to split the school year — the first semester in Pikestown, the second semester in Virginia. So at first I was a weekend warrior. I was home every week up through January, to the end of the first semester. After January it dropped off to an average of twice a month. That lasted for the first two years. Then, when we sold our house in Pikestown and bought a home in Virginia, I stayed on the two trips a month routine.

> I came home every weekend for two years. That's how I got reelected. The two previous congressmen moved their families to Washington and became congressmen. They got to like Washington real fine; but they didn't come back home often enough. Both were defeated after one term. My family stayed in Hopeswell. . . . If my family had moved to Washington, I would have been home less and I would not have been reelected.

Whatever the logic, it is clear that some decisions about home style are family related.

To sum up thus far, the decision to allocate time between home and Washington is affected by seniority — whether his seniority is very high or very low. The decision is affected by the distance from Washington to home — if the distance is very long or very short. It is affected by the location of one's family — whether the family moves to Washington or stays in the district. The electoral margin, objectively measured, has little effect on time allocations. Other factors affecting these allocations, which are suggested by our interviews but for which we cannot collect across-the-board information, will be discussed later.

STAFF ATTENTIVENESS: DISTRICT STAFF STRENGTH. Members of Congress also decide what kind of staff presence they wish to establish in the district. Here, too, we find great variation. Our measure of district staff strength — the percentage of total staff expenditure allocated to district staff — yields percentages for 1973 as low as 0 percent and as high as 81 percent. A question arises as to whether members' decisions about staff vary systematically according to decisions about trips home. Intuitively, it seems plausible that a member whose decision to cultivate "home" is reflected in lots of trips there would display a consistent attentiveness to home by placing a large staff there. A congressman in office one month described his allocative decisions as complementary:

> I'll go home every weekend. . . . Yesterday morning at 6:00 I was at the Bluffton mill. Were people ever pleased and surprised. "We didn't think you'd be back." People get very impressed with themselves around here. I can't wait to get home every weekend. . . . We have eight staff in the district and six here [in Washington]. That's a first; at least we're saying it's a first. And we have three district offices. . . . My predecessor had one person in one office. People are going bananas. They've never seen anything like it.

Yet it is also plausible that a member may view personal and staff allocations as alternative rather than complementary ways of cultivating the district. If he cannot be there, he will allocate a large staff there; if he goes home a lot, he may feel no need to establish a sizable staff presence. "I was so available out there, traveling so much, that I didn't feel the need to beef up the district office. Since I've been in Washington more, I've strengthened the district office." When we correlate staff strength with trips home, however, neither relationship shows up very strongly. Such support as there is tends to favor — but very weakly — the complementary rather than the alternative mode.[13]

In Table 2.5 this relationship is investigated further. The table clusters and cross-tabulates the two allocative decisions. For our measure of district staff strength, we have divided the percentage of expenditures on district staff into thirds. The lowest third ranges from 0 to 22.7 percent; the middle third ranges from 22.8 to 33.5 percent; the highest third ranges from 33.6 to 81 percent. The cross-tabulation of Table 2.5 also shows a weak overall relationship between the decisions on time and staff. Again, the evidence points more toward the complementary than the alternative notion of the relationship. But it is the weakness of the finding that remains striking. If we had information on all 419 districts, on their homogeneity or heterogeneity for example, we might find patterns linking personal and staff attentiveness patterns to perceptions of the district. For now, however, we shall treat the two decisions as if they were made

Table 2.5
Trips Home and District Staff Expenditures

District Staff Expenditures	Frequency of Trips Home			Total
	Low (0–23)	Medium (24–42)	High (43+)	
Lowest third	53 (39%)	42 (31%)	40 (30%)	135 (100%)
Middle third	42 (30%)	55 (40%)	41 (30%)	138 (100%)
Highest third	31 (23%)	32 (23%)	75 (54%)	138 (100%)
Total	126	129	156	411

Note: Gamma = .28

independently of one another and, hence, deserve separate examination.

What kinds of House members, then, emphasize the value of large district staff operations? Once again, it turns out, they are not members in special electoral trouble. Table 2.6 displays the total lack of any discernible effect of electoral situation (objectively measured) on district staff strength. And, as indicated in Table 2.7, seniority also makes no difference in allocative decisions affecting staff. That it does not adds strength to our notion that the relationship be-

Table 2.6
District Staff Expenditures and Electoral Margin

Electoral Margin, 1972	District Staff Expenditures (1973)			Total
	Lowest Third	Middle Third	Highest Third	
Less than 55%	20 (27%)	28 (38%)	26 (35%)	74 (100%)
55–60%	20 (36%)	20 (36%)	16 (28%)	56 (100%)
61–65%	24 (29%)	29 (35%)	29 (35%)	82 (100%)
More than 65%	72 (36%)	61 (30%)	68 (34%)	201 (100%)
Total	136	138	139	413

Note: Gamma = −.04

Table 2.7
District Staff Expenditures and Seniority

Seniority	District Staff Expenditures			
	Lowest Third	Middle Third	Highest Third	Total
Low (1–3 terms)	45 (29%)	54 (35%)	56 (36%)	155 (100%)
Medium (4–7 terms)	44 (29%)	56 (37%)	51 (34%)	151 (100%)
High (8+ terms)	47 (44%)	28 (26%)	32 (30%)	107 (100%)
Total	136	138	139	413

Note: Gamma $= -.13$

tween seniority and home visits discovered earlier is accounted for by career and goal factors rather than electoral factors. If seniority showed equal importance in home trips and staff allocation, an electoral explanation would seem most plausible. But because seniority seems only to affect home visits, an explanation more closely related to home visits (i.e., the partial displacement over time of the reelection goal by the goal of influence in the House) seems most plausible. We shall return to this idea later in the book.

The other variables discussed earlier (family residence and distance from Washington) have no obvious implications for staff allocation. But the variable we used as a surrogate for distance — region — is revealing in its own right. Table 2.8 displays staff allocation patterns by region. It is a twin to Table 2.3, which related region to home visits. Table 2.8 reveals distinctively regional allocation patterns — some similar, some different from those in Table 2.3. Easterners, again, rank highest in the allocation of resources to the district. Far westerners no longer rank lowest; but neither do they appear to compensate strongly for their paucity of home visits with heavy staff allocations. Table 2.8 reveals other regional patterns that did not show up at all in Table 2.3. The southern and border regions emerge with distinctive patterns of staff allocation. To a marked degree, representatives from these two areas eschew large staff operations. If we combine tables 2.3 and 2.8, every region except the Midwest reveals a noteworthy pattern of resource allocation. In the East we find a high frequency of home visits and large district staffs. In the Far West, we find a low frequency of home visits. In the

Table 2.8
District Staff Expenditures and Region

Region	District Staff Expenditures			
	Lowest Third	Middle Third	Highest Third	Total
East[a]	16 (16%)	31 (31%)	52 (53%)	99 (100%)
South[b]	47 (46%)	36 (35%)	19 (19%)	102 (100%)
Border[c]	18 (55%)	8 (24%)	7 (21%)	33 (100%)
Midwest[d]	39 (37%)	34 (32%)	33 (31%)	106 (100%)
Far West[e]	16 (22%)	29 (40%)	28 (38%)	73 (100%)
Total	136	138	139	413

[a] Conn., Maine, Mass., N.H., N.J., N.Y., Pa., R.I., Vt.
[b] Ala., Ark., Fla., Ga., La., Miss., N.C., S.C., Tenn., Tex., Va.
[c] Del., Ky., Md., Mo., Okla., W.Va.
[d] Ill., Ind., Iowa, Kans., Mich., Minn., Nebr., N.Dak., Ohio, S.Dak., Wis.
[e] Alaska, Ariz., Calif., Colo., Hawaii, Idaho, Mont., Nev., N.M., Ore., Utah, Wash., Wyo.

southern and border regions, we find small district staffs. Region, we conclude, has a substantial effect on home style.

PERSONAL AND STAFF ATTENTIVENESS: SOME PATTERNS. Regions, however, are composites of several states. Although regional regularities often reflect state regularities, they can also hide them. Both situations are present in this instance. Table 2.9 displays state-by-state allocation patterns of personal and district staff attentiveness. For each state delegation we have computed the mean number of trips home made by its members in 1973. We have then divided the state delegations into those whose averages fell above and below the median number of trips for all House members (thirty trips). Also, for each state delegation, we computed an average of the percentage of staff expenditures allocated to the district staff by its members. We then divided the state delegations into those whose averages fell above and below the median percentage for all House members (29 percent). The result is a crude fourfold classification of states according to their combined personal and staff resource allocations to "home." The underlined states fall strongly into their particular patterns; the others display weaker tendencies. Each state is further identified by its regional classification.

There are, as Table 2.9 shows, distinctive state allocative patterns.

Table 2.9
Allocation Patterns: By State

District Staff Attentiveness	Personal Attentiveness	
	Above the Median in Trips Home	Below the Median in Trips Home
Above the median in district staff expenditures	Connecticut (E)[a] Massachusetts (E) New York (E) Tennessee (S) Illinois (MW) Maine (E) New Hampshire (E) Pennsylvania (E) Rhode Island (E) South Carolina (S) Vermont (E)	California (FW) Colorado (FW) Hawaii (FW) Idaho (FW) Iowa (MW) Kansas (MW) New Mexico (FW) Wyoming (FW)
Below the median in district staff expenditures	Kentucky (B) Maryland (B) North Carolina (S) Virginia (S) West Virginia (B) Delaware (B) Indiana (MW) Montana (FW) Ohio (MW)	Alabama (S) Arizona (FW) Florida (S) Louisiana (S) Minnesota (MW) Oklahoma (B) Oregon (FW) Washington (FW) Wisconsin (MW) Arkansas (S) Michigan (MW) Nebraska (MW) South Dakota (MW) Texas (S) Utah (FW)

[a] States that fall five trips or more above or below the median *and* whose district staff expenditures fall 5 percent or more above or below the median are underlined. States not listed fall on the median in one or both instances. Regional classifications are in parentheses.

Some were foreshadowed in the regional patterns. For example, the eastern states cluster in the high trips home category; and the far western states cluster in the low trips home category. Southern and border states cluster in the weak district staff category. Other state patterns, however, appear here for the first time. The large number of states clustering in both low trips home and small district staff categories, for example, were totally obscured in our regional data.

The relevance of state delegations to patterns of resource allocation at home will come as no surprise to students of Congress. There is virtually no aspect, formal or informal, of the legislative process on Capitol Hill that has not already revealed the importance of the state delegation.[14] How much that importance is the product of extensive communication among delegation members and how much the product of similar expectations emanating from similar districts has never been definitively answered. Nor can it be here. Most likely both processes are involved. State delegation members probably talk to one another about their allocative practices and follow one another's example and advice. Also, certain expectations and traditions probably develop within states, or within sections of states, so that members feel constrained to make resource allocations that are not too far out of line with those expectations. Perhaps they follow a successful predecessor in these matters.

Explaining distinctive regional and state allocation patterns is a good deal more difficult than discovering them. And only a few speculations will be attempted. The sharp separation between eastern and far western states in trips home is doubtless a function of distance. And, it now appears more strongly, some far western state delegations, particularly California's, do compensate for the infrequency of their home visits by maintaining a relatively large staff presence in the district. But, if California representatives invest heavily in this compensatory allocative strategy, why don't the representatives from Washington and Oregon do likewise? The research of John Macartney into the activity of congressional district staffs in California provides a clue. Macartney finds that the California district staffs are heavily populated by party activists and perform many partylike functions:

> The incumbent's staff, in short, allows him to attract and retain the nucleus of his personal political organization. . . .
> The incumbent fields a publicly paid team of experienced veterans to do a task they have succeeded in before, perhaps many times before, and which differs very little from their everyday jobs.[15]

The suggestion is, then, that in states with weak party organizations (e.g., California) district staffs may be large because they are surrogate electoral organizations. Yet Washington and Oregon are not known as strong party organization states.[16] Why are district staffs in those states smaller than California's? Perhaps Macartney's hunch should be broadened: The more a district staff is called on to perform electoral activity at home (for whatever reason), the larger it will be. Lacking any other studies like Macartney's to tell us what district staffs in particular areas actually do, we shall resist the temptation to roam about in Table 2.9 with this speculative proposition. Students of state politics are, however, invited to do so if they wish.

The decision of most southern and border-state representatives to spend relatively little on their district staff operations provides an interesting puzzle. Maryland and Virginia present special cases, because proximity to Washington allows the Washington staff to be, in effect, the district staff. For the other states we might offer a couple of explanations. One is simply that the demand for district staff services is greater, say, in the northeastern states than in the southern and border areas. The welfare-social services case load may be larger in the older, urbanized areas. And, although there is no absolute reason why heavy case loads must be handled by district staffs, writing to Washington is more difficult and less immediately satisfying than going personally to the district office for help. In a similar vein, district offices may be more likely to become ombudsmen on local matters (i.e., city problems) in older, urban areas, where party organizations traditionally handle all levels of problems and where the representative remains more tied to a local party organization than in the southern and border areas. Local political involvements, that is, will increase the case load of the district office.

A second, not inconsistent, explanation may be the tradition of highly personalized, nonbureaucratized politics in the southern and border areas. People there expect to deal directly with well-known, highly visible public officials rather than with faceless bureaucrats. For the congressman, the problem is not just that tradition runs counter to a big district staff. It is that a large district staff might give the necessary reputation and visibility to an ambitious district staffer, thereby turning him into a political competitor. Where personal relationships are traditional, the congressman must make sure that he monopolizes those relationships. Thus, fear of competition may keep district staffs small and clerical in areas where an entrepreneurial politics is strongest.

If, however, personal attentiveness is a tradition and a necessity in southern and border states, we would expect all states in these regions to rank equally high in this respect. Instead, we find considerable variety. At first glance, the variety seems to be related to distance, with states in the Near South receiving more attention than states in the Far South. But the marked difference among Kentucky, Tennessee, and Alabama would seem to require a more complex explanation, perhaps on a district-by-district basis. That, we cannot do. Finally, speaking of complexity, the similar disposition of resources by the conglomeration of states with low trips home and small district staffs in Table 2.9 defies even an explanatory guess. We shall have to know more about state and local politics and about the actual employment of resources at home before we can develop satisfying explanations.

The variation of allocative practices across regions and states indicates that home style is affected by the congressman's geographical constituency. That constituency, the district, is, after all, the closest thing to a "given" in his nest of perceptions. And we know from our studies of internal House politics that the geographical constituency has an important effect on individual allocative decisions there — on the choice of committee assignments, for example.[17] So we should not be surprised to find that home style is related to place. That raises a larger question about the allocation of resources and, more generally, about home style. Is a congressman's home style imposed on him, by the district he represents, or is a congressman's home style something he chooses and then imposes on his district? We shall consider that question and work our way toward an answer throughout the book. For now, we would only say that despite the evident effect of geographical constituency on home style, there is enough absence of regularity in Table 2.9 to indicate that the allocative aspects of home style are also a matter of individual choice.

Interviews help uncover other dimensions of individual choice. One, in particular, seems noteworthy. House members sometimes choose to allocate their resources to home in ways that deliberately sharpen the contrast between themselves and other members, past or present, with whom they will be compared. That is, instead of acquiescing in a regional or local allocative pattern they deliberately adopt a contrasting pattern in order to gain a stylistic identity for themselves as individuals.

A congressman who shares a metropolitan area with two other House members and has a one-person district staff answered the

question, Why don't you have a highly paid district staff like your
two colleagues? in this way:

> I wanted to submerge the district function. If you have a big
> staff, you create expectations, you encourage people to come
> to you and you get a huge case load. Secondly, I wanted
> to have the image that "Guy does it himself." If people know
> that Lola [the staff] is just a conduit, they will feel that the
> decision is made in Washington and is made by me. . . .
> I don't want anyone speaking for me. Thirdly, I wanted
> the casework done in the Washington office, so I would be
> better informed on who we are helping and how. . . .
> Finally, a little contrapuntal contrast with my two neighbors
> doesn't hurt me in my opinion. They play up district services
> and they have much better identification as the local con-
> gressmen than I could have. No matter what I did, I could
> never achieve the magnificent local identification they have.
> I would always stand in their shadow. They have created
> expectations that people don't have of me. . . . I'm trying to
> gain my identification in another way. So, there are several
> reasons. Put them all together, they spell Lola.

Another House member described his decision to come home a lot
as a self-conscious effort to create an identity different from that of
the powerful, recently retired member he had replaced:

> My predecessor paid no attention to his constituents and did
> not tend the district. His life was back there [in Washington]
> where he was a powerful figure because of his position and
> his native ability. He was terribly important to the major
> interests here. He was powerful and feared here. But he
> couldn't abide coming back here. He hated to fly. When he
> did come, he did everyone a favor, so to speak. And he
> touched the elites — the Chamber of Commerce, the local
> establishment. He would attend ceremonies and cut ribbons.
> But he didn't care about mingling with ordinary citizens.
> Everything I do is in contrast. He came home twice a year. I
> come home every month for a week, hold open houses all over
> the district, and talk to ordinary people. Out here, that makes
> news. It's nothing that lots of others don't do back East.
> But people see me as different because of the contrast with my
> predecessor.

Both these House members made allocative decisions at variance with accepted local practice. And, the point is, they did so as a matter of individual choice.

Even here geographical constraints still apply. The standard by which these two representatives judge their degree of contrast is a local, not a national, standard. The first member's two colleagues have 30 percent of their staff allocation in the district — no better than the median figure nationally. And the second member's once-a-month home visits are far below the national average. They remind us that there is no one national allocative standard against which all House members can be compared. The overall picture is, then, one in which allocative practices result from an interaction between individual choice and geographically related constraints.

CONCLUSION

In Chapter One, we discovered that House members have a fairly complicated set of perceptions of "the constituency." In this chapter, we began to understand how they might come by such perceptions. In brief, they go home to their districts often and spend a lot of time there. Because the members apparently devote a considerable amount of their resources to home activity, political scientists need to devote more of their resources to studying that activity. We have categorized member activity at home as allocating resources, presenting themselves, and explaining their Washington behavior. And we have labeled the combination of these three activities as home style.

Our examination of the allocation of personal and staff resources to the district indicates that we can expect a wide variety of home styles among House members. Among the factors that appear to influence the allocation of a representative's time and money to his or her district are personal goals, family residence, distance, established local expectations, and the desire to create new local expectations. From our aggregate analysis, therefore, we know that the allocative aspects of home style are the product of both personal and constituency factors. There is a lot left unanswered, particularly questions about the effect of electoral uncertainty and of local political patterns on allocative styles. Answers here must await new or different data. But if we take with us our conclusion about the importance of individual choice and contextual constraints in accounting for varieties of style, we shall have a useful perspective with which to study some individual cases in the next two chapters.

NOTES

1. On constituency and voting, see John Kingdon, *Congressmen's Voting Decisions* (New York: Harper and Row, 1973). On the more general point, see David Mayhew, *Congress: The Electoral Connection* (New Haven: Yale University Press, 1974).
2. The basic research was done by John Saloma, and is reported in his *Congress and the New Politics* (Boston: Little, Brown, 1969, Chap. 6; in Donald Tacheron and Morris Udall, *The Job of the Congressman* (Indianapolis: Bobbs Merrill, 1966), pp. 280–88; and in *Guide to the Congress of the United States,* Congressional Quarterly (Washington, D.C., 1971), pp. 532–549. But no one has expanded Saloma's work beyond the Washington context. An intriguing analysis of Washington time budgets, based on an audit of incoming communications to a congressional subcommittee is David Kovenock, "Influence in the U.S. House of Representatives: A Statistical Analysis of Communications," *American Politics Quarterly* 4 (October 1973): 430–33, 440–44. A pioneer work, which would have given us a wider perspective, but which seems to have been neglected is Dorothy H. Cronheim, "Congressmen and Their Communication Practices," unpublished manuscript, Ann Arbor, Michigan, 1957.
3. The "total days home" figure (138) was based on 401 answers. The disparity in figures between my 13 members and the 419 members is probably the result of two factors. First, whereas one-third of the larger group went home every weekend, none of my thirteen members did. The greatest number of trips for them was forty-five. Second, a comparison between records I checked and the replies to the survey question in the same offices (twelve) indicates a consistent tendency for the verbal replies to inflate the actual figures. Number of trips was exaggerated in nine cases, was the same in two cases, and was lower in one case. Total number of days at home was exaggerated in ten cases and was lower in two cases. Because the disparities were much greater with regard to total days spent at home and because, in any case, total days at home is a more difficult figure to pin down, we shall not use this figure further in our aggregate analysis. We shall, instead, use the more reliable figure for number of trips. In some respects the total number of days home is the more informative figure. Any complete analysis ought to take both trips and days into account. In most cases we have not done so. For example, one member made 25 trips home and spent 51 days there, whereas another member made 21 trips home and spent 106 days there.
4. Other kinds of data were collected that might also be useful as an indication of district staff strength. Three of them correlated very highly with the indicator we are using, so we do not seem to be missing much by relying on one indicator. Our measure – percentage of staff expenditures allocated to district staff – correlated at .861 with number of people on the district staff, at .907 with the percentage of total staff members allocated to the district, and at .974 with the dollar amounts spent on district staff. We also have recorded the rank, in the total staff hierarchy, of the highest-paid person on the district staff, as another indicator of district staff allocation practices. We have not utilized that indicator, but we might note that the range is

from first (i.e., the highest-paid district staffer is the highest-paid of all the congressman's staffers) to more than ninth (we stopped counting after nine).

5. There were eleven members who went home every night: eight from Maryland, two from Virginia, and one from Pennsylvania. In computing averages, they were coded at 98 trips (more than anyone else) rather than at 365, to minimize distortion. Also to minimize distortion caused by these cases, I have used the median number of trips in this chapter analysis, rather than the average number of trips.

6. The most common replies were "every week," "once a month," "twice a month," "every other week," "between once and twice a month," "three or four times a month," etc. Representatives placed in the "low" category were those whose staffers were unwilling to go as high as "twice a month." Those whose trips were reported as "once a week" or more fell into the "high" category. But some respondents said, "every week except for a few" or "every week, but maybe he missed one or two here or there." So, we decided to try to capture that sense by including in the "high" category people who were reported to have made somewhat less than 52 trips. (Doubtless those who said they went home every week missed a few too.) Because a sizable group had 40 trips and none had 41 or 42, we cut at that point and made 43 + the "high" category. The middle category were those who remained — people who went home at least twice a month (24 trips) but not as often as 43 times in 1973.

7. Neither does the frequency of 1973 home visits bear any relationship to whether the member's electoral margin declined, increased, or remained the same between 1972 and 1974. The measure of association we have employed for our cross-tabulations is the *gamma*; and we have listed its value beneath the tables where appropriate to give the reader some feeling for the strength of the relationship. Roger Davidson finds, relatedly, that marginality does not affect the budgeting of times between legislative and constituency activities in Washington. Davidson, *The Role of the Congressman* (New York: Pegasus, 1973), pp. 102–03.

8. See Morris Fiorina, *Representatives, Roll Calls and Constituencies* (Boston: Lexington, 1974). The piece of research that dovetails best with my research is Warren Miller, "Majority Rule and the Representative System of Government" in Erik Allandt and Yrjo Littunen, *Cleavages, Ideologies and Party Systems* (Helsinki, 1964), chap. 10. Miller uses subjective marginality as the measure of competitiveness and relates it to the policy attitudes of representatives and their reelection constituencies.

9. The correlation coefficient (Pearson's r) is —.23.

10. Lacking essential data on the physical debilities (real or imagined) of House members, we cannot proceed with our hunches about age. But the correlation between seniority and age is .69, which suggests that the age factor is pretty well accounted for in our seniority calculations. This is most true for the younger members; most of the members under forty-five years of age are also in the one-to-three-term seniority group. Comparing those between forty-five and sixty with those over sixty, we find that the tendency of trips home to decline with seniority is a little bit greater among the older age group. This suggests a slight independent influence of age, but not enough to make it worth pursuing here.

11. As a reminder, however, that money does count, and in nonobvious ways, consider this comment by a member in the high seniority category:

> In the early years, I didn't make many trips home. It was simply a matter of money. . . . I come home more now. I get a bigger travel allowance

and I get asked to speak more. I never pay any of my own money to come home. I can't. But when you speak, your way is paid. . . . I go home much more now than when I first went to Congress. But I don't work as hard as I used to when I'm home.

12. The number of cases is lower here than in the other parts of the analysis because the data were collected in 1975, after a number of the 1973 members were no longer available for questioning.

13. The correlation coefficient is .20.

14. For example, Aage Clausen, *How Congressmen Decide: A Policy Focus* (New York: St. Martins, 1973); Barbara Deckard, "State Party Delegations in the U.S. House of Representatives: A Study in Group Cohesion," *Journal of of Politics* 34 (February 1972): 199–222; John Ferejohn, *Pork Barrel Politics* (Stanford: Stanford University Press, 1974); Donald Matthews and James Stimson, *Yeas and Nays: Normal Decision Making in the U.S. House of Representatives* (New York: Wiley, 1975).

15. John D. Macartney, "Political Staffing: A View From the District," Ph.D. dissertation, University of California, Los Angeles, 1975, p. 195.

16. Indeed, Washington's congressional delegation is very much against strong party organization. See John H. Kessel, "The Washington Congressional Delegation," *Midwest Journal of Political Science* 8 (February 1964): 2.

17. Kenneth Shepsle demonstrates that in applying for committee assignments, a freshman member is very likely to apply for the same committee as his predecessor when there is an identifiable relationship between the predecessor's committee jurisdiction and the geographical constituency — that is, in cases where expectations in the geographical constituency would be well formed. Kenneth Shepsle, *The Giant Jig Saw Puzzle* (Chicago: University of Chicago Press, 1978).

CHAPTER THREE

Home Style: Presentation of Self I

THE PRESENTATION OF SELF

Most House members spend a substantial proportion of their working lives "at home." Even those in our low frequency category return to their districts more often than we would have guessed. Over half of that group go home more than once a month.[1] What, then, do representatives do there? Much of what they do is captured by Erving Goffman's idea of *the presentation of self*.[2] That is, they place themselves in "the immediate physical presence" of others and then "make a presentation of themselves to others." Goffman writes about the ordinary encounters between people "in everyday life." But, the dramaturgical analogues he uses fit the political world, too. Politicians, like actors, speak to and act before audiences from whom they must draw both support and legitimacy. Without support and legitimacy, there is no political relationship.

In all his encounters, says Goffman, the performer will seek to control the response of others to him by expressing himself in ways that leave the correct impressions of himself with others. His expressions will be of two sorts — "the expressions that he gives and the expression that he gives off." The first are mostly verbal; the second are mostly nonverbal. Goffman is particularly interested in the second kind of expression — "the more theatrical and contextual kind" — because he believes that the performer is more likely to be judged by others according to the nonverbal than the verbal elements of his presentation of self. Those who must do the judging, Goffman says, will think that the verbal expressions are more controllable and manipulable by the performer. And they will, therefore, read his nonverbal "signs" as a check on the reliability of his verbal "signs." Basic to this reasoning is the idea that, of necessity, every presentation has a largely "promissory character" to it. Those who listen to and watch the presentation cannot be sure what the relationship between themselves and the performer really is. So the relationship must be sustained, on the part of those watching, by inference. They "must accept the individual on faith." In this process of acceptance, they will rely heavily on the inferences they draw from his non-verbal expressions — the expressions "given off."

Goffman does not talk about politicians; but politicians know what Goffman is talking about. The response they seek from others is political support. And the impressions they try to foster are those that will engender political support. House member politicians believe that a great deal of their support is won by the kind of individual self they present to· others, i.e., to their constituents. More than most other people, they consciously try to manipulate it. Certainly, they believe that what they say, their verbal expression, is an integral part of their "self." But, with Goffman, they place special emphasis on the nonverbal, "contextual" aspects of their presentation. At the least, the nonverbal elements must be consistent with the verbal ones. At the most, the expressions "given off" will become the basis for constituent judgment. Like Goffman, members of Congress are willing to emphasize the latter because, with him, they believe that their constituents will apply a heavier discount to what they say than to how they say it or to how they act in the context in which they say it. In the members' own language, constituents want to judge you "as a person." The comment I have heard most often during my travels is: "he's a good man" or "she's a good woman," unembossed by qualifiers of any sort. Constituents, say House members, want to "size you up" or "get the feel of you" "as a person," or "as a human being." And the largest part of what House members mean when they say "as a person" is what Goffman means by expressions "given off." Largely from expressions given off comes the judgment: "he's a good man," "she's a good woman."

So members of Congress go home to present themselves as a person and to win the accolade: "he's a good man," "she's a good woman." With Goffman, they know there is a "promissory character" to their presentation. And their object is to present themselves as a person in such a way that the inferences drawn by those watching will be supportive. The representatives' word for these supportive inferences is *trust*. It is a word they use a great deal. When a constituent trusts a House member, the constituent is saying something like this: "I am willing to put myself in your hands temporarily; I know you will have opportunities to hurt me, although I may not know when those opportunities occur; I assume — and I will continue to assume until it is proven otherwise — that you will not hurt me; for the time being, then, I'm not going to worry about your behavior." The ultimate response House members seek is political support. But the instrumental response they seek is trust. The presentation of self — that which is given in words and given off as a person — will be calculated to win trust. "If people like you and trust you as individual," members often say, "they will vote for you." So trust becomes central to the representative-constituent relationship. For their part, constituents must rely on trust. They must "accept on faith" that the congressman is what he says he is and will do what he says he will do. House members, for their part, are quite happy to emphasize trust. It helps to ally the uncertainties they feel about their relationship with their supportive constituencies. If members are uncertain as to how to work for support directly, they can always work indirectly to win a degree of personal trust that will increase the likelihood of support or decrease the likelihood of opposition.

Trust is, however, a fragile relationship. It is not an overnight or a one-time thing. It is hard to win; and it must be constantly renewed and rewon. "Trust," said one member, "is a cumulative thing, a totality thing. . . . You do a little here and a little there." So it takes an enormous amount of time to build and to maintain constituent trust. That is what House members believe. And that is why they spend so much of their working time at home. Much of what I have observed in my travels can be explained as a continuous and continuing effort to win (for new members) and to hold (for old members) the trust of supportive constituencies. Most of the communication I have heard and seen is not overtly political at all. It is, rather, part of a ceaseless effort to reenforce the underpinnings of trust in the congressman or the congresswoman as a person. Viewed from this perspective, the archetypical constituent question is not "What have you done for me lately?" but "How have you looked to me lately?" In sum, House members make a strategic calculation that helps us understand why they go home so much. *Presentation of self enhances trust; enhancing trust takes time; therefore, presentation of self takes time.*

Of the many contextual expressions given off in the effort to win and hold constituent trust, three are ubiquitous. They are qualification, identification, and empathy.

Every congressman tries to convey to his constituents a sense of his *qualification* for the job he seeks. Contextually and verbally, he gives them the impression that "I am qualified to hold the office of United States representative." "I understand the job and I have the experience necessary to do a good job." "I can hold my own — or better — in any competition inside the House." It is important for House members to convey this impression. Their campaign brochures invariably list their background, experience, and accomplishments. And between campaigns they seize every opportunity to talk knowledgeably about their work. But it is particularly crucial that any nonincumbent convey this sense of being "qualified." One member described his first campaign:

> It was a brassy thing for a person with no experience to do, and we ran it in a brassy way. On my key card, it said in three places that I was "qualified." By the end of the campaign, people were saying, "at least Bedford is qualified."

For the nonincumbent, qualification is *the* threshold impression, without which he will not be taken seriously as a candidate.

Once, at a "candidates night" in a large church, where he was to face questions by a panel of community leaders, I watched a challenger fail to negotiate the threshold. When he had finished a few remarks, an elderly woman rose and said,

> You don't have any qualification for office. I could do a better job as congressman than you could. My three-year-old granddaughter is better qualified and could do a better job than you. I've lived in this part of the city all my life and I've never heard of you. How much did they pay you to run?

As she sat down, another woman rose to say, "Why should I waste my time"; and she walked out, punctuating her exit with an audible, "Shit." As she went, the candidate commented, "I'm glad that lady only votes once." Thereupon, one of the panelists rose from his seat up front and left, saying as he went, "I'm her husband and I vote too." The meeting dissolved in derision; and no questions were ever asked of the challenger. A new candidate for Congress must display certain credentials that are a temporary warrant of his competence.

He must allay constituent doubts that in running for Congress he is "in over his head."

A less prominent aspect of qualification is honesty. All House members present themselves as personally honest. It is not something they proclaim directly. As one advised, "When a man starts telling you how honest he is, put your hand on your wallet." Indeed, if they do so proclaim, they are probably (like Richard Nixon and "I am not a crook") already in deep trouble. But expressions conveying a sense of their honesty flicker through their statements concerning financial disclosure, limitations on campaign contributions, refusals to go on junkets, return of office allowances to the treasury, appointment of citizen watchdog committees to oversee campaign finances, etc. Honesty is less prominently presented than competence because it is a derivative of the other common expressions. Thus, the most expeditious way to convey one's honesty to constituents is to convey competence, identification, and empathy. When trust is gained on these three bases, honesty will be assumed — unless, of course, dishonesty is disclosed. Qualification (i.e., competence and honesty) will not ensure trust. But neither can trust be established in their absence.

Every congressman also conveys a sense of *identification* with his constituents. Contextually and verbally, he gives them the impression that "I am one of you"; "I am like you"; "I think the way you do and I care about the same things you do." Habits of speech — "we in northern Alabama" or "we in southern Illinois" — convey that impression. So does contextually appropriate humor. One southern member opened his speech at a farm group meeting with broad, rural humor:

> It's pretty strange up there for a country boy like me, and it can go to your head. I went to the White House for breakfast one time. Imagine me from over here on Duck Lake eating at the White House with the President! Well, I reckoned I was getting right important, sure enough — until one of the White House officials came over, put his arm around me, and said, "Joe, how are things in New York City?"

Another member concluded his "support the ticket" pep talk to an urban political club with a drier, more caustic wit: "I hope you'll vote for me, too; frankly, the way unemployment is here, I need the job."

The expression of identification can be verbalized very explicitly, as with a black congressman inspiring responses from a group of black precinct workers:

> "You know me." ("Yes, Yes.") "I could lay out my record, but I know I don't have to." ("No, No.") "You know I've worked hard." ("Yes, Yes.") "You know I've gotten the job done." ("Yes, Yes.") "You know the bills I've gotten passed." ("Yes, Yes.") "You know I've done my best for you." ("Yes, Yes.") "I belong to you." ("Yes, Yes.") "I want you to help me." ("We'll help you.")

The same message, conveyed contextually and nonverbally to a group of supporters, was described by another representative:

> I'm a Christian. And though I never mention it or talk about it publicly, the word spreads fast in the evangelical community — "Hal Spooner and his wife are active Christians." In every town when we went to church, we were recognized from the pulpit.

From these expressions flow the sense of identification, from which flows, in turn, a measure of trust. The message is, "You can trust me because we are like one another."

Third, every House member conveys a sense of *empathy* with his constituents.[3] Contextually and verbally, he gives them the impression that "I understand your situation and I care about it"; "I can put myself in your shoes"; and "I can see the world the way you do." One House member in the group went abroad to learn the native language of a minority of his constituents, and now he gives radio broadcasts in that language. A Gentile with a 5 percent Jewish population in his district took a trip to Israel, and he talks knowledgeably about that country with his Jewish constituents. A white congressman who had come to a black church to address a racially mixed senior citizens group embraced the minister, recently recovered from a heart attack.

> *Congressman:* Whenever I called the hospital, they would say, "He's nearly gone." They were getting ready for the funeral. So I would say "I hope it's a good big one."
> *Minister:* I see you wore your black suit today. How come?

There was a good deal of knee-slapping laughter before the pastor introduced the representative as "a man who always goes to bat for us and always hits a home run."

Verbal expressions of empathy often embroider maiden speeches to unfamiliar groups. To a group of blue-collar bingo players at the Serbian Hall:

> I managed to grow up thirty-five miles down highway 80 in Montrose. So I know this county. My father worked for twenty-six years in this county for U.S. Steel as a member of Local 121, United Steelworkers. So I know something about you and your problems.

To the Board of Realtors in an affluent county:

> You are the essence of America. You are out making a living. You don't have a guaranteed annual wage. You have to hustle to make a living. There's nothing wrong with hustling for a living. You are what makes this system work, and I want to be as supportive as I can.

Again, the expressions given and given off carry a message that seeks trust: "You can trust me because — although I am not one of you — I understand you."

Qualification, identification, and empathy are all helpful in the building of constituent trust.[4] To a large degree these three impressions are conveyed by the very fact of regular personal contact. That is, "I prove to you that I am qualified," or "I prove to you that I am one of you," or "I prove to you that I understand you," by coming around frequently to let you see me, to see you and to meet with you. If, on the other hand, I failed to come home to see and be seen, to talk and be talked to, then you would have some reason to worry about trusting me. Thus do decisions about the allocation of resources affect the frequency of and the opportunity for the presentation of self.

Presentation of self is the centerpiece of home style as we have observed it. We shall devote this chapter and the next to examining it. Once members of Congress are in their districts, what kinds of presentations do they make? How do their presentations differ and why? Can any patterns be discerned — among the elements of presentation, among the presentations to various perceived constituencies, and among the determinants of presentational style? In short, can we generalize about the presentational aspects of home style? We shall work toward answers to these questions by way of some case studies. The first four are arrayed along a spectrum ranging from a style that is heavily weighted toward the cultivation of personal relationships to a style that is heavily weighted toward the discussion of policy issues. These two very different styles — and variants on them — are the most common and most easily recognizable of all presentational styles. Two additional case studies introduce us to common styles that fall outside the personal relationships-policy issue differentiation.

PERSON TO PERSON: CONGRESSMAN A. Although it is probably true that the range of appropriate home styles in any given district is large, it is also probably true that in many geographical constituencies there are distinct limits to that range. Congressman A believes there is a good "fit" between his kind of district and his kind of home style. He thinks of his geographical constituency as a collection of counties in a particular section of his state — as southern, rural, and conservative. And he believes that certain presentations of self would not be acceptable there. As he told a small group at dinner before a college lecture:

> I remember once when I was sitting in the House gallery with a constituent listening to Congressman Dan Flood speak on the floor. Dan is a liberal from Wilkes-Barre, Pennsylvania. He is a former Shakespearean actor, and his wife is a former opera singer. Dan was wearing a purple shirt and a white suit; and he was sporting his little waxed moustache. My constituent turned to me and asked, "What chance do you think a man like that would have of getting elected in our district?" And I said, "Exactly the same chance as I would have of getting elected in Wilkes-Barre, Pennsylvania."

The expressions given off by a former actor with a purple shirt, a white suit, and a waxed moustache would be suicidal in Congressman A's district. Indeed, two days earlier as we got out of the car in one of his county seats, Congressman A said apprehensively, "See my brown shirt? This will be the first time that these people have ever seen me in anything but a white shirt." Brown — possibly; purple — never.

Congressman A sees his geographical constituency as a homogeneous, natural community. And he thinks of himself as totally at one with that community — a microcosm of it. Three generations of his family have lived there and served as its leaders and officeholders. He himself held two elective offices within the district before running for Congress. He has been steeped in the area he represents.

> I should write a book about this district — starting with the Indians. It's a very historic district and a very cohesive district — except for Omega County. Nobody knows it like I do.

> One thing that ties the district together is the dominance of the textile industry and the dependence of the people of the district — employer and employee — on the textile industry. . . . If I were hostile to the textile industry, it would be fatal. But that could never happen because I feel so close to the textile industry.

> I represent a district in which my constituents and I have total mutual confidence, respect, and trust — 95 percent, nearly 100 percent.

Congressman A feels a deep sense of identification with his constituents. It is this sense of identification that he conveys, verbally and nonverbally, when he presents himself to them.

"In my state," he says, "only a person-to-person campaign will work." So, when he goes home, he "beats the bushes" and "ploughs the ground" in search of face-to-face contact with the people of his district. From county to county, town to town, up and down Main Street, in and out of county courthouses, through places of business, into homes and backyards, over country roads, and into country stores, from early morning till late at night ("Anyone who hears a knock on the door after 11:00 P.M. knows it's me") he "mixes and mingles," conveying the impression that he is one of them. In each encounter, he reaches (if the other person does not provide it) for some link between himself and the person he is talking with — and between that person and some other person. There is no conversation that does not involve an elaboration of an interpersonal web and of the ties that bind its members one to the other. In the forefront, always, are ties of family: Congressman A possesses an encyclopedic memory for the names and faces, dates, and places of family relations, and for the life cycle events of family: birth, marriage, moving, sickness, and death. His memory and his interest serve him equally well in finding other common ground, be it rivers, plants,

and trees; farms, crops, and businesses; hunting, fishing, and football; land, buildings, and automobiles; home, church, and country.
He devours the district's history; on one trip he was absorbed in a
county history and genealogy, on another the memoirs of U. S.
Grant. Each evening, he returns home with a purchase or a gift —
turnip greens, pepper relish, chili sauce, books, chewing tobacco —
linking him with others. And he regales his wife with the personal
news of the people he has met during the day. He continually files,
sorts, arranges, and rearranges his catalogue of linkages — person to
person, place to place, event to event, time to time.

One instance of person-to-person "campaigning" (one I happened
to write down) occurred when Congressman A spied a farmer in a
pickup truck turning out of a back road. The congressman stopped
his car and jumped out, waving. The truck stopped, and the "howdying" went like this:

> *Congressman:* "Hey, Bill, how you?"
> *Bill:* "Just fine, how you?"
> *C.:* "Is that your cotton over there?"
> *B.:* "No, I don't do any more row cropping — just cattle and
> hogs."
> *C.:* "How you doin'?"
> *B.:* "Pretty good. I didn't follow your part in it, but I'm glad
> you kicked off that ban on the export of hides. I thought
> that was a mistake."
> *C.:* "Sure enough, I did too."
> *B.:* "The livestock business is about as good as I've ever seen
> it. So things are real good right now."
> *C.:* "I'm mighty glad to hear it."
> *B.:* "I went down to Lamar Johnson's yesterday. He said he
> wanted to have you down to shoot doves. But he didn't
> want you to waste your time if there wasn't any."
> *C.:* "You went on a dove shoot yesterday?"
> *B.:* "Yes. There was a little spread of doves. But dove shoots
> haven't been too good this year."
> *C.:* "I'm sorry I missed it."
> *B.:* "You let me know when you're home in duck season. I
> want you to come over and have breakfast with us and
> we'll go out and shoot us some ducks."
> *C.:* "I sure will. How's your father?"
> *B.:* "Fine, real fine."
> *C.:* "Say hello to him for us, and to Elizabeth, Tom, and
> Deborah. You must be mighty proud of that boy."

B.: "We are."
C.: "And you all come see us, you hear."
B.: "We will."

One of the most delicious fantasies indulged in by a member of Congress will come true when, after retirement, a constituent approaches him saying "I'll bet you don't know who I am?" Whereupon the ex-congressman will say, "No, I don't, and what's more I don't give a damn." While they are in office, however, members must cope with that omnipresent question as good-humoredly as they can. But many of them hate it. Not Congressman A. For him, "the question" constitutes a welcome challenge. Driving home from a Rotary Club speech, he named all forty people present, which table each was at, what each did for a living, where each lived, and other assorted tidbits. At a county fair, a man in a straw hat called out from behind a booth:

> Man: "Hey, Sam, I'll bet you don't know who I am?"
> Congressman: "I sure do, Bob."
> Man: "I'm not Bob, I'm Fred, Fred Haskell."
> Congressman: "Oh, of course, Fred! I didn't recognize you with that hat on."

Congressman A was so chagrined by this uncommon failure, that we had to circle the fair grounds twice so he could bump into Fred at the booth. And we artfully left the fair by way of the booth so he could holler, "You come see us, you hear — Fred."

The congressman muses a lot about the keys to success in person-to-person relationships:

> Do you remember Miss Sharp back in the post office? She had never met me before, but she called me Sam. That's the way people think of me. No person will ever vote against you if he's on a first-name basis with you. Did you know that?

> When I'm campaigning I sometimes stop in a country store and buy some salmon and crackers and share them with everyone there — and buy more if need be. Do you know that a man who eats salmon and crackers with you will vote for you? And if a man takes a bite of your chewing tabacco — or better still if he gives you a bite of his chewing tobacco, he'll not only vote for you, he'll fight for you.

> People feel they can talk to me. When they are talking, they feel that I'm listening to what they have to say. Some people have the ability to make others feel that way and some don't. They feel that if they come to me with a problem, I'll do everything I can to help them.

The expression he tries to give off in all his person-to-person dealings is that he knows them, that they know him as a person, that they are all part of the same community, and that his constituents, therefore, have every reason to make favorable inferences about him. "They know me," he says, "and they trust me."

Because he perceives his geographical constituency as a group of counties, it is natural to find him conveying this sense of identification in terms of counties. In three different counties — none of them his place of residence — he verbalized his relationship with the people who lived there. Chatting with a group of businessmen riding to lunch after a meeting with the officials of Alpha County on water and sewer problems, he said,

> Did you know that an Alpha County man saved my grand-father's life in the Civil War? In the battle of Williamsville, my grandfather was badly wounded and Lieutenant Henry from Henryville picked him up and carried him off the field — just a bloody uniform with pieces of bone sticking out. An orderly stopped him and said, "What are you doing carrying that corpse?" Lieutenant Henry said, "That's no corpse; that's Captain McDonough; and so long as there's a spark of life in him, I'm going to try to save him." He did, and my grandfather lived. My roots go deep in Alpha County.

Giving an after dinner speech to the Women's Business and Professional Club of Beta County, he said,

> I feel as much at home in Beta County as I do any place on earth. I can't begin to describe to you the frustrations I feel when I see these crazy social experiments [in Washington]. . . . These frustrations would make me a nervous wreck or worse if I could not come back home to be with you, my friends and neighbors, my supporters and my constituents. I come home to refresh my spirit and renew my strength, here in the heart of our district, where my family's roots go deep. To me, this truly is "holy ground."

Speaking to a sesquicentennial celebration in adjacent Gamma
County, he began,

> I have never recognized the artificial boundaries that separate
> our two counties. I have felt as much at home in Gamma
> County — our county — among my friends and neighbors as
> if I had been born here, raised here, and lived here every day
> of my life.

Later that evening he reflected on his appearance at the sesquicentennial, which he ranked as the most important event of my four-day
visit: "When Marvin introduced me today and said that there
weren't five people out there, out of 4000, who didn't know me, he
was probably right. And those who don't know me think they do."

His repeated use of the term "at home" suggests that Congressman A perceives the people with whom he meets as his primary
constituency. And he does. When asked to describe his very strongest supporters, he explained, "My strongest supporters are the people who know me and whom I have known and with whom I have
communicated over the years . . . in my oldest counties, that means
thirty to forty years." He does not perceive his primary constituency
in demographic terms, but in terms of personal contacts. In a district
seen as homogeneous there are few benchmarks for differentiation. And the one clear benchmark — race — is one he never men-
tions in public and only rarely in private. His primary constituents
are the rural and small-town whites who know him (or feel that
they know him) personally. He seems to be, as he was once introduced, "equally at home with blue denim and blue serge, with rich
folks and po' folks" — so long as the blue denim is nonunion. Standing around in a dusty brown field swapping hunting jokes with a
group of blue-collar friends and sitting in an antique-filled living-
room talking business with the president of a textile company rank
equally high on his at-homeness index. His primary constituency, as
may be the case in homogeneous districts, is quite amorphous — as
demographically amorphous as V. O. Key's classic "friends and
neighbors" victory pattern. But it is sizable enough and intense
enough to have protected Congressman A, for a considerable number of terms, from any serious primary challenge.

By national standards, and by those of his state delegation, Congressman A does not come home a lot. He made thirteen trips home

and spent seventy-nine days there in 1973. When he does come home, he spends most of his time where it is strategically profitable and personally comfortable — with his primary constituency. There, he reenforces his ties to the group of greatest importance to him in his traditionally one-party district. He explained, for example, why he took time out of a crowded Washington work week to fly home to the installation of officers of a Boy Scout council:

> I wanted to make it because of who they were. They were Boy Scout leaders from six of my counties — the men who make scouting here a viable movement. They have given me some of my strongest support since I have been in politics. And they have never asked anything of me but to give them good government. So when they ask, I sure don't want to pass up the opportunity to meet with ninety to a hundred of them. I knew about 90 percent of them. And the other 10 percent I know now. Some of those I hadn't met were sons of men I had known.

The scout leaders, of course, want more from him than "good government." They want his time and his personal attention. And he, believing these to be the essence of his home style, happily obliges.

When he mentioned that he had also left Washington once to speak at a high school graduation, I asked whether a highly paid staff assistant in the district might relieve him of some of these obligations. (Some members in my group have just such an assistant who attends meetings "in the name of the congressman" when he cannot come.) Congressman A answered,

> It wouldn't work. People want to see the congressman — me. At the high school commencement exercises, I could have sent the most scholarly person I could find to make a more erudite, comprehensive, and scholarly exposition than I made. If I had done so, the people there wouldn't have enjoyed one bit of anything he said. And they would never have forgiven me for not being there.

He has a small district staff — three people, one full-time office, and one half-time office. When he is touring around he is as apt to hear someone's personal problems and jot them down on the back of an envelope as he is to find out about these problems from his district aides. Congressman A, at home, is a virtual one-man band. His home style is one of the hardest to delegate to others; and he has no inclination to do so.

He allocates relatively little of his time to his larger reelection constituency. Omega County, singled out earlier as out of the district's mold, is not rural, is populated heavily by out-of-staters, and has experienced rapid population growth. Of the forty public appearances listed in his 1973 appointment book, four were in Omega County — the district's largest. Congressman A admits he does not feel at home there. Yet he still gets a sizable percentage of Omega County's votes — on grounds of party identification. He explained why he didn't spend time among these reelection constituents:

> It is so heterogeneous, disorganized, and full of factions. . . .
> I don't spend very much time there. Some of my good friends criticize me and say I neglect it unduly. And they have a point. But I can get 50 percent of the vote without campaigning there at all; and I couldn't get more than 75 percent if I campaigned there all the time. If I did that, I would probably lose more votes than I gained, because I would become identified with one of the factions and half the people would hate me. On top of that, I would lose a lot of my support elsewhere in the district by neglecting it. It's just not worth it.

There is another reason besides time costs and political benefits. It is that Congressman A's home style is totally inappropriate for Omega County, and he avoids the personal unpleasantness that would be involved in trying to campaign there. Strategically, Congressman A will accept any increment of support he can get beyond his primary constituency (e.g., "The black people who know me know that I will help them with their problems.") But he allocates very little of his time to the effort.

Congressman A's presentation of self places very little emphasis on articulating issues. The congressman's own abilities and inclinations run to cultivating personal, face-to-face relationships with individuals. When he returns home from a day of campaigning he is likely to go to the telephone and start calling people. The greater the social, psychological, and physical distance between himself and others, the less he is at home, regardless of the situation. And he was clearly least at home at a college, in a lecture-plus-question-and-answer format. He accepts invitations of this sort to discuss issues.

But he does nothing to generate such engagements, nor does he go out of his way to raise issues in his dealings with others at home. On the single occasion when he broke this pattern, he tested out his potentially controversial position with his primary constituents (i.e., the American Legion post in his hometown), found it to be acceptable, and articulated it often thereafter. Congressman A's home style does, however, take place *within an issue context.* There is widespread agreement in the district, and very strong agreement within his primary constituency, on the major issues of race, foreign aid, government spending, and social conservatism. The district voted for George Wallace in 1968. Thus, although Congressman A's home style is apparently issueless, it may depend for its very success on an underlying issue consensus.

There are, therefore, strategic reasons as well as personal reasons for Congressman A not to focus heavily on specific issues. To do so would be unnecessary and potentially divisive. Congressman A is protective of his existing constituency relations and will not want to risk alienating any of his support by introducing or escalating controversy of any kind. He is a stabilizer, a maintainer. And so, when asked to speak formally, he often responds with communitarian homilies: "I believe if ever there was a promised land, that land is America; and if ever there was a chosen people, those people are Americans." "If a man isn't proud of his heritage, he won't leave a heritage to be proud of. And that goes for his family, his community, and his country." These utterances are not the secret of his success. But they do testify, again, to his continuing efforts to articulate a sense of community, to construct and reconstruct a web of enduring personal relationships and to present himself as totally a part of that web. If he gets into electoral difficulty, Congressman A will resort, not to a discussion of "the issues," but to an increased reliance on his person-to-person home style. And, so long as his strategic perceptions are accurate, he will remain a congressman.

THE POPULAR LOCAL BOY: CONGRESSMAN B. Congressman B talks a great deal about public policy when he is home. Mostly, he talks about defense policy. He believes passionately in the strongest possible national defense. And he perceives that it is equally a passion for "the vast majority" of the people of his district.

> A general cross section agree with me on it. You have to elimi-
> nate the liberal people. They think we've just got to love one

another. And the people real low on the economic scale, the
less educated people. They think in more simple terms —
where am I going to get clothes and something to eat. If you
lop off some at both ends, the vast majority agree. The man
who took our poll said this district was more concerned
with national defense than anyplace else in the country. I
don't know how to explain it. We don't have that much
military. . . . People here are more patriotic. They have
more faith in the flag, their country, and their historic values.
They are more nationalistic. Wherever I've been in the
country, there's no place where it's more true than here. . . .
I can go all out on national defense. My people expect it.

During my two visits, two years apart, he did go "all out." At five of
seven speaking engagements he talked about the seriousness of the
Soviet threat and the need for greater military strength. Not only
did he carry this warning to a Disabled American Veterans Convention; he delivered the same message to a women's club awards ban-
quet, to a luncheon meeting of agricultural experts, to a high school
commencement, and to the opening ceremonies of "Girls State."
The subject is not a passing fancy. "I used to give lectures on com-
munism," he says. "I added them up once and they went into the
thousands." Congressman B's presentation of self is, therefore, more
issue-oriented than that of Congressman A.

His preoccupation with national defense dovetails with what Congressman B sees as the ideological conservatism of an otherwise
heterogeneous district.

The district is conservative from the standpoint of philosophy. Aside from that, it is unusual in that it's a conglomeration of districts in general. I've got government type
people — more than most. I've got more students and colleges than most districts. I've got a pretty big farming area
jammed up against the city. I've got factory workers and
high type manufacturing. It's a pretty good cross section and
no one particular slice.

It is not a one-party district. He sees the party breakdown as "21
percent Democratic, 21 percent Republican, and all the rest not in-

clined to either." Party organizations are weak, and split-ticket voting in the district is normal. Although ideology provides a lowest common denominator, Congressman B does not confront the reenforcing homogeneities present in Congressman A's district. Congressman A's reelection constituency is made up of one-party rural conservatives whose livelihood depends a great deal on one industry. Congressman B's reelection constituency is also conservative. But it is politically independent; it has rural, suburban, and urban components; and its members participate in a highly diversified economy.

Congressman B described his reelection constituency best when he lopped off liberals and lower-income people from the "vast majority" of others. He associates "the liberal people" with the educational complex of his district — people connected with the colleges and members of teachers organizations like the NEA. He associates those "real low on the economic scale" with the unskilled factory workers as opposed to workers in what he calls "high type manufacturing": electronics, data processing, and other sophisticated industries in the district. The local area is not heavily unionized; but he counts the unions, also, among his nonsupporters. These three groups, plus those people who "are programmed to vote for the other party," are the constituents whom he believes he "never gets." From the remaining reservoir of constituents — conservative, middle income, and politically independent — he draws his support.

When asked to identify his strongest supporters, he does not speak very definitively. He answers in the language of categoric groups, as if he were reading from the printout of a public opinion poll:

> People who have finished high school and who have made something of themselves as mechanics, or as secretaries, from the female standpoint. Young married people, twenty-five to thirty-five, who work in business, insurance, and industry. Middle-income people. Also, people forty-five to sixty who work in government jobs. And salesmen — people like that. They are all very strong supporters.

He does not perceive his supporters in terms of organized groups. Contrary to our expectation that members in heterogeneous districts would — because it would be easier for them to do so — make sharp definitions of their hard-core support, Congressman B's perceptions

remain amorphous. And, as they stand, they are difficult to embroider. It is not easy to observe him interacting with these kinds of
demographic groupings — much less to detect degrees of at homeness
with them. And because I did not observe him among his intimates,
I could not extrapolate from there.

During my visits we spent most of our time in the farming and
the suburban parts of the district. And from these travels it appears
that the suburbs rank higher on his at-homeness scale than the
countryside. Leaving a large Rural Electrification Cooperative gathering, he commented, "I feel half at home [here]. I've been around
these areas a lot. And I know a little about the things that interest
them — farming, for instance." And he said the Coop members
"would be fairly good supporters." "But," he added, "they aren't as
strong supporters of mine as people like those in Manchester [a sub-
urb], the people who work for Westinghouse and Burroughs." Reflecting on his relationship with the Coop members, he said,

> You have to talk to them colloquially, the way they talk. My
> wife criticizes me when I don't use my English. I was an
> English major. And I tell her, "Honey, you just can't use your
> best college English." They'll say, "What's he talking
> about?" But if I were back in a suburban shopping center, it
> would be different. You have to learn to get along in different
> environments.

Clearly, in his view, the rural and suburban areas are distinctive. The
implication is that he does not have to learn to get along in the
suburbs, that he can act more natural there. We can guess that he
finds some of his strongest support there, too. But it is a guess. He
does not describe his district as dominantly suburban (which, according to census figures, it is), and he never talks about any presentational problems endemic to suburban districts.

Congressman B's district presents a complicated strategic problem.
Unlike Congressman A, who needs only to cultivate a homogeneous
primary constituency, Congressman B must cultivate a heterogeneous
reelection constituency. He does not have to contest primaries. But
he cannot call on party loyalty to help much in the general election.
He has known some close as well as some overwhelming electoral
victories. As we have said, there is a highly visible issue component
to his campaigns. But he regards it as a necessary part of *any* candi-

date's success in that district and, hence, not his special secret. Nor is his policy conservatism generally. He attributes his crucial support, rather, to "personality":

> Contrary to what people say — they say voters are issue-oriented and all that . . . for most of the people I know it's more a matter of personality. They pick out a personality whom they like, who they think is like them, whom they have confidence in, and they trust him to do what's best for them.

He wins constituent trust mostly, he believes, because constituents like him and identify with him.

His national defense posture is by no means irrelevant. It allows him to display his conservative credentials and thereby convey the feeling that "I am one of you; I think like you do." It is a lowest common denominator issue, one that is particularly appropriate for his district because it is a nonpartisan issue. And it also gives him a subject he can speak about easily and naturally. But it is only one element of a more general style, one centering on his "personality." He does not win and hold support because he advocates a strong national defense. Others — like his opponents — advocate that, too. He gets support, he believes, because of the way he presents himself to his reelection constituents as a person.

Congressman B was born, raised, educated, and has lived his entire life in the district he represents. He grew up as a local hero. In high school and college he was an all star athlete and an outstanding young man. He was a captain of teams and a president of student bodies. Like many another politician, he moved immediately from campus success to elective public office. Now, as a member of Congress, he affects a presentational style not very different from that of a campus leader of the 1950s — one combining masculine prowess with personal charm. In the personal résumé he sends in advance to places where he will speak, he lists his high school and college achievements. And he is often introduced with a recital of them. Political success, he believes, depends on being "popular" and "well thought of." He won a state legislative seat against a friend of his because "I was better known and more popular." The congressional challenger who ran closest to him "was a very popular person — good looking, articulate, and well liked." Congressman B, too, is good looking, articulate, and well liked. And he admires politicians who share these attributes. "Some people write off athletics," he says, "but Jack Kemp is one of the most sought-after speakers in the House. He's handsome and articulate. He's well thought of." In Congressman B's district, newspapers publish weekly batting, pitching, and fielding records of every local boy now playing baseball in the major, minor, or semiprofessional leagues. Athletes are remembered, cherished, and "well thought of" in the district.

Defense policy aside, Congressman B seeks support much as if he were running for class president. An election is very much a popularity contest. He is unfailingly nice to everyone, is invariably good humored, and gives off an immense likability as a person. His cardinal rule of campaigning — indeed, a strategy — is one of gentlemanliness: "Never make personal attacks on your opponent." And he is abnormally sensitive to anything that might be construed as a personal attack on him, and hence affect his popularity. A recent critical newspaper story nearly traumatized him. "It gets you right in the stomach and makes you want to throw up all over the floor," he said. He avoids taking controversial positions because he hates controversy. National defense fits perfectly into this pattern. It allows him to talk "issues" while remaining noncontroversial and popular.

With Congressman A, he believes that his supporters want personal contact with him. "People think you aren't around if they don't see you personally," he says. "People expect you to be there at their meetings." So he goes home often to present himself personally. Indeed he goes home substantially more than Congressman A — for a total of 36 trips and 111 days in 1973. When he is there, however, his presentations to others are very different from those of Congressman A. Congressman B displays neither the affection for nor the interest in his supporters that characterize Congressman A's "person-to-person" style. His presentational style is more distant, more impersonal — almost as if he does, indeed, perceive demographic groupings rather than individuals to whom he feels warm-blooded attachments. His preferred technique for presenting himself is a speech. He says, "The main reason I come home is to accept speaking engagements. I take all I can." It is a far more distant technique than the face-to-face encounters sought by Congressman A.

In such face-to-face campaigning as he does, Congressman B does not weave that tapestry of fellow-feeling detail about others that is the essence of a person-to-person style. Congressman B approaches others more superficially. He does not invoke the sense of community that undergirds all of Congressman A's identifications. Congressman B identifies himself not as "one of the family," but as "one of the boys": "You workin' hard or just regular?" "How you doin', about half and half?" "How am I doin'? No use me braggin' this early in the morning, is there?" "Don't step in no stump holes." "If you can't be good be careful." "You've got to serve the needy as well as the greedy." The expressions he gives leave people smiling and in a happy mood. The expressions he gives off convey familiarity but not intimacy. He does not try to touch others with a sense of personal attachment to them.

His presentation of self to women is both illustrative of, and central to, his home style. The first time I flew with him to his district, we were met at planeside by a local radio personality who had brought the congressman four modish new suits. As we walked to the car, the radio man said,

> Rick saw a suit of mine and went ape over it, so I helped him pick out four of them. . . . You'll like Rick. He gets right down to the people. His door is always open. He's not an "I'm the Congressman, who are you?" type of person. And he has the women's vote sewed up. They love him.

The comment about women was one I was to hear often during my visits. Congressman B "loves" the women — in the same good-natured but rather distant way that he likes almost everybody else. But his presentations to women seem to be of special importance to him. Wherever he goes, he is especially attentive to them. He dresses like a peacock, in arresting color combinations; and he preens with frequent wardrobe changes. He greets women with, "Hi, Hon." When he shakes hands with them, he asks, "Can I hold your hand?" By turns, he flatters and titillates. His favorite joke, which he told nearly everywhere (on both trips, two years apart) was:

> I have only two vices, smoking and women. And I like them both. My doctor told me I had to give up smoking. But he said to me, "Let's look at it this way. Why don't you stop one and double up on the other?"

Told by a handsome, smiling congressman — to women from seventeen to seventy — it never failed to draw appreciative laughter.

Even his anti-Soviet, prodefense speeches are spiced with male-female allusions. At the Women's Club in suburban Hayward:

> Russian missiles are only seven minutes away. Either you spend billions and billions for defense or you start deciding how you are going to spend your last seven minutes on earth. You might as well sit under a tree and think about something nice for seven minutes. . . . For me it will be girls.

> I was giving a speech at Midwestern University and I was pouring on the patriotic stuff. There was this little girl shaking her seat like she had ants in her pants. I didn't know if she was signaling that we ought to get together later or what. So I asked her what she wanted and she asked, "What is your definition of freedom?"

Afterward, he bantered with an attractive young woman, a former "Miss Hayward":

> *Congressman:* "I can't help it if I like girls."
> *"Miss Hayward":* Rick, you have a one-track mind.
> *Congressman:* Can you think of a better track?

He began his rousing anticommunist, profreedom speech to 500 high school students at Girls State with a ten-minute flirtation: "You all look so good I could eat you all with salt and pepper — and I never eat anything without salt and pepper. . . . This is hog heaven being here with so many beautiful girls. . . . You look so good, I feel all funny inside. . . . I know I'm supposed to be serious, but I'm wandering around waiting for something to hit me. Nothing has hit me except how good you all look to me." The audience responded warmly. After the speech, the young women mobbed him. For three-quarters of an hour he dispensed autographs and kisses to his admirers. He performs now on the platform instead of the playing field. He is a public rather than a campus celebrity. But female adulation remains a special concomitant of his success.

In Congressman *B*'s world, women seem to be eternal cheerleaders, beauty queens, and "outstanding young women." He ranked the Girls State performance his most important of the weekend because "they are the cream of the crop, the leaders of the future.

And are they ever patriotic." He identifies closely with them; they
are the kinds of people with whom he achieves easy popularity.
Driving home from Girls State he said,

> One girl came up and said, "I don't appreciate your attitude
> toward women." I said, "I love women and I'm not going to
> apologize for it." She was one of them women's libbers. The
> other girls said, "Don't pay any attention to her; she's crazy.
> She doesn't even want to be a woman." I said to her, "Honey,
> you shouldn't be bothering your pretty head about serious
> things like that. You ought to enjoy yourself." But I couldn't
> break her down. You can't get serious with people like that
> — you can't win. You've got to try to turn them off by joking
> with them.

It is not a perception of one's female constituents appropriate for
all congressional districts. But in his district it seems to be a reliable
asset. He opened his "kill or be killed" national defense speech to
the Women's Auxiliary of the Disabled American Veterans with
this story:

> It seems a group of citizens were having a meeting to discuss
> the problem of coyotes destroying their sheep. They were dis-
> cussing ways of getting rid of the coyotes. One of these
> League of Women Voters, Sierra Club, do-gooder type ladies
> spoke up and suggested they capture the coyotes and perform
> a small operation on them that would keep them from
> breeding and multiplying but would save the innocent coyotes.
> When she finished, an old farmer got up and said, "Lady, we
> ain't worried about them coyotes raping our sheep. They're
> killing 'em."

The story makes clear the kinds of women with whom he does not
identify. Public ridicule of the "League of Women Voters, Sierra
Club, do-gooder type ladies" before a women's group requires, however, a pretty sure sense for the social and political conservatism of
his female supporters.

Not once did Congressman B suggest to me that women consti-
tuted a special category of supporters. Yet he obviously works to
cultivate their support. And whether or not he gets it, his efforts
provide us with the clearest picture of his presentational style. It is
a style designed to win trust by making him "popular" and "well

thought of." It is a style that developed naturally out of predispositions and talents that became evident much earlier in life. It is a style that shows much good humor and little personal intimacy. It is a style that can be displayed to all segments of a heterogeneous reelection constituency — a lowest common denominator style. It is a style that does not require sharply honed definitions of a primary constituency. It will work with demographic categories — like "women." And it is a style that, in the end, is only slightly more issue-oriented than that of Congressman A.

Congressman B's presentation to women suggests, also, that his presentational style is distinctively local. Anyone who seeks support by being "popular," "well liked," or "well thought of" becomes heavily dependent on obedience to local mores. The masculine charm with which Congressman B woos feminine support, for example, depends for its acceptance on local male-female traditions. Home styles can be expected to differ widely in the degree to which they reflect distinctive local expectations. Congressman B's style lies, however, at one end of the spectrum. And deliberately so. For although he does not believe (as Congressman A believes) that his presentational style is the only one that will work in his district, he does believe that only a locally derived style of some sort will work there. As Congressman B sees it, therefore, his style must be perceived as a *local* style. The expressions he gives off are especially important, then, in establishing and maintaining his local identification. And, from what we can see, they do. His stylistic instincts are locally imbibed and locally honed. He has held school or public office in the district almost continuously since high school. He is very much the local boy — the local hero, still. And that is the way he wants it. He is most comfortable with that self-image. From it he derives his sense of "fit" with his district — his secure feeling of me-in-the-district.

Nothing exemplifies better his own local orientation, and his belief that his supporters will accept nothing else, than Congressman B's pronounced hostility to the "outsider." When his opponent hired someone from out of state to run his campaign, Congressman B could hardly contain his pleasure:

> My opponent held a press conference and introduced the man they brought in from the outside to run his campaign — some guy from Massachusetts who had run forty-one

campaigns in twenty-one states. I suppose he's a smart fella, but you don't come out and tell people he's from outside! Not people out here! It was amazing! I couldn't believe it — telling everybody he was from the outside! Maybe if he came from someplace nearby you might get away with it, by suggesting he had lived here, too. But Massachusetts! Maybe back in New York it would be different. It might be more cosmopolitan. But I don't think you'd want someone from my state coming back there to tell you how to run things would you? Now, whenever my opponent says anything in the campaign, all I have to say is "That outsider there is giving you bad advice."

Outsiders cannot be trusted. Only local people can. And, believing that his supporters agree, he presents himself to them as the trustworthy local boy. Asked why voters would trust him, he answered,

Mainly because they've known me over a period of years. They know my father and my family's reputation. I'm a known quantity; I'm not an unknown quantity. And that's what people are afraid of — an unknown quantity. . . . People know your general reputation, your family name, your kids. They know you in athletics. People can put their finger on you. . . . They get to know you and your thinking. Here's some fella that never ran, and people worry about him. They don't know what he might do. . . . Someone once said, "The fear of the unknown is the greatest fear." That's a paraphrase, but that's it, I think.

Congressman B sees his reelection constituency as aggressively local — marked by a suspicion of the outsider and a fear of the unknown. It is a view, incidentally, that is also assumed by his national defense posture. If he is correct, the district may have room — as we would suspect all heterogeneous districts do — for stylistic changes. But not for a more outward looking, cosmopolitan home style.

The congressman sees his district changing:

We're growing a lot. That doesn't mean we're unstable. People are moving here from other parts of the state. We are becoming more of a residential area in that people are moving into the rural areas, making bedrooms . . . and pushing the farmers further out.

One-half of the district's population now live in suburbs. But this growth has helped, not hurt, Congressman B at the polls. He feels, as we noted earlier, fairly at home in the suburbs. He is himself a product of the suburbs, living first near the city and then moving outward with the residential tide. And he wins his largest pluralities in the suburbs. So a suburbanizing district holds no terror for him. He says, "Our thinking goes along together. Some things have changed, but I can't see that people have changed anymore than I have or that I have more than they." But, he adds, "The biggest change is that people are becoming more militant." If that trend continues, it will bring more organizations, more issue orientation, more polarization, to the district. And that change could bring the good-natured, personally charming, single-issue, local-boy style under some strain. But before that strain would be endangering, the district would have to become quite different — more like the proto-typical suburban district to which we now turn.

ISSUE INDEPENDENCE PLUS ONE ON ONE: CONGRESSMAN C. When asked how his "constituents" thought of him, Congressman C put his tongue in his cheek and replied, "It's probably wishful thinking — a white knight high on a white horse in gleaming raiments of purest white." It is not a jest that would occur to Representative A or B. It conveys too much remoteness to suit the person-to-person campaigner and too much crusading to suit the well-liked local boy. (And it smacks of too much purity to fit any of the three.) Yet it suggests that Congressman C may inhabit a more demanding district than either of his colleagues. At least, he thinks he does. And he has struggled to develop a suitable presentational style.

The district Congressman C perceives is "a typical suburban district" on the rim of one of America's large cities:

> It is a wholly suburban district, made up of mature suburbs. It is well educated, affluent, white. Although it tends to be Republican, it has a streak of suburban liberalism running through it. It's different from the one I used to have, which had rural and urban pockets. It's very homogeneous. It's all first-, second-, or third-ring suburbs. There are only two communities with any room for development left.

Thus pictured, it is too overwhelmingly suburban to bear much resemblance to the urban-suburban-rural "conglomeration" of Congressman *B.* And it bears a similarity to Congressman *A*'s district only because its homogeneity limits the range of appropriate home styles. The picture Congressman *C* paints of his geographical constituency and of himself in that constituency would never be mistaken for a picture of the other two relationships we have examined.

Congressman *C* thinks of his district as reflecting two distinctive characteristics of the larger region in which it sits. First is the high degree of interest in "the issues" of politics:

> This area is an issue-oriented place. And my district is issue-oriented, particularly compared with [that of] some of my colleagues. I annually query my constituents and they are pretty good about answering. The letters I get don't say yes or no. They show more concern for what should be done. They say, "If you would do thus and so, it would lead to such and such happening and things could be better."

Second, is a tradition of "independence" in politics:

> Politics is different in this area. We have wrestled with the problem of independence in politics. We have many non-partisan elections locally. We have a tradition of people of one party endorsing someone of the other party.

When Congressman *C* thinks of me-in-the-district, he emphasizes his "fit" with these two district-wide characteristics:

> I think I have the image of being independent. There aren't very many people who don't know I'm a Republican. But as my polls say and as my friends say and as I feel it, I'm thought to be independent and outspoken. When people ask me what I think on an issue, I tell them. I think that was true, too, of my predecessor.

Congressman *C* presents himself, then, as issue-oriented and independent. Judging by everything he says, including the comment about his predecessor, it appears that these are necessary elements in any acceptable presentational style in his district.

In thinking about his reelection constituency, Congressman *C* estimates party registration at about 25 percent Republican, 35 percent Democratic, and 40 percent "independent and unknown" —

with "some Republicans lurking among the independents." With his Republican identity clearly established and with the district's Republicans "already sold," his major reelection strategy is "to cross off the Democrats and circle our wagons around the independents to see if we can't hold our strength with that group." Though in one respect — their "maturity" or advanced state of development — he thinks of his suburbs as homogeneous, he makes other distinctions important to him as he constructs a reelection constituency. There are the more affluent suburbs that are strongly Republican. "When you want to harvest Republican votes, you go to Crystal Valley." There are larger suburbs like Appledale, "which makes up one-fifth of my district. We have to pay it special attention for that reason." During the campaign, door-to-door campaigning is restricted to Crystal Valley and the three next most affluent towns plus some sections of Appledale.

On the other hand, distinctions among the suburbs help him to define the limits of his reelection constituency. Tucker and Atlantic Heights are "first-tier suburbs," parts of which are now "like a decaying city" and heavily Democratic. Metropole is adjacent to the blue-collar part of the city and is heavily blue-collar. These are people to whom he pays little attention. He says, "The people I can't reach with a ten-foot pole are the labor unions and the old-line Democrats." Organized labor is strong in the metropolitan area, but "is not strong in the district." "I'm very thin on blue-collar," he says. "The district is not heavily influenced by blue collar." Such a labor vote as there is, Congressman C concedes to his Democratic opponent, happily so:

> My opponent is having trouble getting out of the gate. . . .
> All he has is a lot of labor. So we run him down the canyon
> that says "Big Labor." And when he says that I'm antiunion,
> my district says "good."

By conceding the labor vote he helps consolidate his reelection constituency, particularly because the "Big Labor" he attacks is concentrated more outside the district than within it.

Within his reelection constituency of Republicans and independents, Congressman C sees primary constituents coming from both groups. When asked to describe his "very strongest supporters," he answered,

> He is a businessman and he is fairly liberal, so liberal that
> he is almost a Democrat, but he can't leave the Republican
> party. He's an internationalist. Or else, he's a professional man
> — a doctor, lawyer, engineer. If he's a professional man, he's
> very conservative. He thinks his taxes are confiscatory. He's
> antiunion, more than the businessman. I have other pockets
> of strength, too. I do well among the do-gooders — the
> League of Women Voters, Common Cause, the Nader group.
> That's because I've always been a procedural, structural re-
> former. My women supporters tend to be liberal, active in
> community affairs, and members of several organizations.
> . . . And I have particularly good relations with the mayors
> and councilmen of my cities because of what I did for them
> before I went to Congress.

He tends not to locate his hard-core political strength in specific
suburban towns, but rather in types of people that can be found
throughout the district. And they are more clearly specified than
those of Congressman B. That is largely so because — his description
suggests — Congressman C thinks of his primary constituents as
strongly issue-oriented.

Neither Congressman A or B sees his primary constituency as
issue-based. But Congressman C finds it hard to talk about them in
any other way. He is not linked to his strongest supporters by community ties or by family and personal reputation.

> The big businessmen in my district tend to be quite liberal.
> They are free traders — a lot more interested in export provi-
> sions than in tax law. I'm well situated on a couple of sub-
> committees to help them with that. They are satisfied with
> union politics. The professional men, on the other hand, are
> very antiunion. They take the attitude, "I've made it; every-
> body else can do the same." For them, I take a flint-hearted
> position on federal expenditures. The do-gooders are a little
> nervous with me, but they stay because of the reform missions
> I fly. We've been able to target in on these groups pretty
> effectively.

"Targeting in" clearly has a larger issue component than anything
we have yet seen. Unlike Congressman B, Congressman C is not a
one-issue congressman. Quite the opposite. The expression he gives
off is one of considerable issue versatility. I have listened to him

giving speeches on the effect of energy policy on small business, Middle Eastern policy, tax reform, campaign finance reform, and intergovernmental effects on the housing industry, in addition to several talks on "the job of the congressman." In this region and in this district his issue versatility is evidence of his "qualification."

The supporters with whom his ties of identification are oldest and strongest are the liberal businessmen. When he first entered politics, he and they "thought of ourselves as renegade liberals hiding out in the Republican party." They are his most reliable supporters. But the group he works hardest to keep solidly in his corner is the League of Women Voters. He considers "the editors, the mayors, and the League of Women Voters" as the opinion leaders in his district. And he thinks of the league members as having great organizational and campaign competence. In his parlance, they are the "super gals" who match his "neat guys" from the business world. So he values their support — as individuals, not as an organization — for its own sake. But he values their support even more, it seems, because they typify a larger group of people whose support he seeks — the issue-oriented independent. He construes the intensity of his support within the league as a test of his presentational style.

> The League of Women Voters is important to me because of their interest in issues; and they are strong throughout the district. . . . The only group I speak to regularly is the league. I have a session with them quarterly in which I answer their questions. . . . They ask questions that are designed to test me. That's good for me. . . . Most of them are Democrats, but it's a tradition in this area to cross party lines at least once. I'm their independent vote.

He presents himself to the league "as a person" who is an independent on the issues, and he seeks identification with them on that basis. His success there is a barometer of his success elsewhere. The special place of the league in Congressman C's primary constituency stems, obviously, from vastly different perceptions than Congressman B has of "do-gooder" support and of women in politics.

There is much that is familiar in this picture of an issue-oriented home style — especially in the kind of suburbia pictured here. But, as Congressman C views it, the picture is incomplete. He feels quite sure that only issue-oriented independents need apply for his job; and he feels that probably only issue-oriented independents can secure a dedicated primary constituency. But he knows that being an issue-oriented independent is not enough to win elections. That is, it is not a style sufficient to win and hold a reelection constituency. "Did you ever see a campaign won on issues?" he asks. "Maybe on an emotional issue like abortion. A candidate has to be comfortable talking about the issues. But most campaigns are not won or lost on issues." How are they won?

> The best way to win a vote is to shake hands with someone. You don't win votes by the thousands with a speech. You win votes by looking individuals in the eye, one at a time, and asking them. Very rarely will anyone ask you about how you stand on something.

"Most of my campaigning," he says, "is one on one." The congressman must be thoughtful, comfortable, frank, and versatile in dealing with issues. But that is not enough. There must be something of the personal relationship that both Congressmen A and B have with their supporters.

Suburbia's characteristics, however, make one on one or "one at a time" presentations difficult. The district is homogeneous, but it lacks the sense of community of Congressman A's district. Though he has lived in it most of his life, its networks are cosmopolitan and not local like Congressman B's. There is, for example, constant population change. "There is about a 30 percent turnover in bodies every two years — even though the type of bodies remains the same . . . [It's] a game of musical houses." Furthermore, within each household, there is constant motion. "My district is a typical suburban district in a frenzy. Susie has to be taken to her piano lesson, mom has to sing in the choir, dad's on a business trip." This hypermobility renders even the census bureau statistics suspect. Besides the one-third turnover, "there's a lot of double job holding. And they go bowling at night, fishing on the weekends. So, nobody's home most of the time." It is a district in which it is impossible to exploit the local continuities that underpin the presentational styles of either Representative A or B. Congressman C's greatest strategic problem is not how to present himself. It is how to find people to present himself to.

As a matter of personal preference, he wants personal contact with "the folks." His early allocative decisions were designed to create a contrast with his predecessor in that respect.

> My office operation is very different from his. It is much more oriented toward the home folks. I hired all people from the state, as he did not. . . . I came home a lot more than he did. And when he did come home, he tended to stay out where he lived, with the wealthy group. I tend to hang around more and listen to the folks.

"I like to come home and it's fun to campaign," he says. And he adds, "I hold a lot of office hours so people can come to me directly with their problems." Actually, he spends less time at home than either Congressman A or B. In 1973, he came home eighteen times for a total of fifty-one days in the district. (Among his state delegation, however, he ranks about average.) His personal relationships are neither as intimate as those of Congressman A nor as continuous as those of Congressman B, both of whom are a lot more surefooted in dealing with "the folks" than Congressman C. But he wants his supporters to think of him as personally attentive.

> I hope it [the way people think of me] has something to do with the qualities I think I have — that I have a concern for the people of the district, that I'm someone who is around a lot and pays attention to what people are saying.

He tries to present himself to others as someone interested in individuals as well as issues. But it is a struggle.

I visited Congressman C's district twice — once during a campaign, once not. In the noncampaign year, the problem of finding people centered on establishing contact with groups, so as to meet group members "one at a time." He sees the district, like many suburban areas, as "shot full of community groups." He says, "There are a lot of clubs in each community and there's an overlay of clubs from the city that cover the metropolitan area. It's a very active place." Congressman C's home schedule is much more crowded with appearances than that of either Congressman A or B. In 1973, he had 104 public engagements, compared to 40 for Congressman A and 50 for Congressman B. Thus, he averages two scheduled appearances each day he is home, whereas Congressman A schedules one appearance every two days, and Congressman B schedules one appearance every three days. Even from Congressman C's perspective, "It's very hard to get people to sit down in groups to be assaulted by a politician." During my three-day, off-year trip, he "assaulted" six of them. Afterward, he ranked them for me in terms of the opportunity they provided to present himself effectively "as a person" interested in others.

At the top of the list, he placed his forty-five-minute lunchtime visit to the cafeteria of a small technical business, where he ate, table hopped, shook hands, and talked with about seventy-five employees.

> It was excellent. Those were people who didn't know me, who had never met me. There was a childlike quality about meeting the congressman. It was a real event for them. And they were surprisingly talkative. It was an ice-breaker. That's the best kind of meeting.

In second place, he ranked his "job-of-the-congressman" talk to about fifty Sears, Roebuck employees before their shopping plaza store opened — a part of Sears' continuing political education program. On the way in, he said,

> You like to make contact with people where they live, work, pray, and play. It's hardest to find them where they work. But it's a good place. It's their turf. They feel comfortable. . . . These people are really unsophisticated. They don't track well. They can't get their questions out. It's neat because it lets me get exposure to people I wouldn't have contact with otherwise. If they meet the congressman, they might find he's not so scary and they might ask me for something.

Later he compared it to the luncheon:

> It was good, but not quite as good as the other. It was more formal with me up there behind the podium. But they were new people. And I got a chance to move around a little before it began. The kind of meetings I like are those that give me a chance to mingle briefly instead of orate.

His third best presentation opportunity came at a Sunday morning breakfast with thirty-five members of the men's club of a small orthodox Jewish synagogue. He spoke about Middle Eastern policy, basing his comments on a recent trip to Israel, and answered questions. "That meeting was a ten strike," he said as we left.

> I was exposed to a group of people that I had never met before. They were smart, thoughtful, up on things and had certain things they were interested in and wanted done. It was especially good afterward when several came up and had specific information they wanted to get from me. I was especially glad to meet the Rabbi. He's very active and I had heard of him, but had never met him. You can't accomplish anything in this district except one on one. So I was happy to have the chance to sit with him, eat breakfast with him, and get to know him. I think we may have something going now. That was a real score.

When he was ranking the meetings, I reminded him of this enthusiasm and asked why he didn't rank the breakfast higher. "Though I didn't know many of them," he said, "they all knew me. They are well informed. They knew who I was. So while it was good, I didn't meet as many people as I did at either [of the other two places]."

Well below this top cluster of three presentations, he ranked his speech on tax reform to 150 members of the American Association of University Women and his party pep talk to 75 people at a Women's Republican Club — both held in the city. Each group contained many nonconstituents. But the others he already counted among his primary constituents. Far and away the least beneficial presentation was a "current issues" speech to fifty people at a B'nai B'rith couples club luncheon. He explained,

> That was a waste of time — a washout. Nothing happened between us — no communication. I couldn't fit them into the community at all. They weren't interested. They had no questions. No one came up to me before or afterward. There didn't seem to be anything they wanted from me, so they will be of no help politically. It was hard for me to get interested in my speech; and it was like a sleeping pill for both of us. Finally, as we left, one guy came running in my direction and I thought that finally someone was going to ask me a question. But he was on his way to the men's room!

Even mention of his trip to Israel did not stir the group. He had no sense of having had personal contact, of having "met" anyone there.

Congressman C wants to present himself as someone with a personal concern for what other people are thinking and what they want. First, he must reach out to make contact. Then he must try to get to people one at a time or one on one. Making contact is so difficult a threshold in this "mobile," "active" district that meetings where he meets new people — people who do not know him, and people out of the political mainstream — rank highest with him. Then, among such meetings, those which give him the most opportunities to present himself to others one on one are the best. In nearly every meeting, success is measured by the opportunity to have some personal contact with another individual. Particularly important to him is a request for help of some sort — any sort. That is the most effective way, he believes, of presenting himself as a person who is concerned about others. It is Congressman C's effort to achieve an equivalent of Congressman A's person-to-person style in a context where such an achievement is impossible. So one on one is at best a poor equivalence of person to person.

Still, Congressman C's efforts at personal contact are quite conventional. What is unique — among the districts studied so far — is the sheer difficulty of reaching others. In this kind of "typical suburban district in a frenzy," the politician suffers more competition for people's attention than elsewhere. Competition is most acute at election time. During my campaign visit, Congressman C constantly emphasized the root necessity of gaining visibility. On TV: "You need it so people will know you're running for Congress." On billboards: "Billboards let people know you're in the race." On flyers: "It isn't what you say on the flyer that counts; it's just getting them out." On his opponent: "He hasn't even surfaced. Nobody knows he's in the race. . . . It looks to me like the people in the know have decided he can't win and have cut off his money." In 1973, a noncampaign year, Congressman C scheduled fifteen media appearances — TV talk shows, radio interviews, meetings with editorial boards — as opposed to one for Congressman A and four for Congressman B. Visibility in the suburbs is not just necessary and hard to come by. It costs a lot of money. That is why, among my various House members, Congressman C ranks with two others, both of whom have heavily urban-suburban districts, in their preoccupation with the problem of raising money.

At campaign time, he continued to advocate one-on-one campaigning as the best way to get and hold a reelection constituency:

> You need the speeches and the press to let people know you're in the race. But the most effective way to win votes is going door to door. There's something very flattering when a person comes to your house to ask you for a vote. . . . We make selected forays into a few neighborhoods – and to plant gates and shopping centers.

Aside from these "forays," Congressman C faces the same old problem of finding people to present himself to. During the campaign, the symptom of his problem is that he cannot reach beyond his primary constituency. On the way to a Jaycee pancake breakfast the morning after a Republican party dinner in the same town, he fretted,

> I hope we won't see the same people today that we saw last night. I'm afraid we will. If you subtracted all the candidates, their wives, and their managers, there wasn't a "people" at the dinner. . . . You can see what's troubling me. Everywhere we go, we see the same people – the hard core.

"Between campaigns I meet new people," he says. "During campaigns I see the same old faces."

Congressman C has chosen a mix of presentational styles, a blend of the issue-oriented independent and the person seeking one-on-one contact with constituents. The constraints of his geographical constituency compel the issue-related element of his style. But district homogeneities create difficulties for the addition of some personal attentiveness to that style. His thoughtfulness, comfortableness, and versatility on the issues will bind his primary constituency to him. His reelection constituency, in view of the difficulty in reaching it, will be more problematical. After several terms in Congress, his name identification rests at 44 percent – up only 26 percent (from 18 percent) after ten years of home activity. Since one early scare, he has won by margins near 60 percent. There are other ways to cultivate a reelection constituency besides the rather conventional methods he employs. At best, he will continue to struggle to make contact in his way. At worst, someone else may find another combination of issue-related and attentiveness-related presentations of which a majority in this ever-changing district will approve.

ARTICULATING THE ISSUES: CONGRESSMAN D. If Congressman D's geographical constituency places any constraints on an appropriate home style, he is not very aware of them. He sees his district as heterogeneous:

> It is three worlds — three very different worlds. . . . It has a city — which is urban disaster. It has suburbs — the fastest growing part of the district. . . . It has a rural area which is a place unto itself.

> We spent all afternoon talking to the Teamsters in the city; and then we went to a cocktail party in a wealthy suburb. That's the kind of culture shock I get all the time in the district — bam! bam! bam!

The "three worlds" are not just different. They are also socially and psychologically separate.

> Actually the people in the three worlds don't know the others are even in the district. They are three separate worlds. In the city, they call it the city district; in the rural area, they call it their district. And both of them are shocked when they are told that they each make up only one-quarter of the district.

The other half are the suburbs, which are themselves very disparate. A few suburbs are linked to the city; most are not. Some are blue-collar; others are affluent. Some are WASP; others are ethnic. The district is, then, perceived not only as diverse but, unlike any others discussed so far, *segmented* as well. The possibilities for an acceptable presentation of self would seem to be limitless.

Congressman D's past associations in the district do not incline him toward a style indigenous to any one of "the three worlds." His district ties are not deep; he is a young man who went to college, worked, and got his political feet wet outside his district and his state. Nor are they strong; he grew up in a suburb in which he probably feels less at home ("We lost that stupid, friggin' town by 1000 votes last time.") than anywhere else in the district. When he first

thought about running, he knew nothing about the district. He
says,

> I can remember sitting in the living room here, in 1963, look-
> ing at the map of the district, and saying to myself, "Franklin?
> Webster? I didn't know there was a town called Franklin in
> this district. Is there a town called Webster?" I didn't know
> anything about the district.

Furthermore, he didn't know any people there. "We started completely from scratch. I was about as little known in the district as
anyone could be. In the city, I knew exactly two people. In the
largest suburb, I didn't know a single person."

His campaign began when he, plus two people he had recently
met, rented a motel room.

> We didn't know anybody. We thought we knew how to run
> a campaign, but we didn't know anybody to help us run it.
> The phone would ring and Mary would say "Welch for
> Congress." And she'd say, "I don't know whether he's here
> or not." Then she'd put her hand over the phone and say,
> "Are you here?" It was wild and crazy. And that's the way the
> campaign began.

Unlike the other three congressmen we have discussed, he has absolutely no sense that "only a person like myself," or that someone
like him in some respects, can win in his district. Indeed, he thinks
the opponent he first defeated was better suited to the district and
should have won the election. He says, "If I were he, I'd have
beaten me." In terms of an individual's immersion in his geographical constituency, it is hard to imagine two more different perceptions of me-in-the-district than those of Congressmen A and D —
with Congressmen B and C falling somewhere in between.

Congressman D has not been in office very long. Not only did he
begin from scratch, but he has been scratching ever since. He lost
his first race for Congress; he succeeded in his second; and he now
represents an objectively (and subjectively) marginal district. His
entire career has been spent reaching out for political support. As
he has gone about identifying and building first a primary and then
a reelection constituency, he has simultaneously been evolving a
political "self" and methods of presenting that self to them.

His earliest campaign promises were about the allocation of resources. He pledged to return to the district every week and to open three district offices, one in each of the "three worlds." These commitments about home style were contextually appropriate, if not contextually determined. For a candidate who neither knew the district nor was known there, pledges of attentiveness would seem almost mandatory. Furthermore, they allowed him to differentiate his proposed style from that of the incumbent, who was not very visible in the district and who operated one office there staffed by two people. Also, these pledges allowed him to elaborate his belief that "a sense of distance has developed between the people and the government" necessitating efforts to "humanize" the relationship. And, finally, his pledges gave him a stylistic lowest common denominator in a district with palpably diverse substantive interests. In 1973, Congressman *D* made thirty trips home, spent 109 working days there, operated three district offices, and assigned half of his total staff of fourteen to the district. Promises have turned into style: "We have given the impression of being hardworking — of having a magic carpet, of being all over the place. It's been backbreaking, but it's the impression of being accessible."

Congressman *D*'s actual presentation of self (what he does when he goes home) has evolved out of his personal interests and talents. He was propelled into active politics by his opposition to the Vietnam War. And his political impulses have been strongly issue-based ever since. He is severely critical of most of what has gone on in American public life for the last ten years. And he espouses a series of programmatic remedies — mostly governmental — for our social ills. He is contemptuous of "old-line" politicians who are uninterested in issues and who campaign "by putting on their straw hats and going to barbeques." Riding to a meeting at which he was to address one of his aging town committees, he shouted, "We don't want any old pols or town committees. Give me housewives who have never been in politics before." Thereupon, he rehearsed the opening lines of "the speech I'd like to give" to the town committee. "It will be a stirring speech. 'My fellow political hacks. We are gathered together to find every possible way to avoid talking about the issues.'" This comment, together with his running mimicry of the "old pols," exemplifies what Goffman calls a performance in the "back region," i.e., behind the scenes, where the individual's behavior is sharply differentiated from, and serves to accent, his presentation of self to the audience in the "front region." [5]

Congressman *D* presents himself in the "front region" (in public) as a practitioner of an open, issue-based, and participatory politics. It was his antiwar stand particularly, and his issue-orientation generally, that attracted the largest element of his primary constituency. This was made up of the antiwar activists — young housewives, graduate students, and professionals — who created, staffed, and manned the large volunteer organization that became his political backbone. In the end, his volunteers became skilled in the campaign arts — organizing, coordinating, polling, canvassing, targeting, mailing, fund raising, scheduling, advancing, leafleting — even "bumper-stickering." He said, "We organized and ran a campaign the likes of which people in this district had never seen. Neither party had done anything like it." Lacking a natural community to tie into and lacking any widespread personal appeal (or basis for such), Congressman D turned to the only alternative basis for building support — an organization. The "strongest supporters" in his organization did not support him because they knew him or had had any previous connection with him. The bond was agreement on the central issues and on the importance of emphasizing the issues. That agreement was the only "qualification" for the office that mattered to them. Within this group, the sense of identification between candidate and supporters was nearly total. He was "one of them." They trusted him. And they, with some trade union help (especially financial), gave him a victory in his initial primary.

In reaching for broader electoral support, Congressman D has been guided, not only by his commitment to "the issues," but by a personal penchant for talking about them. That is, he is an exceptionally verbal person; and he has evolved a suitably verbal home style. He places special emphasis on articulating, explaining, discussing, and debating issues. In each campaign (whether he be challenger or incumbent) he has pressed for debates with his opponent; and his assessment of his opponents focuses on their issue positions and their verbal facility. For example, he said of one opponent, "He's very conservative and, I understand, more articulate than the last guy. I felt sorry for him; he was so slow." For Congressman D, issue articulation is the essence of his presentational style. And it is so because he chose to make it so. Thus, he differs from Congressman C, whose issue-oriented style was thrust on him and who, in any case, has chosen to place equal stress on reaching people one at a time. On a continuum ranging from the most to the least person-to-person oriented style, or from the least to the most issue-oriented style, Congressman D stands at the opposite end from Congressman A, with B and C ranged between.

In his first two campaigns the main vehicle for presenting himself to his prospective election-reelection constituency was "the coffee." He would sit in a living room or a yard, morning, afternoon, and evening (sometimes as often as eight or ten times each day) with one or two dozen people, stating his issue positions, answering their questions, and engaging in give and take. At the verbal level, the subject was substantive problems. But Congressman D knew that expressions given off were equally important.

> People don't make up their minds on the basis of reading all our position papers. We have twenty-six of them, because some people are interested. But most people get a gut feeling about the kind of human being they want to represent them.

Thus, his display of substantive knowledge and his mental agility at the coffees would help convey the impression that "as a human being," he was qualified for the office. And, not relying wholly on these expressions given off, he would remind his listeners, "No congressman can represent his people unless he's quick on his feet, because you have to deal with 434 other people — each of whom got there by being quick on his feet." Coffees were by no means the only way Congressman D presented himself. But it was his preferred method. "The coffees are a spectacular success. They are at the heart of the campaign." Strategically, they were particularly successful in the suburban swing area of the district. But he tried them everywhere — even in the city, where they were probably least appropriate.

Once in office, he evolved a natural extension of the campaign coffee — a new vehicle that allowed him to emphasize, still, his accessibility, his openness, and his commitment to rational dialogue. It is "the open meeting," held twice a year, in every city and town in the district — nearly 200 in each session of Congress. Each postal patron gets an invitation to "come and 'have at' your congressman." And, before groups of 4 to 300, in town halls, schools, and community centers, he articulates the issues in a question-and-answer format. The exchanges are informative and wide-ranging; they are punctuated with enthusiasm and wit. The open meetings, like the coffees, allow Congressman D to play to his personal strengths — his issue interests and his verbal agility. In the coffees he was concerned with conveying threshold impressions of qualification; now his knowledge and status reenforce that impression in the open meetings. But, in the open meetings he is reaching for some deeper underpinnings of constituent trust. He does this with a presentation of self that combines identification and empathy. "I am not exactly one of you," he seems to tell them, "but we have a lot in common, and I feel a lot like you do." He expresses this feeling in two ways.

One expression given and given off in the open meetings is the sense that the give-and-take format requires a special kind of congressman and a rather special kind of constituency, and involves them, therefore, in a special kind of relationship. In each meeting I attended, his opening remarks included two such expressions:

> One of the first pieces of advice I got from a senior member of my party was, "Send out lots of newsletters, but don't mention any issues. The next thing you know, they'll want to know how you vote." Well, I don't believe that.

> My colleagues in Congress told me that the questionnaires I sent you were too long and too complicated and that you would never answer them. Well, five thousand have been filled out and returned already — before we've even sent them all out.

At the same time that he exhibits willingness and ability to tackle any question, explain any vote, and debate any difference of opinion, he massages the egos of his constituents by indicating how intelligent, aware, and concerned they are to engage with him in this new, open, rational style of politics. At the conclusion of an emotional debate with a right to life group — whose views he steadfastly opposed, he summed up: "I don't want to pat myself on the back, but there aren't too many congressmen who would do what I am doing here today. Most of them dig a hole and crawl in. I respect your opinions and I hope you will respect mine." The "pat on the back" is for *them* as well as him. And the expression given off is that of a special stylistic relationship. From that relationship, he hopes, will flow an increasing measure of constituent trust.

A second, related, expression given off is the sense that Congressman D, though he is a politician, is more like his constituents than he is like other politicians. It is not easy for him to convey such an impression, because the only thing his potential reelection constituents know about him is that he is a politician. They do not know him from any prior involvement in a community life. So he works very hard to bind himself to his constituents by disassociating himself from "the government" and disavowing his politician's status. He presents himself as an antipolitician, giving off the feeling that, "I'm just as fed up with government and the people who run it as you are." Because he is a congressman-politician, he is unrelentingly harsh in his criticism of Congress and his fellow legislators:

> As you know, I'm one of the greatest critics of Congress. It's an outrageous and outmoded institution.

> All Congress has ever done since I've been in Congress is pass the buck to the president and then blame him for what goes wrong. . . . Congress is gutless beyond my power to describe to you.

> Most members of Congress think that most people are clods. . . . Most of the guys down there are out of touch with their districts. . . . We aren't living in the 1930s anymore. Of course some members of Congress are. . . . I could never understand the lack of congressional sensitivity to the problems of the elderly. There are so many of them there.

A politician seeking to convey the impression that he is not a politician, Congressman D hopes to build constituent trust by inviting them to blend their cynicism with his.

The presentation of self at the open meetings — as an accessible, issue-oriented, communicative antipolitician — is a lowest-common-denominator presentation. It can win support in each of the three worlds without losing support in any. For it is the style, not the issue content that counts most in the reelection constituency. Congressman D is completely comfortable in the setting. "That was fun," he says after each open meeting. And, occasionally, "It's more fun when there's some hostility." But it is the format more than the individuals in attendance with which he is really "at home." He is not a person-to-person campaigner.

> Two of my friends in Congress hold office hours and see people one at a time. That would be a horribly inefficient use

of my time. I can see fifty at once. Besides, they don't want
to get involved in a give and take.

He, on the other hand, keeps his distance from the personal problems of his constituents, inviting them to talk with the staff members who accompany him to the open meetings. Of course, he meets
people face to face all the time. But he does not know or seek out
much about them as individuals, not much that would build anything more than a strictly political connection. An aptitude for
names and faces, a facility with tidbits of personal information and
small talk, an easy informality in face-to-face relations — these are
not his natural personal strengths. But they are not the keys to his
success with his reelection constituency. He has evolved a home
style that does not call for person-to-person abilities in large supply.

The open meetings remain the centerpiece of his home style.
"They are the most extraordinary thing we've ever done," he says,
"and the most important." He sees them as vehicles that help him
reach out to and expand his reelection constituency. He remains a
builder instead of a stabilizer in his constituency relations.

> Politically, these open meetings are pure gold. Fifty may
> come, but everybody in town gets an invitation. . . . I do
> know that none of our loyalists come to the meetings. They
> know the meetings are nonpartisan. Maybe one or two of
> them will show up, but mostly they are new faces.

They have given him entree into the least supportive, rural areas
of his district, where he recruits support and neutralizes the more
intense opposition. "At first," he says, "in some of these towns they
didn't know what to say to a Democrat. They probably hadn't met
one except for people who fixed their toilets." Yet, at the open
meetings, "we've had better turnouts, proportionately, in the rural
area. . . . And we get a lot of letters from people there who say
they disagree with us but respect our honesty and independence. We
get one-half of our mail from there." In time — but only in time —
interest and respect may turn into the supportive inferences that
connote trust.

But as Congressman D spends more and more of his time at home
cultivating an expanding reelection constituency, his oldest and

strongest supporters have felt neglected. So Congressman *D* has a complex strategic problem, in terms of allocating his time.

> When we began, we had the true believers working their hearts out. It was just like a family. But the more you gain in voters, and the more you broaden your constituency, the more the family feels hurt. Our true believers keep asking me, "Why don't you drink with us?" "Why don't you talk to me personally anymore?" I have to keep talking to them about the need to build a larger majority. I have to keep telling them that politics is not exclusive; it is inclusive. It is not something that can be done in the living room.

The true believers are not threatening a total loss of support; but declining enthusiasm would present a serious support problem. One way Congressman *D* may deal with the problem is to come home more, so that he can give the necessary time to the true believers. He does come home more than Congressman *A* or *C*, partly because his strategic problems at home require it. Still, Congressman *D*'s emphasis is on identifying and building support beyond the primary constituency in the three worlds. In 1973, he allocated his home engagements in faithful proportion to the population of the three worlds — spending 50 percent of his time in the suburbs, 26 percent in the rural area, and 24 percent in the city. He finds the open meetings the most effective (and most comfortable) vehicle for him. "What more could anyone ask," he says, "than to have the congressman come to their town personally?" His primary constituents do ask something more. And, so long as he gives it to them, he will remain a congressman.

NOTES

1. Fifty-six percent — 72 of 129.
2. Erving Goffman, *The Presentation of Self in Everyday Life* (New York: Doubleday, 1959). The language I have quoted appears in the Introduction and the Conclusion.
3. A helpful discussion of empathy is that of Daniel Lerner in his study of modernization in the Middle East. Daniel Lerner, *The Passing of Traditional Society* (Glencoe: Free Press, 1958), pp. 47–52, 69–75.
4. David Leuthold concludes in his study of House campaigns that voters are looking for ability, concern, and similarity to themselves. In the somewhat different language we have used — qualification, empathy, identification — that

is what my representatives also think the voters want. See David Leuthold, *Electioneering in a Democracy* (New York: Wiley, 1968), pp. 23–24.
5. Goffman, *Presentation of Self*, chap. 3, esp. p. 128. Often, comments made in the "back regions" provide clues for at-homeness estimates. For example: "We're having breakfast tomorrow with a businessman's group. They're really a bunch of hoodlums." "We don't want to expose Dick to any of these knee-jerk liberals — the whites who are going to save us blacks in the city." "Smell that stench. That's the mill. Those sons of bitches have polluted the air so that ducks won't come in here anymore." "Labor is mad at my opponent because they think he's selling them out to these nature fakers." "Now there's a bunch of consumer advocates. That car dealer — what a schlock. He's been unloading lousy cars on people for years. . . . And that engineer, all he wants to do is sell boilers. Hell, he doesn't give a shit if the thing leaks around the faucets." "Those people are affluent, well educated and idle. They think of themselves as totally unselfish, idealistic, and right. They think they are separate and apart from everyone else. They come from the do-gooders and crybaby groups — disillusioned McGovernites and Republican liberals. These crybaby groups bruise easily. If you deal with them too harshly or too abruptly they will go home and sulk and drop out."

CHAPTER FOUR

Home Style: Presentation of Self II

THE PRESENTATION OF SELF

Every presentational style contains both person-to-person and issue-oriented components in some degree. And every presentational style contains a third element, too — service to the district. Many activities can be incorporated under the rubric of "district service," or "constituent service," but the core activity is providing help to individuals, groups, and localities in coping with the federal government. Individuals need someone to intercede with the bureaucracies handling their veterans' benefits, social security checks, military status, civil service pension, immigration proceedings, and the like. Private groups and local governments need assistance in pursuing federal funds, for water and sewer projects, highways, dams, buildings, planning, research and development, small business loans, and so forth. Sometimes, service benefiting individuals is known as "casework" and service having a larger number of benefactors is called "project assistance." Sometimes both are lumped together as casework.[1] Whatever it is called, all House members and their staffs engage in it.

For the congressman's staff — whether located in Washington or at home — constituent service is the most time-consuming activity.[2] For the member of Congress, it is a highly valued form of activity. Not only is constituent service universally recognized as an important part of the job in its own right. It is also universally recognized as powerful reelection medicine. "What political scientists have to understand," said one member, "is that an incumbent congressman can get reelected by the services he is in a position to do for people." Nonetheless, the prominence of district service in the presentational styles of House members varies widely.

SERVICING THE DISTRICT: CONGRESSMAN E. Congressman E is by no means the purest example one could find of a service-oriented congressman. But of the eighteen we have observed, he comes closest. In the importance he attributes to casework as an ingredient of his home style, he stands first among the members of our "sample."

As Congressman E views his geographical constituency, there is nothing about it that would constrain him to adopt a particular home style. He thinks of it as just about as heterogeneous as it can be. "This district," he says, "is a microcosm of the nation."

> We are geographically southern and politically northern. We have agriculture — mostly soybeans and corn. We have big business like Union Carbide and General Electric. And we have unions. We have a city and we have small towns. We have some of the worst poverty in the country in Delta County. And we have some very wealthy sections, though not large. We have wealth in the city and some wealthy towns. We have urban poverty and rural poverty. Just about the only thing we don't have is a good-sized ghetto. Otherwise, everything you can have, we've got it right here.

In thinking about his district, therefore, he perceives no commanding source of stylistic expectations. Moreover, Congressman E is not a native of the area. He moved there after college and went into business. So he does not view the district with Congressman B's ingrained local-boy sensitivity — a sensitivity that might help him imbibe some locally acceptable lowest-common-denominator style. Congressman E, therefore, most closely resembles Congressman D, who also faces a heterogeneous district without any guiding personal roots. In neither case is there that sense of fit between the congressman and the district that exists for the other cases we have examined.

Nor has Congressman E had any prior political experience that would predispose him toward some familiar formula for political survival. When he was recruited to run for Congress by a group of local businessmen and politicians, he was a political innocent.

> I was home one day when the phone rang. It was former Congressman Carl Schmitz, who said, "Can you come down to the Anthracite Club? There's a group of us here who have

> something very important to ask you. . . . We want you to run for Congress on the Republican ticket." When I heard that, I said, "Absolutely not, that's the silliest thing I ever heard of." And I hung up. I didn't even think it was important enough to mention to the family. I had the normal disdain for politicians and politics that many businessmen have. I was a registered Republican, but I had done nothing whatever politically. I had helped run all the good guy civic functions — Boy Scouts, Red Cross, United Fund — but had never turned a finger in politics. . . . Well, the same group kept coming back and hitting me hard. . . . [So] three days before the filing date, I went down and signed up. Absolutely and in every sense of the word, I was drafted into politics.

As a congressman, he continues to think of himself as nonpolitical. "I'm not a politician. I came to the job without any experience in politics. People on my staff half my age have had twice as much political experience as I have. . . . I'm no politician. I'm probably the most nonpolitical congressman around." Congressman E's distaste for politics only accents his lack of fit with his district, because he sees it as an extraordinarily "political" district:

> This district has traditionally been known as "The Bloody Third," the home of the most vicious, brutal politics in the state. This is a very political state and this district has the reputation of being the most bone crunching of them all.

By background and attitudes, therefore, he would incline toward a style whereby he could present himself "as a person" who is nonpolitical. One obvious possibility is a style emphasizing constituency service. Partly by design and partly by trial and error, this is the style he has adopted.

To say that Congressman E has little taste for the politics of his district is not to say that he is without a political philosophy. When asked why the men at the Anthracite Club came to him, he replied,

> I had done a great deal of speaking in the area . . . speaking in praise of the free enterprise system. They knew I thought as they did philosophically – that we should increase productivity, live within our means, cut down on welfare. They also thought I was electable.

Just why they thought him "electable" is not clear. Probably it was because he was articulate and people-oriented, having been an "outside" rather than an "inside" businessman. It is not likely they thought his philosophy would attract a reelection constituency. Surely, he did not.

> This is a marginal district. I always win by less than 55 percent. No landslides here. It's a Democratic district and a liberal district. My predecessor, who was around a long time, always had high ADA ratings. They thought he was wonderful.

Congressman E never linked his emphasis on constituency service to the marginality of his district or to the liberalism of his predecessor. But, for a congressman facing the prospect of close elections in a district opposed to him philosophically, the appeal of a constituency service emphasis would have to be strong. Constituency service is totally nonpartisan and nonideological. As an electoral increment, it is an unadulterated plus. It is all the more appealing to a nonpolitical congressman who finds the milieu of his adopted heterogeneous district bewildering from an issue standpoint. "The leadership tells you to support the president but vote your district. What is your district on these questions? It's hard to say."

His earliest allocative decisions indicated a strong interest in emphasizing service to the district. He talked about his staffing decisions:

> I wanted a good liaison man who would go out and see people in the district who had problems. I got Dennis Hooper who had been with Congressman Stu Brown, who had just retired. Dennis has an office in his home out in Clarksburg. So the first thing I wanted was an experienced guy. Then I got a uniquely qualified gal to head up the city office. Like Dennis Hooper, she was an older person. And she had a sympathetic ear. Both of them were good and experienced at casework.

The decision to hire a professional district aide, one who had not even lived in the district, was evidence of serious intent, particularly because it ran counter to his predecessor's decision to name a prominent party official to the position. Congressman E did not set out deliberately to create a contrast with his predecessor. He is just not comfortable with nor respectful of local party officials. (Of the party official who wanted to be his district representative, he commented, "Just between you and me, I'm sure he's a crook. And I don't know why he hasn't landed in jail.") Nor was his decision to handle more casework in the district than his predecessor a conscious effort at contrast. But field representative Hooper does something that has never been done before. He rides circuit weekly to hold office hours in three of the larger towns in the rural part of the district. In addition, he makes "house calls" throughout the district, and runs a district office in his home. These visits advertise Congressman *E*'s desire to help, and they encourage people to seek that help, thus inflating the congressman's reputation for service to the district.

A second, related allocative decision was to keep his family in the district and to return home every weekend. He thinks of that decision as adding a crucial increment to his first reelection margin. "If my family had come to Washington," he says, "I would have been home less. And I would not have been reelected. I won reelection by only two or three points the first time." Congressman *E* comes home appreciably more often than any other of the eighteen we have studied. In 1973 he made 42 trips home and was in the district for a total of 49 weekends and 165 days. That is, he spent 45 percent of the year at home. "I doubt that I've spent more than ten weekends away from the district in eight years," he says. When he is home, he makes himself totally accessible to constituents. He holds office hours each weekend. He goes to any function to which he is invited. And, "I keep a listed phone number, and it rings constantly when I'm home. We don't discourage it."

He describes his weekend routine:

> I hold office hours here every Friday morning. I used to come in Thursday night till they took the plane off. Now I come in Friday morning, Sally meets me at 9:00, and I can be at the office by 9:30. On rainy days, I'll stay in the office till about 11:00, go over to the Anthracite Club for lunch and bridge till about 1:00, and come back to the office. On sunny days, I'll stay in the office till 11:59 and then go out to the golf course.

> I come home every weekend. As soon as the congressional business ends, I head for the district. I have at least four

> separate engagements every weekend. Once, I had eleven. I
> go wherever I'm asked. If someone calls months ahead, I
> put it on the calendar. I don't do the way some people do and
> say "I don't schedule that far ahead," while they wait to see
> what the biggest invitation will be. I take the one that asks
> first, big or small.

Frequent home visits and frequent public appearances there do not
necessarily indicate a service-oriented presentational style. But when
coupled with a strong emphasis on casework — both by staff and in
person — home trips and home appearances can be fairly construed
as further evidence of the congressman's desire to help his constituents.

The service image is even further strengthened by Congressman
E's devotion to securing federal money for his district. "I've been
very successful in getting things for the district," he says.

> Before I was elected, there were exactly seven miles of inter-
> state highway built in this district. Now, just look at that vista
> up and down I-40, "Brought to you by courtesy of your
> member of Congress, the O'Connor highway."

> We got $1 million in above the budget for a dam in the
> district that will enable us to get going early. I think it was
> the only item in the bill above the budget. I've also gotten
> some money for river bank erosion projects — the only two
> new ones in the bill.

> My main issue is inflation and holding down the cost of
> government spending. We've been so successful at getting
> money for this district — the year-by-year graph for FHA
> [Farmers Home Administration] money goes shooting up —
> that I'm embarrassed to mention it. My opponent will accuse
> me of talking out of both sides of my mouth.

But Congressman E is not so embarrassed that he would prefer to
present himself to others as issue-oriented rather than service-
oriented — or close his mouth.

After he had been in office four years, a poll told him that it was
precisely the service image that was gaining him identification with
the voters.

> We had a very high recognition factor. And of all the things
> said about me, none of them said, "He's a conservative or a

liberal," or "He votes this way on such and such an issue."
None of that at all. There were two things said. One, "He
works hard." Two, "He works for us." Nothing more than
that. So we made it our theme, "O'Connor gets things done";
and we emphasized the dams, the highways, the buildings,
the casework.

It has been his theme ever since. Two years later, he repeated, "I'm
not identified as a person interested in national problems. I'm identified for my interest in local problems. This is what we're going to
make the theme of our campaign." His campaign brochure listed
not a single issue position. At the top, it headlined, "O'Connor
Works for Us!" At the bottom it said, "Tim O'Connor works hard
to serve his constituents in _____." In between, it listed six summary results of his years in office: 14,000 individuals helped "with
problems involving the federal government," 25,000 "incidental requests" filled, 20,000 letters concerning "national issues" answered,
700 community "projects" assisted, weekly visits and office hours,
plus a 93 percent voting record and sponsorship of 100 pieces of
legislation. The service emphasis in this literary presentation of himself is clear.

Congressman E's perception of his various constituencies makes
it clear that he thinks his service activities do provide a winning
electoral increment. When asked "Who votes for you?" he replied,

> If you get over 50 percent, that means you must get a little
> something from everybody. The labor leaders fight me tooth
> and nail, but I get some votes from the rank and file. I lead
> the ticket in Democratic counties, but I win much bigger
> in Republican counties. It would not be fair to say I get the
> most conservative counties . . . because the most conserva-
> tive counties are Democratic. We took a poll and the one
> image they had of me was that I was a hard worker. So I
> get a broad base of votes. I think I get a lot of votes because
> of casework.

He "never gets" the union-oriented workers: "Every union hall has
a 'Beat O'Connor' sign in it. I'm a prime target of organized labor."
Nor does he ever get those conservative Democratic counties: "On
all the issues they agree with me, but they are German Catholics
and they are Democrats by religion." But the reason he gets some
rank-and-file union votes and the reason he leads the ticket in Demo-

cratic counties, he believes, is because of his constituency service —
casework. "The biggest part of getting reelected is casework. I have
the best case workers anywhere, in the district and in Washington."
   When asked, further, "Who are your very strongest supporters?"
he replied,

> Financially, my strong support comes from the Chamber of
> Commerce types, business and professional people. They
> finance my campaigns. But if you are talking about grassroots
> support, the most loyal followers are the people for whom
> we have done casework. "You helped Bessie Whiteside
> with her Social Security check, and our whole neighborhood
> is going to vote for you." I hear that all the time. And
> then there are the veterans groups and the civic and social
> groups. . . . These groups don't endorse candidates, but they
> identify with me.

He believes that his constituency service brings him primary as well
as reelection constituents. And, though he doesn't speak explicitly
about the value of this presentational style in his kind of district,
he clearly does not believe the district could be held by his party
without it. "Could the Republicans hold the seat if you retired?" he
was asked. "The Republicans wouldn't stand a ghost of a chance to
win it. My strength is the result of the casework and all the visits."
"It's an individual franchise you hold," he says, "not a political
franchise."
   During the time I traveled with him, Congressman E survived.
But, save for the year he ran against "an incompetent [who] didn't
know his knee from his elbow," he has teetered on the brink of
defeat. Perhaps we should conclude this description by expressing
wonderment at his staying power and attributing it to his service-
oriented style. That conclusion is surely valid. But we might ask ourselves briefly why Congressman E, unlike so many other House
members in recent years, has been unable to consolidate his electoral hold. For that, too, is an accurate generalization.
   We have already commented on the electoral potency of district
service. As Congressman E says, "We get forty requests a week for
help. Half of them we can't do anything about. Some we can. But
they all get a sympathetic ear. That's what people want more than
anything else, a sympathetic ear." If we grant that service always
helps, the question is: How much does it help? If we equate constit-

uent service with "the power of incumbency," our best present estimate is that incumbency, or extra constituent service, adds an *average* of 5 percent to a House member's electoral total.[3] Our guess is that those who exceed the average and thus consolidate their districts are not only those who are especially service-oriented, but those whose personal qualities and personal predispositions strongly reenforce their service-orientation. As a presentational style, service to the district is available to all representatives. Indeed, it is the most available. That is why it is a residual component of every member's home style. But it is exploited more intentionally and more effectively by some than by others. Congressman E, despite his intentions, does not exploit it to the maximum. That is why, early on, we said that he did not represent the purest case of the service congressman. Perhaps, if he did, he would have secured for himself a more protected reelection constituency.

"I love the job. I love the casework," he says. Yet he also says, "Others do it for me. I'm the worst caseworker around. The best work is done when I stay completely out of it." He worries a great deal about the most productive use of his time. And surprisingly often he concludes that his time is better spent in some form of activity other than direct contact with constituents. One might expect to find a service-oriented congressman presenting himself to others person to person as Congressman A does or one on one as Congressman C does. But we do not find Congressman E doing this, not consistently. And it is this lack of consistency in expressions given and expressions given off that makes his style difficult to fathom. There are probably many reasons why he has not gotten a firm grip on his district. But one of them, we think, is stylistic.

He campaigns, for example, in the rural half of his district by driving around in a van blaring music, in a caravan of cars, which stops in each little town while the volunteers in their O'Connor hats distribute literature and the congressman shakes any hands he can find. But it is not at all personal. When he grabbed one man's hand, the man said, "I'm a member of the caravan." Congressman E replied, "I can't tell the people in the caravan from the customers." He philosophizes, "The purpose of the campaign is to get hundreds of people involved at the grass roots. A caravan of forty cars in a town of thirty people — that's involvement." He creates more hoopla later in the campaign by blitzing the larger rural towns in a helicopter.

But there is a very different kind of home style that he deliberately does not employ in the rural areas.

> I was talking to Jack Evans [the neighboring congressman] the other day, and I told him I was having a hard campaign. He asked me what I was doing, and I told him I had these vans with the loudspeakers, and the helicopters. He told me that he gets in the car, all by himself, and drives to a little town and goes into the grocery store to talk. He says that by the time he works his way up to the hardware store, the guys say to him, "We heard you were in town." He says the small towns don't like the oompah, the noise. He says that it's all over town when he goes.

Congressman A, and several other person-to-person campaigners present themselves in exactly this way. Congressman E does not.

When asked to select the most important event of a busy campaign weekend, he chose walking in a parade. "Whenever you see 10,000 people, that's important." But he continued, "The most productive use of my time was my news conference. That got me more coverage — all the TV stations and two newspapers." Here again is an alternate style in dealing with the media, one he eschews.

> When the governor comes to town, he visits each one of the newspapers and each one of the TV stations and talks with them personally. I hold a news conference, write up a press release, and send it to those who weren't there. I do in twenty minutes what it takes him a whole day to do. But he believes in the personal touch.

Congressman E deliberately sacrifices "the personal touch" for a quicker, broader exposure.

Despite his office hours, he frequently chooses not to use person-to-person approaches to his constituents. The same is true with the less personal one-on-one approach. Surely he meets people individually during his various formal appearances. And he recognizes its importance:

> In this area, the man who wins is the man who shakes the most hands. People will vote for you if they can say "I know him" or "I met him." And they will say that if they have shaken hands with you. The only Republicans who win

around here are the ones who shake every danged hand in every danged county.

On one occasion, I saw him do some handshaking in a Fourth of July fireworks crowd. When he attends church festivals, he says, "I stand at the beginning of the line and say, 'I'm the federal complaint officer.'" Yet during his toughest campaign, he repeatedly rejected handshaking — the opportunity for soliciting casework — in favor of other activity. "The most productive way to spend an hour of my time is to hold a news conference, or send a radio bleeper," he said. And that is what he did.

> Next week, there's St. Theresa's Festival, the biggest thing of the year on the East Side. You can walk up and down Main Street and meet thousands of voters. My staff thinks I should be there. What they don't understand is that I'm better off in Washington, having my picture taken with Henry Kissinger on Tuesday, complaining to him about foreign aid. On Wednesday I'm going to get the Small Business Award. I'll take the trophy or whatever they give me and have my picture in the paper with it. I think I should be doing those things; my staff doesn't. How do you know what you should be doing?

He went to Washington to have his picture taken instead of staying home to shake hands. It is a productivity calculus at odds with his own prescription for winning and with his own comment that his constituents identify with him because of what he does about local, not national, problems.

A possible answer to this puzzle may be found in Congressman E's personal preferences. For despite his extroverted appearance and his cheerful "Hi, how are you," he is not personally comfortable in unstructured, face-to-face relationships with others. At the fireworks fair, he commented, "These are the people I don't normally come in contact with. They are blue-collar workers, the people who work at Sylvania. You just don't meet these kinds of people at the chamber of commerce or the country club." Yet his handshaking was surprisingly unaggressive. When I asked him why, he said,

> I'm shy. Maybe not shy — but yes you could say I'm shy. I don't like to go up to someone and stick my hand in his face.

If I were either of our state's senators, I would start at one end of this area and shake every single hand till I got to the other end. They both go to basketball games and start at the top row, circle the stadium shaking every hand, then drop down a row and go around again. To me that's just bad manners. If a person goes to a basketball game, he wants to see the basketball game, not have some idiot politician sticking a hand in his face.

A couple of days later, while waiting to be served in a country restaurant, he said, "If either of our state's senators were here, they would have gotten up and shaken every hand in the place." Again, he distinguished himself from the "idiot politicians" who stick their hands in other people's faces. Unlike Representative A or B or C, he is not an experienced politician, and he remains personally uncomfortable with some of the established practices of politics in his highly politicized area.

For whatever reason, Congressman E often chooses to present himself in ways that do not seem calculated to reenforce his presentation to others as someone who wants to help with their problems. His ways seem, to the contrary, fairly remote from such a purpose. The efficient, businessman side of Congressman E inclines him toward a public relations activity that is out of phase with the constituent service elements of his style. It is this inconsistency or lack of reenforcement, we speculate, that keeps him from capitalizing on the full potential of his service-oriented presentational style. When asked why he thought people trusted him, he replied,

> People are impressed by my TV image. I'm not a polished speaker, and I've tried not to become one. I don't enunciate my words carefully or train myself to use perfect diction. I look right into the camera and talk to people like it's over the back fence. My skill, if I have any and people seem to think I have, is in responding to questions. People trust a guy that will immediately respond to some question and come right out and answer it.

If, indeed, he believes that his TV image is the primary source of constituent trust, all those calculations which sacrifice personal relationships for broad exposure may be rational. But if he wishes to reenforce his service-oriented presentation to others, it would be more rational to choose to close the social and psychological distance between himself and his constituents instead of widening it. Too much stylistic ambiguity is not helpful electorally. So long as Congressman *E*'s home activity contains these ambiguities, he will remain a very marginal congressman.

Very little has been said about local political organizations and their relationship to the presentation of self. We can assume that every House member has the rudiments of an organization to help with the tasks of a campaign. But in none of the cases discussed so far have local party organizations shaped the home styles of the members. We know there have been some such cases — in the Chicago of Richard Daley, for example.[4] But the research of Avery Leiserson in the 1950s and David Olson in the 1960s has told us that most members of Congress are neither the creatures of, nor constrained by, local organizations.[5] Chroniclers of "the new politics" of the 1970s have made even stronger assertions about the change from party-based to candidate-centered campaigning.[6] As voters, party loyalists are assumed to provide the foundation for every reelection constituency. But permanent party organizations are said to be giving way to transient, candidate-centered campaign organizations as the most effective electoral vehicle.

Our observations dovetail with these conclusions. Only two of the eighteen members studied were originally recruited by the local party organization. And eight began their careers by challenging the party organization. Most of the eighteen coexist with the party — because of party indifference to the congressional office or because the party leaders value the proven independent strength of the congressman as a resource. Most primary constituencies consist of people whose loyalties are to the congressman rather than to the party. And in only two or three cases is there an integrated working relationship between the congressman's personal organization and the local party organization. That is exactly the way most of our House members want it — separate organizations pursuing separate tasks. The task of the congressman's personal organization is to keep him in Congress. The task of the local party organizations is to keep the party in control of local offices.

Most members of Congress work to preserve this separation of congressional from local politics. They prefer to remain minimally involved in local politics, not to become local political leaders. Said one,

A congressman has to make a conscious choice, whether he
wants to be a local political leader – to be a big cheese in
local politics – or whether he wants to tend to business in
Washington and do what the local leaders ask of him in local
politics. I deliberately chose the second course.

And so have most of his colleagues. Four of the eighteen (all Democrats) campaign loyally — year in and year out — for the entire party
ticket, top to bottom.[7] In the final analysis, however, they, like the
others, are in business for themselves. In Congressman E's words,
"It's an individual franchise you hold, not a political franchise."
But it remains open to a member of Congress to pursue a different
course — to involve himself heavily in local politics, became a local
political leader, and, of course, be perceived as such by his supportive
constituencies. Of the eighteen we have observed, one member follows this course. And it is to his example that we turn to elaborate
a different home style.

THE POLITICAL LEADER: CONGRESSMAN F. It would not be correct
to say that Congressman F ever deliberately chose to become a local
political leader — certainly not to the extent that he now is. But a
black congressman from a dominantly black district does not have
much choice. At the very least, his high-status job gives him extraordinary local prestige. At the very least, too, he exerts more leverage
on the world outside his district than almost any of his constituents.
So, willy-nilly, his support and his spokesmanship will be valued
locally. At a time of rapid politicization, with black citizens reaching
for a larger share of political power, the congressman can hardly avoid
becoming first an exemplar and then a leader of that process. And
because that transformation, like all other American political change,
must be wrought locally, from the ground up, a sensitive congressman
will find it impossible to remain aloof.

And Congressman F is sensitive. The very first time I saw him at
home, he was singing the Negro National Anthem at the dedication
of an Afro-American Cultural Center at a local college. The very
last time I saw him at home, three visits later, he was preaching in
church, saying,

Three hundred people have been killed, shot — men, women
and children – in Soweto. And you know, those people look
just like you do. Our roots are in that part of the world. And

> we, as church people, have an obligation to be concerned about our brothers and sisters in that part of the world.

He is sensitive to all the common experiences and common aspirations that bind black people one to the other. The term he uses, always, is "the black community." And he works every chance he gets to deepen the sense of community among blacks. His own identification with the black community is obvious and total. Every expression he gives or gives off conveys the idea "I am one of you." His view of me-in-the-district begins, then, with a feeling of total immersion in the black community. Congressman *F* sees himself as a microcosm of that community. He says, "When I vote my conscience as a black man, I necessarily represent the black community. I don't have any trouble knowing what the black community thinks or wants." Nothing less, he believes, than a microcosmic relationship of this sort — a perfect fit — can bring success in this district. It is a perception very much like that of his white colleague from the rural South, Congressman *A*.

Congressman *F*'s district is urban and northern. It is roughly two-thirds black and one-third white. He thinks of his reelection constituency as "the whole black community." He will take whatever white support comes his way. And he knows some will. But he does not count on any when he calculates. Reflecting on an upcoming redistricting, he said,

> If they packed my district with whites from Southgate, as some say they might, that would kill me. . . . I need a black base — 55 percent at least. With only 40 percent black, I don't believe I could win. I don't mind having whites in the district, so long as I have enough black support to begin with. That's the way it has to be for me.

Because the district — black and white — is heavily Democratic, all Congressman *F* has to worry about is a primary. And when he thinks of his primary constituency, he also excludes whites. That is, he does not depend on any white votes to win.

He has faced two serious primary opponents. Both were black, and both courted white support. He described the first one:

> He was a black man who was popular with the white community. And the reason was that he was always criticizing the

black community. He would tell them just what they wanted
to hear — that black people were hoodlums and bums and
all that sort of thing. They thought he was a wonderful
person. He ran with the help of the Democratic party, the
unions, the city newspapers, and one black church group.
I had the endorsement of every other black church group
and all the organizations there were in the black community.
I beat him two to one.

This primary victory secured his seat. And his superior identification
with the black community won for him a primary constituency
among its elites.

Congressman F's first primary victory was one of several local
political successes that produced fresh leadership, increased con-
sciousness, and heightened aspirations within the local black community. And in time-honored fashion, their leaders asked for a
larger share of political power within the urban area as a whole.
They pressed their claims through the Democratic party structure,
of which they were a part — claims for a greater share of candidacies,
appointments, contracts, and jobs, a share commensurate with their
growing importance within the party. But they were rebuffed. And
in retaliation they decided to organize the black community as an
autonomous political force, to endorse and elect candidates of their
own choice across party lines. They hoped thereby to demonstrate
the fact of black power to the white politicians in the metropolitan
area and use that demonstration to advance black interests.

Thus was the South Side Community Caucus born — an independent black political organization of Republicans as well as Democrats, working outside the framework of the established political
parties. Congressman F was only one among a number of leaders
in this effort. But because he occupied the office with the greatest
prestige and territorial scope, and because most of the area's blacks
were in his district, he soon became the formal head of the South
Side Community Caucus. And the caucus became his, as well as
the community's, organizational backbone.

When I first visited the district, the caucus was undergoing its
first test of strength. It had endorsed some Republicans — black and
white — for local office. And it had energized the local community
to a level of volunteer activity unmatched by anything I observed
in the other seventeen districts. The idea, of course, was more auda-
cious than the mere election of a congressman, because it involved

teaching the most sophisticated kind of cross-party, split-ticket voting patterns to an entire electorate, many of whom were altogether new to political activity. In this context, Congressman F was organizer, energizer, and educator. Everywhere he went — candidate's night in a church, neighborhood improvement association dinner, fund-raising cocktail party — he articulated the concept of the caucus:

> The Democratic party has had the black vote in its pocket for years. And what have they given us in return? Nothing. Why should they? They had our vote. Of course they handed out a few menial jobs. . . . This year the Democratic Committee said to us, "We've got a chairman, a vice-chairman, a secretary, and a treasurer and not one of them can be black. We've got the election board and not one of them can be black. . . ." We have 25 percent of the vote, and the Democratic Committee won't put one black man on their slate. . . . Well, we told them they could take their party and stick it some place else. The bosses can still make their decisions in the back room, but we want no more of it. . . . Party labels are taboo. That's what the South Side Community Caucus is all about. We screened all the candidates . . . and endorsed those candidates we felt would be most responsive to the needs of this community . . . some black and some white, some Democratic and some Republicans. When a Bill Carter [Republican councilman] can sit down with a Carol Benson [Democratic councilwoman] and decide, regardless of party, what's good for this community, that's beauty! We're asking you to vote that way — some here, some there. Cross the street. Teach the Democratic party respect. . . . No one ever gives up power. You have to seize power. That's why we're asking you to support the caucus and what we're trying to do. . . . With the caucus you can stand tall, not, as Flip Wilson says, crawl small. This is not Art Brooks's caucus or anyone's caucus. It's bigger than any one of us because it's all of us. The caucus is you. It's the unity of the whole black community.

This is the language of identification combined with the language of leadership. "I am one of you; I am standing up for you." From this combination flows constituent trust. "The more active I am working for them in the caucus," he says, "the more popular I become, the more they trust me and are proud of me."

Political ambition came neither quickly nor obsessively to Congressman F. He is a long-time resident of his city, a member of a well-known family, and active in the civic affairs of the middle class — NAACP, Urban League, church. "For a long time," he says, "I had very little interest in politics. . . . I was not interested in running for public office." He was recruited to run for Congress by some fellow civic activists.

> After a great deal of praying and thinking and lots of family confabs, I decided to run. And here I am. I'm in it and I like it. But I would have been perfectly happy without it.

He comes home regularly.

> I come home more often than a lot of the guys. Not like the Philadelphia people who go home every night. But I'm home on the average once a week. I meet with church groups and other groups. And I let people see me, let them know that I haven't lost touch with them.

In 1973, he made thirty trips home. A majority of them included meetings related to caucus affairs. Otherwise, the presentations he prefers are set speeches to community organizations. "I try to speak everywhere I'm asked in the district." Seven of the twelve events at which I observed him were formal speeches. And on five of the nine days I spent in the district, his entire schedule consisted of a single speech. In these speeches he covers the spectrum of black concerns — education, health, housing, poverty, drugs, welfare, and, throughout, the underlying theme of black political action. He works hard on speeches, and they drain a lot of his energy. The pace of his public schedule at home is greater than that of his colleagues A and B, but slower than that of Representatives C and D. His 1973 schedule called for seventy-five appearances during his ninety-four days at home.

He has never acquired a taste for the mundane routines of politics. He does not promote one-on-one contacts with his constituents, as, for example, Congressman C does. He holds as few office hours as possible.

> Mac and the staff try to do all they can for them and put them off. But if they insist, and Mac has gone all the way

> with them, then I will see them. It's their right. . . . Congressman Nix of Philadelphia goes home every Saturday and sits in his office talking to his clients. I don't do that and I don't want to.

Nor does he like it when he gets caught up in the daily crises of the caucus. "Tomorrow I'll have to sit with all the local politicians and hold their hands. The way they have me doing this is ridiculous." He professes neither knowledge about, nor appetite for, "ward politics." Unlike Congressman A, he says, "The thing that bugs me the most about politics . . . is the guy who comes up to you and says, 'What's my name? . . . I'll bet you don't know who I am.'" He reacts strongly to suggestions that he stay home more and engage in more one-on-one activity:

> I get on the plane after five days' work in Washington and come home for two more. . . . What do you want me to do — stand on the corner of 33rd and Chestnut, jive talking and slapping hands and giving the African handshake bullshit all week long, or do you want me to spend my time working for you in Washington?

He does not think of himself and he does not present himself as either a person-to-person politician or as "one of the boys."

It is not just that one-on-one politicking does not appeal to him. His supporters do not seem to expect it from him. He is an established celebrity in the black community. "They did a survey and found that my name recognition was 99 percent. I'll bet face recognition is just as high." As we drove through the district, during each of my visits, people waved as they passed, or, at stoplights, they rolled down the car window to call to him — something I did not see elsewhere.

> People recognize the car and they want to pull alongside and say hello. It makes them feel proud; and you can see the smile break over their faces. They feel important, too, to see and talk to the congressman.

Certainly, he feels under no political pressure to get out and meet people as, for example, Congressman C — with less than half that recognition — feels driven to do.

More important, Congressman F's idea that people are and want to be proud of him calls for a dignified, exemplary presentational style more than for an intimate or familiar one.

> People in the black community read avidly about what I'm doing, and almost everyday there is something in the paper. They read it and they feel proud. Almost anything I do makes them feel proud. They know that I'm a black man standing up for the black man.

His supporters interpret much of what he does symbolically. And symbolic presentations do not require person-to-person activities.

When he walked into the hall to give a speech to 1000 members of a women's educational sorority, he was given a standing ovation. He was introduced as "our leader," as "a man who has known poverty and overcome it, a man who knows what it is to be part of an oppressed people — our people," and as "a man admired for his many, many awards and accomplishments, for his many qualifications." At the end of the speech, he received another standing ovation. Then dozens of women crowded forward to get his autograph. Afterward, he explained why the speech was important:

> A large group like that does something to me. It makes me want to prepare more and do a better job. But I'm relieved when it's over. They are all from my district. They are a good cross section of concerned people — schoolteachers and administrators mostly. Some of them are campaign workers — more now than they used to be, with more black awareness. These people were the types who used to want to stay out of things and keep to themselves.

The South Side Caucus had brought these people into politics. And they recognized, in Congressman F, a leader they would not have recognized a few years earlier.

The autograph-seeking of Congressman F's audience is reminiscent of Congressman B's experience at Girls State. Both enjoy celebrity status at home. The similarities do not end there. Congressman F explains the trust of his supporters in much the same language as Congressman B uses:

> I have to go way back. I worked in the community for eighteen years. People knew who I was and knew I was involved in the community — the NAACP, YMCA, Boy Scouts,

you name it. That way people know you. You aren't an
isolated name. They know you from the personal relationship
they had with you. If you did business with them, they know
you are able and that you didn't pull any deals on them. . . .
People in the community feel a kinship to our family. They
know where we came from. They know what our circumstances were. . . . People take pride in our accomplishments.
They like what we've stood for, and they know what abuse
we've taken when we've stood up for the black community.

Congressman F, like Congressman B, is a local hero, with extensive
local roots. By local standards, both men have "made something of
themselves" and, hence, are "well thought of." Both are "known
quantities." Both believe they have won constituent trust. Congressman B has won it because people know him and like him. Congressman F has won it because people know him and are proud of him.
But Congressman B acts always to close the social and psychological
distance between himself and his supporters. Congressman F acts
always to maintain some social and psychological distance between
himself and his supporters. Congressman B presents himself as a
trustworthy "one of the boys." Congressman F presents himself as
a trustworthy "community leader."

The South Side Community Caucus has had a turbulent and
byzantine organizational history. It won its initial test of strength,
electing some candidates of both parties who were opposed by the
Democratic organization. And its leaders won increased power
within the party. In success, however, the caucus lost the unity it
found in adversity. Conflicting ambitions and conflicting philoso-
phies eventually cost the caucus the support of most of its Democratic politicians. They returned to the Democratic party fold. The
caucus remains an organization of Democrats and Republicans who
still believe in the idea of an independent, bipartisan black political
force. But it lacks the muscle to act on that belief. Congressman F
is still the caucus leader. And although the caucus has diminished
in communitywide political importance, it has grown proportionately in importance to him as "my political lifeline." It is his personal
organizational protection against the ambitions of other local leaders
and his personal hedge against the uncertain support of the Democratic organization.

The beauty of having twenty-five elected black officials sit
around the table and make decisions on the basis of what's

best for the black community — that beauty is gone.
Obviously I've got to keep my own political organization.
And people want to organize around me. I have to do it for
my own protection every two years. . . . If I didn't have
the caucus I'd be in bad shape in terms of support for me.
The people in the caucus will be loyal to me. They will rally
around me. Nobody can take that away.

The caucus can still turn out 3000 people for a picnic. And its
leader remains a major force in local politics.

The South Side Caucus is Congressman F's primary constituency.
Having lost its other politician-members, the organization has been
reduced to its hard core. And that hard core is the black church.
In his first primary, Congressman F drew his base of support from
them.

I have always been very fortunate in having the strong support of the churches. In the black community, ministers
are very influential. Their members will do what the minister
says they will do. And if the minister stands up on Sunday
and says, "You've got to support Art Brooks," they say, "Yes
sir," "Yes Reverend." And then they go out and do it. If the
minister speaks for you, why that's better than being there
yourself.

The blending of political and church activity seems totally natural
and naturally total.

Congressman F's appearance at Freedom Grove Baptist Church
ranked highest on his at-homeness index. "Freedom Grove is like
home for me," he began his talk there,

I know so many of the people here. My roots go back so far.
I look out and see Ruth and Rose Harper, with whom I went
to South High School and whose mother was a mother to me.
And I'm pleased to see so many members of the South Side
Community Caucus here. We had 3000 people at the picnic
two weeks ago. These are the people who make it worthwhile for me to go through what I go through day after day.
. . . Whatever I have achieved, it's because of my church
background. You know sometimes people forget from whence
they came. They reach the heights and they think they did it
all by themselves. Men like Reverend Johnson have been my

inspiration. Many black folks have felt they should be in the white church, the integrated church. When I rassled with that question, I decided that my roots are in the black church.

Following a talk in which Congressman F discussed the "concentration of social problems, health care, education, housing" in the district, Reverend Johnson praised the "unselfish and dedicated" congressman, warned of our "collapsed society," and then offered the benediction: "Well, may God bless you all and may Congressman Brooks keep getting elected to Congress. May you continue your unselfish work. I'm proud of you and I'm pullin' for you." Driving away, the congressman ranked this event as the most important and the most comfortable of the weekend:

> I get the greatest enjoyment out of something like this. I like the church. I enjoy the ministers. They have been so important to the black experience. And they are my strength. I enjoy being around them and with them. And the people there are people of warmth, sincerity, and appreciation.

They are his primary constituents.

Congressman F's relations with the local Democratic organization will continue to resemble a Virginia reel. The two will come together when their interests merge and will peel off when they do not. The Democratic organization withheld endorsement from him on one occasion — to no effect. He maintains his independent strength, yet worries that "I don't have the control over finances and over the jobs that the guys in ward politics have." So he alternately endorses Democrats and threatens them that "If you do that, I'll tear up the party." They joined him in fighting to win his second major primary — under a neutral organizational banner. Of that contest, he explained,

> I set my strategy. My opponent figured if he got the whole 35 percent of the white vote, he would need only 16 percent of the black vote to win. So I was determined to hold my strength in the black community. . . . The first thing I did was get the ministers. I called a breakfast meeting and 125 ministers came. That's all of them! There is a group of ministers who have to work at other jobs, because their parishioners are too poor to pay them — some of the store-

fronts for instance. Fifty of them came. Once I had the ministers cemented in, I called a similar meeting of all the black elected officials. Twenty-three of the twenty-four showed up for that. Then I had it all. When you have the ministers and the black elected officials, you have the black community. . . . In every black ward, I beat him at least twelve to one, and I got almost half of the white vote. Overall, I beat him four to one.

With his support in the church-based South Side Caucus and his ability to rally the black politicians when he most needs them, Congressman F remains the preeminent political leader in his district.

PRESENTATION OF SELF:
SUMMARY SPECULATIONS

CONTEXT, PERSONAL PREFERENCE, AND STRATEGY. Six presentational styles have been described. As a group, they capture something of the variety of possible home styles. But we have no way of knowing how nearly they have captured the stylistic universe. From our own examination of the twelve other House members, we know that the six cases do not exhaust all possibilities. Later on, we shall add one or two more to our complement of cases. On the other hand, the six cases are representative of a large proportion of the presentational styles we have observed. Although we cannot know what lies beyond our observational range — and lack a sample size sufficient to reassure us — the six cases do provide a basis for a few summary speculations.

I have taken each member's presentational style as I have found it, and have attempted to describe it as best I could. The guiding theme has been that each House member's style is understandable in the light of his or her perceived constituencies. And so the description has centered on these constituencies. In further understanding why a particular member presents himself or herself the way he or she does, I have emphasized three factors, *contextual*, *personal*, and *strategic*. Each House member's presentation of self is, we think, explainable largely in terms of these three kinds of variables. And, in each description, I have tried to see how these three elements fit together, in the light of member perceptions of their constituencies. I have tried to combine interview and observational material to produce a consistent, patterned description — one that would be convincing to us. Yet the reader must be aware that the meshing of context, "personality," and strategy is less ambiguous and more convincing in some cases than in others. The jigsaw puzzle portraits of Representatives *B*, *C*, and *E* have more pieces missing than do our pictures of Representatives *A*, *D*, and *F*. The explanation for differences in results could lie in the objective situation of the member or in the abilities of the observer. But it needs to be noted here that our descriptions are not, and probably cannot be, equally complete, satisfying, or persuasive.

It should come as no surprise, however, that we have been able to discern a stylistic pattern in most cases. Representatives try to behave that way. They want their supportive constituents to perceive a patterned style. As we speculated in the case of Congressman *E*, the lack of a pattern may be puzzling and damaging. A successful home style is very much a matter of reenforcement — of stylistic elements that mesh with one another and of stylistic continuity over time. We should not think of a member's presentation of self as a cameo performance or as a snapshot personality projection. Their presentations are consistent and durable; they are repetitive and reenforcing. And deliberately so — which is, of course, a reason why it is doubly prudent, when in doubt, to "do just what we did last time." It may take time for a member to work out a stylistic pattern that is comfortable for him and recognizable by his supportive constituents. But once he has achieved that synthesis, he is more likely to reenforce it than change it. We shall return to this subject in Chapter Six.

Contextually, members of Congress think about their constituency relations, first of all, in terms of me-in-the-district. This perception predates their service in Washington, and it cannot be understood by drawing inferences from their Washington behavior. Part of the content of that perception involves a sense of fit with the district — not all of the district, of course, but a very sizable proportion of it. Representatives *A* and *F* feel theirs is a good fit; Representatives *B* and *C* think of theirs as a fair fit; Representatives *D* and *E* think of their situation not as a bad fit, but simply as a nonfit.[8] A member's sense of fit will, in turn, be affected by whether he or she sees the district as homogeneous or heterogeneous. Good fits are most likely in homogeneous districts. Representatives *A* and *F* (our "good fits") see their districts as homogeneous; Representatives *D* and *E* (our "nonfits") see theirs as heterogeneous; Representatives *B* and *C* (our "fair fits") are split in this respect.

The chief contextual question is: "How much latitude do I have in choosing a presentational style?" When the district is perceived as homogeneous, and when the congressman feels that he is a microcosm of the district, he is not likely to have much choice of presentational styles. That is, if Congressman A or F did not represent his district, someone who performed similarly at home — with a person-to-person or a political leadership style — probably would. The range of acceptable styles is narrower in a district perceived to be homogeneous than in one perceived to be heterogeneous. In districts perceived to be heterogeneous, and where the member expresses no strong feeling that "I am like my district," presentational style is likely to be a matter of individual choice. Representatives D and E have developed presentational styles different from those of their predecessors. The range of acceptable styles is fairly broad in such situations. Again, Congressman B and C do not fit these generalizations entirely. In his heterogeneous district, Congressman B nonetheless believes that a locally derived style of some sort must be adopted there. And, in his homogeneous district, Congressman C has been only partly constrained. He has followed his predecessor's issue-oriented style but has exercised choice in terms of his concern for personal attentiveness.

Nevertheless, in answering the question as to whether a congressman's home style is imposed on him by his constituency or whether he imposes a home style on the constituency, we suggest — for the presentational aspects, at least — that the result will vary with the perception of the geographical constituency and the congressman's own sense of fit in that milieu. The congressman in the homogeneous district is not likely to feel imposed on. His style will be one that is taken for granted in the district and will probably have been a key to his earlier recruitment. The idea of choosing a style, therefore, would not occur to him. The congressman in the heterogeneous district is freer, if he wishes, to consider the alternatives and choose, possibly through time, an acceptable presentational style. Nonfit, heterogeneous districts, in sum, give a congressman more latitude in choosing a presentational style than do good fit, homogeneous districts.

It is tempting to speculate whether this proposition holds, also, for the allocative elements of home style. If it does, we should expect to find, in any district by district breakdown of the state allocation patterns of Chapter Two, that the most idiosyncratic patterns within each state would appear in poor fit, heterogeneous districts. Thus perceptions of district homogeneity or heterogeneity might help us to understand the more baffling allocative patterns of Table 2.9 in Chapter Two. Our six case studies suggest other possible relationships between perceptions of the district and allocative style. For example, because the three members in heterogeneous districts spend more time at home than the three in homogeneous districts, we might speculate that the poorer a congressman's sense of fit — most likely in heterogeneous districts — the more time he will need or want to spend at home cultivating supportive constituencies. If this were so, the congressman in poor fit, heterogeneous districts might have less latitude in the allocative than in the presentational elements of his home style. Our other twelve cases do not lend much support to this thesis, however, so it remains speculative.

Allocation patterns, we suggested in Chapter Two, are partly a matter of geography, or context, and partly a matter of individual choice. The same is true of presentational patterns. Every House member has some latitude in deciding how to present himself or herself as a person. Within whatever constraints are set by the member's perception of the district and the feeling of me-in-the-district, *personal preferences* and talents shape his or her presentational style. "We all have different operations," observes one member, "and each suits a particular personality. You do what you like."

The chief personal question is: "What presentational style am I most comfortable with?" When they are at home, members of Congress tend to do what they are experienced, comfortable, and talented at doing and tend not to do what they neither like nor do well. This does not mean that House members enjoy everything they do at home. Far from it. But they all engage in public activity of some type. Insofar as they have a choice, they will emphasize, out of the array of possible public activities, those which come naturally. Those activities will then become central to each member's home style.

Congressman A seeks out person-to-person relationships, but does not encourage issue-oriented meetings. Congressman D seeks out issue-oriented meetings, but does not encourage person-to-person relationships. Congressman B closes the psychological and social distance when he presents himself to others. Congressman F maintains a psychological and social distance when he presents himself to others. Representatives C and E both claim that handshaking is the best way to win votes. Yet Congressman C struggles to meet "the folks" one on one, whereas Congressman *E* often chooses presentational techniques that avoid face-to-face relationships with others. These differences are traceable in part to differences in personal predispositions.

Strategically, each congressman must decide whom he will present himself to when he is home. It is helpful to think of this strategic problem in terms of his perceived constituencies. In subsequent studies, more attention will have to be paid to the actual choices a congressman makes when at home, e.g. "Why did you decide to go here rather than there?" For now, we can only conclude that he will present himself most often, we would guess, to those constituencies where he feels most in need of electoral support. The chief strategic question is: "To whom must I present myself in order to win renomination or reelection?" A congressman who worries only about a primary contest will spend a disproportionate amount of time and energy cultivating his primary constituency. Such is the case of Representatives *A* and *F*, for whom the strategic problem is to ward off primary challengers. Congressman *A* does not "campaign" in Omega County; Congressman *F* spends little time in the white section of his district. Although the primary constituency is smaller than the reelection constituency in each district, it is not always more easily bounded. That is why we have relied so heavily on our at-homeness observations to help with the mapping. And in a district protected in the general election, a primary constituency can encompass a large number of people. Thus a strategic concentration of effort in the primary constituency does not mean that any less time or effort will be required to cultivate it.

A congressman who is protected in the primary and who worries only about the general election will spend a disproportionate amount of time and energy presenting himself to his reelection constituency. He will spend time expanding that constituency, partly on the assumption that his strongest supporters have no inclination to go elsewhere. Such is the case with Representatives *C* and *D*. Yet neither can neglect his primary constituency unduly, because their loyalty and intensity of commitment are necessary to sustain his reelection campaign. Indeed, all the evidence we have accumulated suggests that a congressman's strongest supporters demand more, not less, of a congressman's time than his other constituencies. The congressman who is unprotected in the general election faces, then, a problem of balancing his efforts across different types of constituencies, a problem not faced by the congressman who is unprotected only in the primary.

It might be wondered whether presentational styles differ according to the constituency being cultivated. Are there certain styles which, for strategic reasons, are more likely to be employed in dealing with a primary constituency than a reelection constituency? On the basis of our six (or eighteen) cases, we can make no such connection. First, styles are partly a matter of personal predilection. Second, there is too much variation within each type of constituency. For example, a primary constituency in a homogeneous district tends to be large and amorphous, whereas a primary constituency in a heterogeneous district tends to be small and well bounded. It is not likely that any single presentational style will be deemed strategically necessary in both cases. There is, however, one fairly common presentational choice, which House members face in calculating the use of their time at home. Although their decision cannot be connected to the type of constituency being cultivated, it nonetheless has enough strategic importance to be noted here.

Some kinds of presentation are calculated to reach large numbers of people even if they produce lukewarm support. Other kinds of presentation are calculated to produce devoted support, even if they do not reach many people. This is not a dichotomy; but the contrast captures a dilemma that often confronts members at home, as we can see in these two examples:

> I could meet more voters by standing in front of the Handy Andy Supermarket for thirty minutes than I did riding all over Lewis County all day today. Maybe I met only forty voters, but there were fifty good Democrats in the motorcade, all of whom will work harder for me because I showed up.

> *Congressman:* Sunday afternoon's reception for the minister is one of my two big spots this week. It's the largest church in my district.
> *District Staff Member:* There will be 800 people there.
> *Congressman:* Am I going to be introduced? Do you suppose they'll ask me to say something? How will I meet 800 people?
> *Staffer:* You'll be in the receiving line.
> *Congressman:* That's good. . . . Who was that kid who

arranged the thing last weekend? I never want to see him
again. He said there would be 1000 people there. One
hundred showed up. How come we make such mistakes as
that? . . . And why did I ever agree to go to that breakfast in the city tomorrow?

Staffer: It's the biggest breakfast group in the city. They say
300 people will be there.

Congressman: I'll tell you how many people will be there —
forty-six. I can't believe I ever agreed to go.

The two illustrations show different resolutions of what members
call the "quality-quantity problem" or the "name-recognition approach versus the small-group approach." During campaigns, with
time scarce, the problem can become acute; and it may be solved
on a day-to-day, ad hoc basis. At one time or another, every congressman will try for name recognition and for intense support, depending on his judgment of electoral necessity. But the dilemma may
also be seen as involving a more long-term choice about the kind of
presentation and the kind of self one wishes to emphasize, a choice
that becomes controlling in most specific situations. For instance:

I have always based my political survival on the enthusiasm
of a few people rather than recognition by the many. That
may not be good politics. But I'd rather rely on people who
have some personal involvement with me and not on name
recognition. . . . I really cast my bread upon the waters
tonight. The people [about ten] who stayed after the party
were so interested that I gave them a lot of the inside stuff.
I want them to feel a sense of personal identification with
me. So I stayed late and gave them much more of myself
than I ordinarily would. Every one of those people now
feels he knows me and has a personal relationship with me.

This congressman has given priority to the cultivation of a primary
constituency, and has chosen what he considers an appropriate
presentational style. But there are other presentational styles equally
effective in cultivating primary constituencies. So, again, we cannot
connect particular styles with particular constituency circles. But we
can identify one kind of presentational choice that members often
face, the resolution of which has both tactical and strategic importance.

We have not said much about the strategic problem of presenting
oneself to one's strongest opponents — to the people each congress-

man believes he "never gets." House members handle the problem differently. Representatives *B, D,* and *E* spend more time at home than the other three, and stress their willingness to speak to any group, anywhere, at any time. Others are more selective. But most will accept opportunities to present themselves to unfriendly constituents. The strategic hope is that displaying themselves "as a person" may reduce the intensity of the opposition, thus neutralizing its effect within the district. Intense opposition is what every congressman wants least of. "There's nothing worse than intense opposition for a politician," says one. Any time spent warming up personal relationships may cool the intensity of the opposition. To neutralize the opposition is to stop them from talking against you. It is to win their silence, not their support. It is to reduce the intensity of support for the challenger, to reduce the size of his primary constituency. Functionally, the same accents used in presenting one's self to supporters apply to a presentation to opponents. That is, the process of allaying hostility differs little from the process of building trust. It is not, therefore, especially difficult, except psychologically. Besides, it is easier to maintain the trust of one's own supporters when no active hostility exists anywhere in the district. Thus it makes sense for every House member to allocate some time to a strategy of neutralization.

ACCESS. House members believe it is necessary for them to make presentations of themselves to their several constituencies if they are to achieve renomination and reelection. If they did not hold this belief, they would not devote so much time, energy, calculation, and worry to presentational matters. Chapters Three and Four rest on this assumption. Behind this assumption, however, lies another assumption — about just what it is that constituents want or expect from their elected representatives. It is the belief of House members that constituents want their congressman to be accessible to them. This belief is a common denominator running through all of the cases discussed and all of the cases not discussed. Constituents want *access* to their congressman. They — or better some sizable proportion of them — want to feel that they can reach their congressman, that he is or can be available to them, that they can — if they wish — see him, listen to him, talk to him. The congressman, for his part, satisfies this expectation when he presents himself to them. Members will, of course, choose different styles, for reasons already discussed. As a general proposition, however, it does not matter what presentational style the congressman adopts. It is the fact of presentation — at home — that is crucial. It is the act of presenting one's self to them that satisfies the constituent desire for access. So, at least, House members believe.

Access is not the only expectation constituents hold for their congressman. How access ranks with other expectations we cannot say. But House members themselves invariably rank what they do at home as more important to their electoral success than "the issues" or than "my votes." Recall Congressman *B*'s comment that "issue-oriented" did not apply to "most of the people I know," or Congressman *C*'s query, "Did you ever see a campaign won on issues?" or Congressman *D*'s statement, "People don't make up their minds on the basis of reading all our position papers." Congressman *E* put it this way:

> A person could have the same district as I have and hold very different views. It happens. Look at Charley Frisch in the next district. Both our constituencies are against government control. I vote against it; he votes for it. . . . Our political philosophies are different, but our people are pretty much the same; and we both get elected. Issues don't have one dang thing to do with it.

More important than "the issues" is the presentation at home. And common to all presentations is the granting of access.

Not all constituents have direct access to their congressman, of course. And among those who do, the quality of that access varies. But House members believe that they can, by their presentations, convey the possibility of access to a larger number than actually take advantage of the opportunity. Directly, there is access; indirectly there is the promise of access. Access is most direct and of the highest quality within the personal constituency; it is most attenuated and of the poorest quality in relation to the geographical constituency.

Commenting about his relationship with the most important member of his primary constituency, a borderline intimate, one member said,

> What he wants from me is attention. He's very powerful and very rich, and there's nothing I can do for him. He doesn't want anything from me but recognition. Human beings want

> to be recognized, no matter how powerful they are. . . . All
> he wants is to be able to say, "Oh, the Congressman was here
> Sunday afternoon," or "when I was talking to the Congress-
> man Friday evening. . . ." That's all he wants. And so I
> talk to him every time I come home.

As we waited to dedicate a massive housing project, an urban congressman talked about the community leaders there whom he counts
among his primary constituents:

> These people are leadership types. What they want is to be
> able to have a call on me, to have me present at their func-
> tions. In a sense, I let myself be used – or my office be used
> – to give them what they want. It boosts their ego. . . . If
> you ask me which is more important, my vote or my work
> in the community, the latter is much more important. People
> will vote for you when you attend openings like this. You
> asked me once if one vote could kill me. If you attend all
> the openings, no vote will matter.

Two other representatives talked about the importance of access to
the reelection constituency:

> If you can talk to people in groups, if they identify with you
> and if they know you care about their problems, they'll sup-
> port you and they won't care how you vote.

> I'd hate to think of the reasons why people vote for me. But
> none of them has anything to do with what I do in Washing-
> ton or how I vote on the issues. Mostly, I think, it's because
> they think of me as a nice guy who will come to the Cross-
> town Tavern for a party, someone who will be jolly with them,
> someone they can be comfortable with. People don't want
> a leader; they want a buddy. They want a man who will come
> and have his picture taken with his arm around the dumpy
> old lady without being patronizing about it.

Finally, a fifth member spoke of the value of access to a strategy of
neutralization within the geographical constituency:

> People want to know that you've been around. Sometimes
> there's a story in the paper. They don't expect to see you,
> but they'll know you were in town. Even if people disagree

> with you, you can disarm them that way so that they won't
> be against you.

At this point, accessibility means little more than keeping visible. But visibility carries with it the promise of better access. The desire for some kind of access, House members believe, is present in every one of their perceived constituencies. They further believe that providing access at home is more important to their electoral success than providing votes in Washington.

The importance that members of Congress place on their accessibility differs from an emphasis on public policy issues as most important to election outcomes. But we should not think of access and issues as an either-or proposition. Access is important because it is the precondition for the presentation of self. Presentation of self is important for winning and holding constituent trust. House members, however, may choose to place a great deal of emphasis on the issues in presenting themselves to their constituents. Our six members varied considerably in this respect. Issues, therefore, may be very important to the presentation of self and hence to conveying the impressions of trustworthiness that produce supportive constituencies.

In this view, however, issues have little autonomous effect on election outcomes. Rather, issues are vehicles that some House members choose to convey their qualifications, their sense of identification, and their sense of empathy. It is not the statement of an issue position that wins elections, but the presentation of self by the candidate as he states his issue position. When members worry about a challenger, they do not worry about what he is saying on the issues, but how he is saying it and how he is "coming across" as a person. "Debates on the issues" are, in this view, debates between candidates, each of whom uses certain issues to convey his trustworthiness to his prospective constituents. A good issue for a candidate is, in this view, one that allows him to present himself as a person in a favorable light. One member said:

> Watergate was the number one ingredient in my election. Not just because of Watergate, but because of the things it allowed us to say — that I was not going down there and vote anybody's party line, that I was not going to be a party hack, that I was an independent thinker, unlike my opponent who

had followed Nixon blindly to the end. . . . I'm going down
to think for myself and not follow anyone or play by the old
rules. Watergate helped us get that message across.

This same member summed up, "Most voters vote more on style
than they do on issues." But for those House members who choose
to make issue presentations central to their home style, a better
summary would be that voters vote for style on the issues. This
formulation preserves the primacy of presentational style — and of
access — while acknowledging the importance of issues to some presentational styles. That is a view which these eighteen members
hold and which these six cases would support.

NOTES

1. See T. Edward Westen, "The Constituent Needs Help: Casework in the
   House of Representatives," in *To Be a Congressman: The Promise and the
   Power*, ed. Sven Groennings and Jonathan Hawley (Washington, D.C.:
   Acropolis, 1973), pp. 53–72.
2. John Saloma, *Congress and the New Politics* (Boston: Little, Brown; 1969),
   p. 185; John Macartney, "Political Staffing: A View from the District," unpublished Ph.D. dissertation, University of California, Los Angeles, 1975, p.
   93.
3. Robert S. Erikson, "The Advantage of Incumbency in Congressional Elections," *Polity* 3 (Spring 1971): 395–405.
4. Leo Snowiss, "Congressional Recruitment and Organization," *American
   Political Science Review* 60 (September 1966): 627–39.
5. Avery Leiserson, "National Party Organization and Congressional Districts,"
   Western Political Quarterly 16 (September 1963): 633–49; David M. Olson,
   "The Congressman and His Party," unpublished manuscript, Athens, Georgia,
   1970.
6. Robert Agranoff, *The New Style in Election Campaigns*, 2nd ed. (Boston:
   Holbrook, 1976), pp. 3–47.
7. It remains a weakness of this study that no strong party organization congressman of the pro-Daley, Chicago type is represented here.
8. For none of the eighteen is there the feeling of a bad fit, expressed by that
   House member who refers to his district as "Outer Mongolia."

CHAPTER FIVE

Home Style: Explanation of Washington Activity

EXPLANATION AND MEMBER GOALS

When House members are at home they do something that is closely connected to, yet separable from, the presentation of self to their constituencies. They *explain* what they have done while they have been away from home. By explaining we mean to include the *description*, the *interpretation*, and the *justification* of their behavior. We speak about their explanation of past behavior rather than their promises of future behavior, although the two are sometimes hard to disentangle. And we speak about the explanation of their past behavior in Washington. All House members spend time at home explaining to others what they have done in Washington and why. A representative's explanations to his or her various constituencies can be treated as a distinctive aspect of his or her home style.

We cannot be as knowledgeable about explanatory activity as we are presentational activity, because too many components of explanatory style lie beyond our observational range. A great deal of explanation takes place by telephone, by letter writing, by private conversation, by selective mailings, by press releases, by radio "beepers," by television appearances, and by newsletters. A complete treatment of explanatory styles would monitor the totality of congressional communications practices. That is a subject, an important subject, for another study. Still, some proportion of congressional explanation does occur at home; and we can help to open up the subject of explaining with a brief discussion here.

When most people think of explaining Washington behavior to

constituents, they think of explaining votes. But explanations cover a broader range of activities than that. A House member will explain any Washington activity that is relevant to winning and holding support at home, for the objective of explanation, as of presentation, is political support. All House members, we would argue, try to achieve, in varying combinations, three basic personal goals: re-election, power inside Congress, and good public policy.[1] As they seek reelection at home, their explanations will pertain mostly to their efforts to achieve their other two goals. That is, when they are at home they describe, interpret, and justify their pursuit of power and their pursuit of policy in Washington. Explanations concerning their power pursuits focus on their legislative effectiveness. Explanations concerning their policy pursuits focus on their votes and their positions.

EXPLAINING POWER

When House members talk to their constituents, one rhetorical staple is a description and an interpretation of "Congress at work" or "the job of the congressman." Every congressman carries a speech or a minispeech of this sort around with him — usually in his head — to be delivered at a moment's notice to students of all ages, to organizations, and to the media. Sometimes "the speech" is a civics lecture. Sometimes it is spiced with inside dope — how Congress "really" works. Often it is cast in the form of "a day in the life of the congressman." Always, it manages to convey to the audience some feeling for the distribution and the use of power in Congress and some idea of the representative's own exercise of power therein.

It is hard to separate out the presentational and the explanatory aspects of this kind of performance. Clearly, one purpose is to convey the impression that the member is thoroughly knowledgeable about the system and comfortably conversant with its procedural intricacies. Thus, he presents himself as "qualified" for the office he holds. Indeed, the opportunity to make a presentation of a qualified self is a potent incumbent advantage. But there is also an explanatory element here as well. That is, there is a straightforward discussion of how the nation's business is conducted, interlarded with comments about the representative's own contribution. To the extent possible — even if it requires a bit of imagination — members will picture themselves as effective users of inside power. Key committee assignments obtained, special recognition from the leadership, floor amendments passed, floor attendance records, meetings with high-level officials, benefits obtained for the district, the length of the working day, the volume of work handled — almost anything a member does can be used back home as evidence of his effectiveness in Washington. All members do not have sparkling records of inside achievement. But they will use whatever they can.

A senior representative opened every one of the thirteen campaign speeches I heard as follows:

> I have represented this district for the last twenty years. And I come to you to ask for a two-year renewal of my contract. I'm running because I have a twenty-year investment in my job and because I think you, as my constituents, have an investment in my seniority. In a body as large as the House of Representatives with 435 elected, coequal members, there has to be a structure if we're ever going to get anything done. And it takes a long time to learn that structure, to learn who has the power and to learn where to grease the skids to get something done. I think I know the structure and the people in the House better than any newcomers could. And I believe I can accomplish things for you that no newcomer could.

Obviously, he is making a "presentation of self" to others — as experienced and qualified. But he is also describing the working of the system and his own place within it.

As his speech proceeded he would become more explicit. Claiming credit for them in varying degrees, he would list the three district-related environmental bills that had passed in the last session of Congress. "I'm feeling pretty smug right now, because the three pieces of legislation I have been sponsoring passed into law this year." The most important of these he called "the greatest achievement in my twenty years of service." "If anyone had told me," he elaborated, "that we would get a complicated bill involving 50,000 acres and $125 million through the House and Senate in twenty-four hours, I wouldn't have believed it. It was a minor miracle, but we did it." In oblique reference to the jurisdictional and personality problems plaguing the bill, and to the newspaper stories about how he "flew back to Washington to save the bill," he would sometimes add, "No newcomer could have accomplished what I did." He attributed it to "my low-key effectiveness." And he interpreted him-

self to his audiences as "a low-key effective member of the House." Not all members, of course, have as much grist as this. But it is this kind of discussion of what goes on in Washington — both general and specific — that we have labeled "explaining power."

House members explain their use of power in Congress because they believe it will help them win renomination and reelection. Members believe that their supporters want their representative to be influential in Congress, and that they take a certain pride in having an effective congressman — the more so when he is effective on their behalf. One standard line of attack that challengers use against incumbents accuses them of being insufficiently effective or influential inside Congress. "He's a nice enough guy, but he's an ineffective congressman." Such accusations create serious explanatory problems at home. By stressing the importance of seniority in the House and his ability to capitalize on it, the congressman just discussed was trying to stay on the offensive against his challenger.

Another member found himself on the defensive in countering press reports that he had lost a committee assignment of importance to his district because of his lack of power within the House.

> Nothing is more damaging to a congressman in his district than to have his constituents believe he doesn't have the power to get something he wants of that nature. . . . It might have been the only issue in the next campaign. . . . That would have been all that was needed — and only that — to defeat me. . . . No one in the world would believe my explanation, so I had to try for the next vacancy on the committee and I had to win. [Which he did, before the next election.]

"I worked my head off to get that building," the same man said, as we drove by a new federal building in one of his localities. "The people here were fixing to run someone against me if I hadn't produced it. People think you just have to wave a magic wand to get an appropriation, when most of it is just standing in line waiting your turn." Obviously, such an explanation of "how Congress really works" would not have satisfied his constituents in that part of the district. So, again, he had to produce. Then his credit-claiming explanation afterward would shore up his home support. For a congressman in this kind of home situation, explaining his power in the

House (or lack of it) may be more crucial to his reelection success than explaining his votes.

House members seek inside power in many ways. Congress is a complex, decentralized structure providing countless opportunities to affect decision-making. Members seek inside power, too, for many reasons — most of which political scientists find hard to plumb. Whatever their reasons and their methods, when they are home they justify their pursuit of power by claiming to have used it on behalf of their constituents. The message is not just "I am effective." It is also "I am effective *for you.*" Members particularly like to be able to claim credit for bringing tangible benefits to their constituents, because it proves their concern for others as well as their effectiveness. The senior congressman who explained his "low-key effectiveness" in Washington ended the standard "pitch" quoted a moment ago by telling his audience, "You have an important investment in my seniority." Explaining to his constituents that he was getting close to a committee chairmanship, another member said everywhere he went, "When I become chairman of the _____ Committee, the mantle will be draped not only on my shoulders, but on the shoulders of every man, woman, and child in the First District." Explanation involves legitimation. When representatives explain their quest for influence in the House, they do so in ways that will legitimize their power pursuits in the eyes of their supporters. I do what I do "for you" is one such legitimating formula.

As they go about "explaining power" at home, House members talk a great deal about the institution of which they are a part, the United States Congress. They have the opportunity, if they wish to avail themselves of it, to enlighten their several constituencies on the most complicated and, hence, the least understood of all our national political institutions. With the opportunity to enlighten comes the opportunity to evaluate. That is, House members can, if they care to do so, help their constituencies assess the strength and weaknesses of Congress as an institution. Because of the low public esteem in which the Congress has been held during the period of this research, the opportunity to point out the redeeming strengths of the institution (of which they are, after all, a part) might seem particularly inviting. Although they have such a set of opportunities, House members do *not* customarily encourage any of their supportive constituents to think about Congress as an institution, and particularly not about its institutional virtues. Their explanations tend to be more individualistic than institutional. Indeed, the more elaborate, sustained, and complex the explanation is, the more likely it is to focus on the individual member rather than the institution. Such virtues as are discussed will be those of the individual member of Congress and not of the Congress itself. We shall have more to say about this explanatory pattern later in the chapter.

EXPLAINING POLICY

The range of Washington activities requiring a home explanation extends well beyond voting. Nonetheless, voting *is* the Washington activity we most easily recognize and most often generalize about. It is the activity we shall treat most extensively here. From John Kingdon's splendid discussion of "explaining," [2] we know that at the time House members are called on to vote they are very aware that they may be called on to explain their vote to some of their constituents. Moreover, says Kingdon, the anticipated need to explain influences their decision on how to vote. They may cast a certain vote only when they are convinced that they have a satisfactory explanation in hand. Or, they may cast a certain vote because it is the vote least likely to require an explanation. Kingdon is interested in finding out why House members vote the way they do, but he also helps make the case for finding out why House members explain the way they do. If the anticipated need to explain has the effect on voting that Kingdon suggests (i.e., if it makes voting more complicated and more difficult than it otherwise would be) then the act of explaining must be as problematical for House members as the act of voting. They believe that they can win and lose constituent support through their explanations as well as through their votes. To them, therefore, voting and explaining are interrelated aspects of a single strategic problem. If that is the way members of Congress see it, then it might be useful for political scientists to look at it that way as well — to spend a little less of our time explaining votes and a little more of our time *explaining explanations*.

House members are called on to vote much more often than they are called on to explain. That is, they are never called on to explain all their votes. They cast 400 to 500 votes each year, and no constituent knows, or wants to know, what each was about — let alone seek explanations for it. Our Congressman C, for example, whose suburban district appears to be the most issue-oriented of all those visited said, "I don't think people could specify anything of my voting record. . . . I once printed it and offered to send it to anyone who wanted it. No one did. It was too complicated to understand." Two other issue-oriented members made the same point: "People don't care about my votes. They are indifferent. It's amazing to me." "People write me and say they like the way I vote. But if we sat down and went through them, they would disagree with me on six out of twelve." Of course, every congressman will cast many votes on which he and his supporters are in complete agreement anyway.[3] The number of such votes is largest in a homogeneous district. As Congressman C noted, "A congressman who comes from a homogeneous district like mine will vote the way his district wants most of the time because he's so much like them." In such cases, there is no need to explain. So, if we ask ourselves just how many of their votes House members will "need to" explain, the answer probably is not many. "If your conscience and your district disagree too often," members like to say, "you're in the wrong business." But that does not make the explanatory process any the less problematical. Members believe that it would not take many unacceptable explanations to cost them dearly at the polls.

Members will stockpile more explanatory ammunition than they need, because they are uncertain as to just which votes they will be called on to explain. It is not the omniscient constituent armed with information on all their votes that concerns them. It is the individual or group armed with information and feeling deeply aggrieved about one vote or one cluster of votes that is most worrisome. "There isn't one voter in 20,000 who knows my voting record," said one member, "except on that one thing that affects him." And another said, "Only a few discerning people know my voting record: labor, the environmentalists, and the Chamber of Commerce." But it is, of course, the voter dissatisfied with "that one thing that affects him" or the "few discerning people" who will press for explanations. The member must be ready for these requests when they come. There are other kinds of constituents, too, who make it their business to call for explanations — particularly the local media. And, above all, there are the explanations that will be demanded by the electoral challenger in the next campaign. The challenger's task is to probe for the votes that are most difficult for the incumbent to explain. And the member cannot be sure before the actual campaign just which ones they might be. "You know your opponent will pick on one vote or two, but you don't know which one it will be." The same uncertainty that the challenger produces for the perception of a reelection constituency, the challenger also brings to the problem of explanation.

Members of Congress can, however, help to determine just what it is they will need to explain. Mostly they do this by the way they vote. Members know pretty well, for example, just which votes will be most difficult or impossible to explain, consistent with reelection. If, of course, the representative agrees with his reelection constituency on such survival votes, neither voting nor explaining presents a problem. Said a Jewish congressman from a dominantly Jewish district, "If I voted against aid to Israel — well, that's inconceivable of course. . . . [But] that would be it! If I did something absurd like that and voted counter to a massive opinion in my district, I would lose." When, however, the member disagrees with the bulk of his supporters on what is good public policy, some calculation will be necessary. And in deciding how he will vote, the member also decides what he will need to explain back home.

One member talked about two such decisions:

> On gun control, I believe we should have it. But my district — a rural district — is overwhelmingly against gun control, 80 percent to 20 percent. So I decided a long time ago not to hassle that issue. I am against all gun control.

> On environmental issues, most of my district goes one way and I go the other. The environmentalists are mostly in the cities. People out here are afraid of losing their land and their jobs. But I keep taking many more proenvironmental stands than my district would support.

In both cases, he knows that if he votes contrary to district opinion, "I'll have a lot of explaining to do." And in deciding to vote as he does, he decides to eliminate the need to explain on gun control and accept the need to explain on environmental matters.

When House members think about controlling their explanatory agenda back home, they think not just about specific votes but about their overall policy record. Typically, members ask for electoral support in these general terms: "I've cast 4000 votes, so I'm sure you don't agree with me on every one of them. But if you think the total record is a good one, if you approve of my overall performance, I hope you'll support me." Two-thirds of the eighteen members believed that although no single vote could defeat them, voter disapproval of their "total," "overall" policy performance could. One congressman said,

> I don't think any one vote would defeat any congressman anywhere. I hear some of my colleagues say that, but I don't believe it. If you get too far away from your district, you'll lose it. But on any one vote, the important thing is that you be able to explain why you did it.

The idea that "if you get too far away from your district, you'll lose it" is one that all members believe. Whether or not they also believe it constitutes a more serious electoral problem than "any one vote," they do not wish to have to defend themselves back home against any such suspicion. So they face another kind of voting-explanation calculation.

Getting "too far away from the district" is not the result of a single vote but of an accumulation of votes — of "a string of votes" in John Kingdon's terms.[4] Members worry about their "string of votes" because they believe that more voters think in these terms than think in terms of specific votes. This larger group of voters may get their information secondhand from the smaller group. For example,

> People have a sense of a person's voting record — that I am a progressive Democrat. I am one of eight who got 100 percent from the environmental groups. I was one of 20 who got 100 percent from ADA. People see these articles in the paper and they leave an impression.

Or the information may come firsthand from the member:

> People have an idea of what I'm like that comes from . . . hearing me talk about it — whether I'm for Vietnam or big spending. What they know is based more on what I say than my voting record.

When members are called on to "explain" in open forums at home, they are more often asked to explain their general "policy positions" than they are asked to explain specific votes: "What is your position on the energy problem?" "What are you doing about unemployment?" Sometimes, the answer will incorporate elements of the member's voting record. Sometimes it will be pure "position taking" — bills introduced, speeches made, administration officials contacted, "Dear Colleague" letter written, and so on.[5] In a variety of ways, then, some constituents come to have a "sense" or "impression" or "idea" about a member's "overall voting record" or "voting patterns," or "policy positions." It is a summary judgment about the member's past pursuit of good public policy. And it is when members act to cause revisions in these summary judgments that they believe they are in danger of getting "too far away from the district." If they do get into this situation, they will face a serious explanatory problem. But — and this has been our main point — it is one they can control, if they wish, with their votes.[6]

We say "if they wish," because members of Congress strike quite different postures with regard to explaining. How they choose to control their explanatory agenda depends heavily on their personal inclinations in the matter. Some are aggressive and confident; they will create opportunities to explain policy wherever possible. Others are passive and timid; they will avoid policy explanation wherever they can do so. These differences of personal preference exist above and beyond any differences in perceived constituencies.

Congressman D, the issue articulator, comes from a district that he perceives to be both heterogeneous and marginal. He bends over backward to explain any vote that might be considered controversial by anyone in the district. His "open meetings" are designed to maximize the likelihood of explaining. He eagerly debates with his opponents, to the same end. "We have explained every difficult vote," he says. "Anyone who gives a twit about how I vote has the opportunity to know it. We have explained our vote on all the toughies." He is impatient with anything less than an explanation of specific votes. "I hate the labels conservative and liberal. My attitude is 'Cut the shit and tell me what votes you like and what votes you don't like and why.' "

Service-oriented Congressman E also perceives his district to be heterogeneous and marginal. But he follows the congressional adage that "If you have to explain, you're in trouble." Whenever he confronts a strongly held opinion in his reelection constituency, he bends to it rather than explain the contrary position — with which he frequently agrees.

> I got more mail, by far, in opposition to gun control legisla-
> tion than on any other thing since I've been in Congress —
> 400 letters a day. If I voted against restrictive legislation, I'd
> better not come home. . . . [And] this is a very heavily
> Catholic district. A vote against aid to parochial schools
> might defeat me. That and gun control together would do
> it, and either one separately might. . . . Anyone who advo-
> cated busing would be ridden out of my district on a rail. . . .
> Prayer in the schools is another one. If I get on the wrong
> side of any one big emotional issue, I'll lose a whale of a lot
> of votes. . . . People are not aware of the issues, but they will
> get up on one damn thing and raise hell. My personal opinion
> is that abortion is a matter between a woman and her doctor.
> . . . But so many people feel so strongly about it that I will
> support the right-to-life amendment. . . . I sponsored a bill
> to increase the size of trucks on our highways. But I got an
> awful lot of mail on that and it would have lost me a lot of
> people. . . . Confidentially, I tell you it was a good bill; and
> I'm still in favor of it. But because so many people were
> opposed to it, I decided not to support it. I'm not here to
> vote my own convictions. I'm here to represent my people.

These are not just voting calculations. They are explaining calculations as well. Congressman E votes so as to minimize the need for explanation — except to himself. He will not debate his opponents.
He will explain if he has to; and, as we noted earlier, he thinks he
is good at it. But, unlike Congressman D, he tries to avoid both the
tough explanations and the tough explanatory situations. House
members, in short, will adopt different explanatory styles.

EXPLANATION AND PRESENTATION

We can expect personal factors to affect the explanations, just as
they do the presentations, of House members. The question for the
member is the same in both cases. Here, it is: What explanatory
procedure do I feel most comfortable with? We might also expect
to find that a member's choices concerning style would tend to produce a compatibility between his or her explanatory and presentational styles. There is, for example, a compatibility between the

articulate, issue-oriented presentational style and the aggressive-confident explanatory style of Congressman D. Members who talk a lot about policy issues will produce a large volume of policy explanations. On the other hand, there is a compatibility between the service-oriented presentational style and the passive-fearful explanatory style of Congressman E. A member whose presentation of self does not emphasize policy will produce a correspondingly small volume of policy explanations.

We cannot catalogue the many possible interrelationships between presentational and explanatory styles. But at the least we would expect to find a "strain toward compatibility" between them and, hence, some consistency between the elements of each House member's home style. It is our further guess that the presentational style — as the centerpiece of home style — would dominate the relationship. As for what underlying factors actually produce the strain toward compatibility, we would assume they are the same factors that shape presentational styles — personal, contextual, and strategic. Having touched on the personal factor, we turn now to the contextual and strategic ones.

We would expect the broadest perception of me-in-the-district to underlie the choice of explanatory styles, just as it underlies the choice of presentational styles. A good illustration of this contextual influence lies outside my particular group of House members — in the explanation of their historic impeachment vote by two members of the House Judiciary Committee.

In the face of extraordinary constituency interest, two Judiciary Committee Republicans took to statewide television and radio in the summer of 1974 to explain their decision to vote in favor of impeaching their own party's president. Representative Lawrence Hogan of Maryland cast his explanation heavily in terms of voting his individual conscience against the acknowledged wishes of many prospective constituents — primary and reelection — in his announced try for the Maryland governorship. To accent his act of conscience, he acknowledged the grave risks to his career.

> I know that many of my friends, in and out of Congress, will be very displeased with me. I know that some of my financial contributors (who have staunchly supported Richard Nixon and me) will no longer support me. I know that some of my long time campaign workers will no longer campaign for me.

But to those who were my campaign workers back in my first campaign, I want to remind you of something. Remember, I was running for Congress as a Republican in an area that was registered three to one Democratic, and in an effort to convince Democrats that they should vote for me, a Republican, I quoted John F. Kennedy who said, "Sometimes party loyalty demands too much." Remember that?

Well, those words have been coming back to haunt me in recent weeks. Clearly, this is an occasion when "party loyalty demands too much." To base this decision on politics would not only violate my own conscience, but would also be a breach of my own oath of office to uphold the Constitution of the United States. This vote may result not only in defeat in my campaign for governor of Maryland, but may end my future political career. But that pales into insignificance when weighted against my historic duty to vote as my conscience dictates.[7]

Representative William Cohen cast his explanation in terms of voting as the people of his state of Maine would vote if they were in his shoes. He did not say they were pressuring him to vote, but that he and they, as members of the same community, thought alike on fundamental matters.

I have tried to put all of these events into the context of a political system that I know well, that of the state of Maine. I have asked myself some questions.

What if the governor of Maine ordered his aides to keep a list of those people who supported his opponents? What if he tried to have the state treasurer's department conduct audits of those who voiced dissent? What if he ordered the state police to investigate those who were critical of his policies or speeches? What if he asked aides to lie before legislative committees and judicial bodies? What if he approved of burglaries in order to smear and destroy a man's credibility? What if he obtained information that was to be presented to a grand jury for the purpose of helping his advisors design a strategy for defense?

What would the people of Maine say? You and I both know that the people of Maine would not stand for such a situation, for it is inconsistent with our principles and our constitutional system of government.[8]

Hogan and Cohen offered their listeners very different explanations for the same vote. It is our hunch that underlying the difference in their explanatory styles are different perceptions of me-in-the-district. Cohen sees himself, we would guess, as part of a fairly homogeneous reelection-plus-primary constituency. He identifies strongly with it; and he has a comfortable sense of fit with this broad constituency. That being so, he would neither perceive nor explain his vote in terms that set his conscience against theirs. His explanation was, therefore, communitarian: "I am one of you and the issue is our conscience as a community." Hogan, we would guess, perceives his geographical constituency to be heterogeneous, and has no strong sense of fit with any large or differentiable element of it. Almost surely, he feels uncertainty about his prospective statewide constituency; but it seems that he feels uncertainty, even, about his relationships with the primary constituency in his district. It is hard, therefore, for him to find any communitarian bases for explanation. His explanation was individualistic: "I am following my conscience and disregarding the opinions of my constituents."

Neither explanation is inherently "better" than the other. Each had an element of strategic calculation to it. That is, each man chose his words deliberately; and, I presume, neither wanted to lose the next election by virtue of his explanation. If that is the case, the acceptability of the two explanations by the Maryland and Maine constituencies becomes a question of some moment. We lack sufficient information to assess the actual impact of the two explanations on each man's political support. But we can try a more general answer.

To the degree that Maryland voters already perceived Hogan to be "a man of conscience," and to the degree that Maine voters already perceived Cohen to be "one of us," their explanations probably would have been accepted. On the other hand, to the degree that Maryland voters had already come to view Hogan as a self-serving opportunist, and to the degree that Maine voters had already come to view Cohen as a spineless follower of the herd, their explanations probably would not have been accepted. That is, the credibility of any given explanation probably depends less on the content of the explanation itself than on its compatibility with some previously established perception of the explainer, "as a person." It is also true, however, that in the act of explaining and by his manner of explaining, a congressman can help create and reenforce the perception others have of him. That is, explanation is one form of presentation. And some constituents probably want access to their congressman so that they can hear him explain and size him up as he does so. Thus we probably should think of Hogan and Cohen as building and reenforcing credibility at the same time they were drawing on credibility already established. Putting the relationship most generally, therefore, we can say that the acceptability of explanations depends on a compatibility between explanatory and presentational styles.

I did travel with another Republican member of the House Judiciary Committee — although I did not join him until after President Nixon's resignation. From everything I observed, however, his presentation of self as an independent-thinking, issue-oriented member was completely consistent with his high volume of explanations and his Hogan-like position that he did what he thought best on the impeachment matter. Over and over he told his reelection constituents, "I didn't give a damn what my constituents thought about impeachment. It was a matter of intellectual judgment." And in terms of personal predispositions, he is an intellectual. "I don't like politicking," he says privately. "I'd rather be off somewhere reading a book about our problems." He stopped reading his mail on the subject of impeachment in March. (This was in marked contrast, I should add, to the actions of several other Republicans with whom I traveled: they were nervously taking polls and weighing their mail on the subject up to the very last gasp.) "I don't apologize for a single thing I did in the impeachment hearing," he would say, as he explained his "position" on the matter.

This posture on explaining impeachment was entirely consistent with his presentation to others as someone with "a willingness and a record of standing up to pressures and saying, no." As he developed his extraordinarily thorough explanations of his various policy positions, he would ask his audiences everywhere,

> Do you want the kind of guy with guts to stand up and say no? I hope so, because that's the kind of guy you're going to get if you vote for me. . . . I'm going to offer you something and you can take it or leave it. I'm not going to change. If you approve my record, I hope you will support one who has the guts not to make promises. If you do not approve of my record, vote for someone else.

And in response to criticism, he would reply, "That's the cross I have to bear. I live by the sword and I die by the sword." There was, in sum, a reenforcing consistency of explanatory and presentational styles — of being thoughtful and independent on the issues and of aggressively explaining policy — that increased the likelihood that his impeachment explanation would be accepted. This is exactly the situation Congressman Hogan hoped he was in when he explained to the Maryland electorate that he was going to follow his conscience.

Members elaborate the linkage between presentation and explanation this way: There are at most only a very few policy issues on which representatives are constrained in their voting by the views of their reelection constituencies. They may not *feel* constrained, if they agree with those views. But that is beside the point; they are constrained nevertheless. On the vast majority of votes, however, representatives can do as they wish — provided only that they can, when they need to, explain their votes to the satisfaction of interested constituents. The ability to get explanations accepted at home is, then, the essential underpinning of a member's voting leeway in Washington.

So the question arises: How can representatives increase the likelihood that their explanations will be accepted at home? And the answer House members give is: They can win and hold constituent trust. The more your various constituencies trust you, members reason, the less likely they are to require an explanation of your votes and the more likely they are to accept your explanation when they do ask for it. The winning of trust, we have said earlier, depends largely on the presentation of self. Presentation of self, then, not only helps win votes at election time. It also makes voting in Washington easier. So members of Congress make a strategic calculation: *Presentation of self enhances trust; trust enhances the acceptability of explanations; the acceptability of explanations enhances voting leeway; therefore, presentation of self enhances voting leeway.*

Our Representatives A and F, who present themselves as microcosms of their large homogeneous primary constituencies, cast seemingly unconventional votes on the Voting Rights Act of 1970. Each discussed his voting leeway and his explanatory activity in the terms we have just discussed. Said Congressman A, the white southerner,

> I have more freedom in voting than almost anyone I know. Sometimes I vote in ways that are not popular with my constituents and I know they aren't popular. They know how I vote but they will listen to me and let me explain. *They trust*

me. For instance, I voted for the Voting Rights Bill. It was a liberal vote — not all southerners voted for it. But I did it because it equalized treatment instead of singling out and discriminating against the South. When I explained that to my constituents, they all said, "If I were in your place, I'd have done the same thing."

Said Congressman *F,* the black northerner,

When I come home, I go to the church groups and tell them what's been going on in Washington and explain to them why I voted as I did. For instance, I explained to them that I voted against the Voting Rights Bill because it was a fraud. Nixon wanted to get the fifty-seven registrars working in the South out of there. After they heard me on the Voting Rights Bill, they went home mad. I know my people will agree with me. . . . The fact is that I have the freedom to do almost anything I want to in Congress and it won't affect me a bit back home. My constituents don't know how I vote, but they know me and *they trust me.* . . . They say to themselves, "everything we know about him tells us he's up there doing a good job for us." It's a blind faith type of thing.

In Chapters Three and Four, we spelled out at length how each of these two representatives wins and holds primary constituent trust. One of the payoffs of their presentational activity is the ease with which they can give acceptable explanations at home, and hence, have voting leeway in Washington.

Neither Congressman A or F has as much freedom as he thinks he has. That is, although neither may feel constrained, each none-theless is. Members cannot cast any vote at all and then come home and explain it successfully. In order for a presentational style to be helpful in explaining policy, a member must have established a general policy position or voting record sufficiently close to that of his supporters to allow constituent trust to operate. If a member "gets too far away from the district" or casts "a string of votes" at variance with supporter sentiment, then no amount of presentational activity can compensate. Congressmen A and F cannot imagine that any such policy distance would ever open up between them and their constituents. But a degree of proximity on policy in general is none the less vital to their success in explaining policy in particular. Two additional examples may help illustrate the presentation-explanation relationship.

LIBERAL VOTES AND CONSERVATIVE SUPPORT: CONGRESSMAN G. The relationship is most visible when the member acts less as a microcosm of his or her constituency. When I asked Congressman G whether he wasn't more liberal than his district, he said,

> Hell yes, but don't quote me on that. It's the biggest part of my problem — to keep people from thinking I'm a radical liberal. How do you explain to a group of Polish Catholics why you voted to abolish the House Internal Security Committee or why you voted against a bill to keep Jane Fonda from going to North Vietnam? How do you explain that? You can't.

He sees his reelection constituency as made up of farmers, blue-collar workers, and academic liberals. The latter group, the smallest, does not present an explanatory problem. "The liberals are happy with my votes, happier than they are with me personally," he says. "I vote in a way that makes university types happy, but personally I feel more comfortable with farmer and labor types." He sees his farm and labor supporters as mostly interested in "bread and butter issues," and on those issues he has established a general policy position much like theirs. About his farm supporters, he said, "They don't know how I vote. All they ask of me is that I take care of farm problems. Otherwise they trust me to look out for 'the poor little bastard.'" In general, he says, that is just the way his supporters do think of him:

> They don't know much about my votes. Most of what they know is what I tell them. They know more of what kind of a guy I am. It comes through in my letters: "You care about the little guy." And I'm associated with some reform stuff. The labor guys know generally that I support working people's legislation.

So long as Congressman G works for "the poor little bastard" or "the little guy," or for "working people's legislation," he is in no danger of getting "too far away from his district" in terms of his overall voting record or general policy position.

When that degree of policy proximity is established, his presentational style can then help him to alleviate his explanatory problems. "Most of the time people will allow you. If they have confidence in you and if you haven't gone off half-cocked, they will give you the benefit of the doubt." How does he win confidence? Partly, by the expressions he gives off when he presents himself. He says, "A lot of it has to do with your personal demeanor. If you're not shouting and screaming, if you are casual, even boring, people think you're not going off half-cocked." He does not present himself as a "radical liberal" — as someone who is "half-cocked." And when he was asked on a TV interview to comment on his opponent's charge that he was "ten times more radical than George McGovern," his expression given was a low-key appeal to identification and trust. "If he means," answered Congressman G, "that I'm some kind of wild-eyed radical, people around here know me better than that." After the interview, he mused about managing his explanatory problem:

> It's a weird thing how you get a district to the point where you can vote the way you want to without getting scalped for doing it. I guess you do it in two ways. You come back here a lot and let people see you, so they get a feel for you. And, secondly, I go out of my way to disagree with people or specific issues. That way, they know you aren't trying to snow them. And when you vote against their views, they'll say, "Well, he's got his reasons." They'll trust you. I think that's it. If they trust you, you can vote the way you want, and it won't hurt.

A vote in favor of gun control, he believes, will be his most difficult, costly one. "It will be hard to sell, but I think I can sell it." Because he has a general policy proximity to his supporters, Congressman G's presentation of self builds the trust necessary to "sell" his explanations at home and, hence, to cast votes more liberal than his district in Washington.

URBAN VOTES AND RURAL SUPPORT: CONGRESSMAN H. It is sometimes said that representatives from heterogeneous districts enjoy a special degree of voting leeway because no single constituency interest controls their electoral future. As one member put the argument,

> It's a mixed up district. People split seventeen ways on every issue. No matter how I vote, as many people agree with me as disagree. So I am a totally free agent. I can't vote according to pattern. I am completely independent, as independent as any congressman I know.

This argument is rarely brought full circle, to encompass the ability to explain at home and the presentational activities that underlie explanatory success. For it is not the sheer mix of interests that provides independence; it is the activity of the member above and beyond the act of voting. If it were not, the member would always be in jeopardy at the hands of a coalition of minorities.[9]

Congressman *H*, for example, describes his district as "heterogeneous — one-third urban, one-third suburban, one-third rural." His primary constituency is the rural area, where three generations of his family have lived. It is the rural area he has in mind when he says, "I was born in my district; I grew up in my district; and I have a very close identification with the people in it. I know what their values are." At the very moment we turned off a four-lane highway onto a back road on our way to a small-town fair, he said,

> It must be terrible to be without roots, without a place to call home. I have a profound sense of identification with these rural people. My wife still worries about me a little bit in this respect — that I'm too much of a country boy. But life's too short to play a role or strike a pose. This will be fun. I'm really going to enjoy myself.

Because we had just come from a labor union meeting in the city ("I can't make any nickels with labor. But I won't run away"), he was moving from the bottom to the top of his at-homeness index.

Not only is the rural part of the district the part he feels most at home in, but it casts a disproportionate 50 percent of his party's primary vote. "If these city people [in my party] with their slick city ways think they could go out to Mrs. O'Leary's cow pasture and get the farmers to throw out the local boy, they're crazy," he says. "My strength in the rural areas is so great, that people from the city think I'm unbeatable." His off-season presentation of self is skewed toward his primary constituency. During his 35 trips and 100 working days at home in 1973, his scheduled appearances were allocated as follows: 41 in the urban area, 38 in the suburban area, and 70 (or about 50 percent) in the rural third of the district. "I'm there so often they think they own me," he says. When he is there, he displays a person-to-person presentational style.

> In the urban area, I'm a captive of the party. I go to rallies and stand up and make platitudinous proparty solidarity

statements. I'm not allowed to be independent, to be myself.
People in the rural areas wouldn't be satisfied with this. They
expect whole relationships with people, not fragmentary relationships the way city people do. I like whole relationships,
and that's why I do so much better in the rural area than in
the urban area.

Congressman *H* believes that his personal accessibility and popularity — "I'm unpopular with those who don't know me, but popular
with those who do" — is the source of his political strength. "I have
a few dedicated supporters who create an atmosphere in which
others come to support me."

He believes that his person-to-person presentational style is what
wins him constituent trust:

> Sometimes I do my talking to the same people over and over
> again. But they talk to others and they speak favorably about
> me. They tell others that "Old George" is always available
> and accessible. And I get a reputation in that way. That's
> how I succeed in this kind of district. People think of me as
> a nice guy, one of the boys, and they make presumptions in
> my favor because I'm a nice guy.

The "presumptions in my favor" represent, of course, trust. When
asked whether one vote could defeat him, Congressman *H* makes
the argument about voting leeway in heterogeneous districts: "No,
not in my district. It's too diverse, not all urban ghetto or Idaho
potato farmers. That gives me a chance to balance interests in my
votes. There really aren't any dominant interests." But he completes
the argument by noting that despite the heterogeneity of his district, he still must be able to explain his voting pattern to his constituents and have that explanation accepted. This is especially true
in the case of his rural primary constituents.

> If I want to vote for an urban program, I can do it, and the
> people in the rural area will say, "He does have an urban
> constituency and he has to help them, too." And they will
> still vote for me so long as they think I'm a nice fella. But
> if I had no urban constituents — if I had all countryside —
> and I voted for an urban program, people in the rural areas
> would say, "He's running for governor and he's forgotten
> who his friends are." The same is true in the urban area.

> They know I'm a country boy and that I have a lot of rural area. So they say, "He gives us a vote once in a while; he's probably all right."

Congressman H is not unconstrained. He would, he says, lose his primary constituency if he voted consistently for urban programs. In that case, he would have gotten "too far away from his district." But he will also lose his primary constituency if they stop thinking of him as "a nice fella" and no longer "make presumptions in my favor."

If we are to understand a congressman's voting patterns in Washington, it seems that we must also understand his presentational and explanatory patterns at home — his home style.

Listening to Representatives G and H describe their explanatory behavior at home gives us a broader perspective on the congressman's unending quest for political support there. He cultivates home support not just because he wants to be reelected. He cultivates support at home, also, because he wants voting (and other) leeway in Washington. It is an incomplete notion to think of constituent support as useful only for reelection purposes. It is important well beyond that. Political support at home guarantees the congressman some freedom of maneuver on Capitol Hill.[10] Better, perhaps, it can *if* he so desires — if, that is, he wants to pursue the goals of power or policy. For such a congressman, an inquiry into the acceptability of his explanations at home provides a clue to his survival locally *and* to his performance nationally.

EXPLANATORY CONSISTENCY

In view of the commonly held notion that elective politicians "talk out of both sides of their mouths" or "try to be all things to all people," I had expected to find members of Congress explaining their Washington activity differently to their various constituencies. The likelihood seemed especially strong in heterogeneous districts, where the opportunity and the temptation would be greatest. Erving Goffman discusses this possibility in terms of performances before "segregated audiences." But I have found little trace of such explanatory chameleons in my travels. House members give the same explanations for their Washington activity before people who disagree with them as they give before people who agree with them —

before nonsupporters as well as supporters, committed as well as uncommitted, and from one end to the other in the most segmented of districts. It should be emphasized that we are talking mostly about explanations after the fact and have not focused on promises made concerning future Washington activity. Such promises may well produce more ambiguity than explanations, partly because of the politician's desire to preserve his or her future options and partly because of the politician's reluctance to antagonize people until it is absolutely necessary.

As for explaining, however, the lack of demagoguery and the patient doggedness with which most members explained their votes or their voting record before unsympathetic reelection constituents surprised me. A white member explained his strongly pro-civil rights voting record to his majority lower-middle-class white supporters in the same way he did to his small minority of black supporters. A supporter of President Nixon on Vietnam explained his position to the dovish majority in his district in the same language he used to explain it to his small band of conservative supporters. A western member explained his votes on water distribution measures in the same way to those supporters who stood to lose water by his votes as to those supporters who stood to gain water by his votes.

Viewed in isolation, each of these instances of explanatory consistency could be expected to drive away normal electoral support. We shall not try to understand why each member behaved as he did. Clearly, however, each believed that he could minimize any prospective losses because of the cushion of trust he had already developed with his supporters. The civil rights advocate noted, "Our poll showed that I'm a little more liberal than my district on civil rights. It also showed that they tolerate that because they agree with me on most other issues and because they think I work hard." The Vietnam hawk said, "Let's face it: it doesn't make any sense for me to have been elected in this district. I guess people have confidence in me. So long as they have confidence in me, I can keep my independence." And the westerner commented, "My constituents are tolerant with me because I'm tolerant with them. . . . There's no animosity toward me anywhere in the district. . . . People are tolerant and they ask me to explain. They don't say, 'You're a ding dong.'" To a degree, then, House members are not explanatory chameleons because they do not have to be — not to survive. They can win and hold electoral support in ways that do not depend on their explanations.

This does not mean that members go out of their way to find disagreement, though many welcome a little disagreement because of the opportunity it gives them to demonstrate a degree of independence. It only means that when disagreement is present and explanations are called for, members offer the same explanations for their vote or for their established policy positions as they offer when no disagreement is present.

As we have already indicated, disagreements do not constantly attend members when they are at home. Usually there is a general policy agreement between members and the people to whom they talk. Many of a member's appearances are intended to celebrate individual, group, or community achievement and thus produce only reenforcing sentiments — "smooching," or "playing butter" as two members call it. Furthermore, in the most heterogeneous of districts — in segmented districts anyway — any temptation to alter explanations may be blunted by the lack of any necessity for doing so. People in one part of the district neither know nor care about explanations given elsewhere.

> That's the thing about this district. That part of the district is so isolated and cut off from the rest of the district. I could survive down here and be in a lot of trouble there — as I am. No one here knows what's going on there. It's a local issue and it's confined. There aren't any reverberations or shock waves. It's an explosion without tremors in the rest of the district.

Besides the lack of necessity, the member has some control over his explanatory agenda at home, by directing constituent attention to subjects he feels most comfortable and knowledgeable and persuasive in explaining, or by talking to each constituent group only about that which interests them in particular or by adopting a generally low-output explanatory style.

Of course, a member's presentation of self may vary from group to group in the sense that the basis for demonstrating identification or empathy will have to differ from group to group. Said one member,

> I don't have any trouble talking to blacks and then talking to the Italians who live next to them. You don't start with the same priorities. But you interface with them where you can and go on from there. I don't happen to think there's

anything wrong with that. If you don't start communicating
somewhere, you don't get anywhere.

As they try to relate to or "interface with" each group in a manner
appropriate to that group, members may, then, take on some local
coloration. But, for all the reasons we have mentioned, they rarely
alter their explanations of their past Washington activity in the
process.

EXPLANATION AS LEGITIMATION

Explaining Washington activity, as said at the outset, includes justifying that activity to one's constituents. The pursuit of power, for
example, is sometimes justified with the argument that the representative accumulates power not for himself but for his constituents.
In justifying their policy decisions, representatives sometimes claim
that their policy decisions follow not what they want but what their
constituents want. Recall the member who justified his decision
not to support his own highway bill with the comment, "I'm not
here to vote my own convictions. I'm here to represent my people."
Similarly, the member who decided to yield to his constituent's
wishes on gun control said, "I rationalize it by saying that I owe it
to my constituents if they feel that strongly about it." But this is
not a justification all members use. The independent, issue-oriented
Judiciary Committee member mentioned earlier commented (privately) with heavy sarcasm,

> All some House members are interested in is "the folks."
> They think "the folks" are the second coming. They would
> no longer do anything to displease "the folks" than they
> would fly. They spend all their time trying to find out what
> "the folks" want. I imagine if they get five letters on one
> side and five letters on the other side, they die.

An alternative justification, of course, is that the representative's
policy decisions are based on what he thinks is good public policy,
regardless of what his constituents want. As the Judiciary Committee member told his constituents often, "If I were sitting where
you are, I think what I would want is to elect a man to Congress
who will exercise his best judgment on the facts when he has them
all." At a large community college gathering in the heart of his

district, a member who was supporting President Nixon's Vietnam policy was asked, "If a majority of your constituents signed a petition asking you to vote for a date to end the war, would you vote for it?" He answered,

> It's hard for me to imagine a majority of my constituents agreeing on anything. But if it did happen, then no, I would not vote for it. I would still have to use my own judgment — especially where the security of the country is involved. You can express opinions. I have to make the decision. If you disagree with my decisions, you have the power every two years to vote me out of office. I listen to you, believe me. But, in the end, I have to use my judgment as to what is in your best interests.[11]

He then proceeded to describe his views on the substantive question.

To political scientists, these two kinds of policy justification are very familiar. One is a "delegate" justification, the other a "trustee" justification. The two persist side by side because the set of constituent attitudes on which each depends also exist side by side.[12] Voters, that is, believe that members of Congress should follow constituents' wishes; and voters also believe that members of Congress should use their own best judgment. They want their representatives, it has been said, to be "common people of uncommon judgment." Most probably, though we do not know, voters want delegate behavior on matters most precious to them and trustee behavior on all others. Nonetheless, both kinds of justification are acceptable as a general proposition. Both are legitimate, and in explaining their Washington activity members are seeking to legitimate that activity. They use delegate and trustee justifications because both are legitimating concepts.

If, when they are deciding how to vote, House members think in terms of delegates and trustees, it is because they are thinking about the terms in which they will explain (i.e., justify or legitimate) that vote back home if the need to do so arises. If members never had to legitimate any of their policy decisions back home, they would stop altogether talking in delegate or trustee language. We cannot, therefore, make full use of the ideas of delegate and trustee until we see them as categories that pertain primarily to the explanatory-legitimating end of the voting-explaining sequence. Unconnected to the explanatory part of the process, the concepts have little behavioral content. This realization may help us get more mileage out of a conceptualization that will not die but that has had a low payoff in explaining actual behavior. The behavior to be explained by the conceptualization, we suggest, may be explanation — in its legitimating sense. To put the matter more broadly still, empirical theories of representation will always be incomplete without theories that explain explaining.

EXPLANATION AS EDUCATION

Our idea of explaining — as describing, interpreting, and justifying — has a largely defensive connotation to it. That is so because we have linked it, ultimately, to the problem of constituent support. But there is an aspect of explanation that cannot be so directly linked to the necessity for electoral support. That is what we might call "education." All explanation is, from one standpoint, educational. But we think of education as an effort to persuade people to change their attitudes when the effort itself cannot be seen, in the short run anyway, as electorally beneficial. Education is something you do to your supporters — not your nonsupporters. Education involves the willingness to spend electoral capital — votes, even some trust — in an attempt to alter supporter attitudes about member activity in Washington. Few members would deny the importance of "educating your constituents" in the abstract. Some members extol it: "Educating your constituency is the most important job we have." "I have the best platform from which to educate of anyone in the country. To me, there's no difference between leadership and education. You know what the Latin meaning of education is — 'to lead out.' What is politics if it's not teaching?" But if education is a home activity that by definition has to *hurt a little*, then I did not see a great deal of it.

A representative cannot educate his or her supportive constituents constantly. That would hurt too much. At best, then, constituent education will be occasional, and will cover a very few subjects. I did see a few instances. During a question period after a Rotary Club speech, club president Fred Baxter denounced the sale of American grain to India amidst supportive catcalls — "Cut 'em off," "knock it out" — from the audience. Thereupon the congressman, a deep-dyed conservative, jumped up to say that as members of the world community, we have the responsibility to send wheat to where people are starving and that we could not turn our backs on India. Later that afternoon he referred to the incident as one of his "minimal education efforts":

> I tell you the truth; I'm not campaigning any harder than I have to. . . . I would much rather have a conversation with someone like Fred who introduced me this noon. He barely concedes that roads are a government function. He doesn't concede schools. He's a real right-winger, and I'd rather spend a lot more time trying to talk some sense into him instead of handshaking.

Another time, I watched as a far western congressman told his supporters why he wasn't backing their preferred legislation: because it could not pass. "A legislative body has to represent conflicting interests and we have to recognize other points of view," he told them.

> We could put the bill in now, demagogue it, and take credit for it, but it wouldn't get anywhere. So I think we should build a base of support for it first, and that's what I'm doing. People in the cities, you know, aren't in favor of it as we are.

Education here centered more on the pursuit of power than policy, as he tried to tell his regionally minded supporters that "Since I've been in Congress I've come to realize that Congress is a microcosm of the United States, with diverse and conflicting interests." There were other instances of education, too. At their best, these educational efforts carried the message that it was necessary to temper parochialism in order to balance interests and to surrender stereotypes in order to entertain policy options. But, again, the only generalization supportable by the evidence is the apparent paucity of educational effort.[18]

Earlier we noted the reluctance of representatives to explain power in terms of the Congress as an institution. They prefer to discuss their power as individuals. The extent to which this individualistic preference dominates the entire explanatory process was, to me at least, a surprise. From years of exposure to the literature on party government — which has taught us that our national parties are weak and decentralized and that our congressional parties are not cohesive or disciplined — I fully expected to observe a highly individualistic politics in the congressional district. I expected to find individually customized home styles. It was more with a sense of proof than enlightenment, therefore, that I listened while every member with whom I traveled — whatever his or her background, philosophy, talent, or effectiveness — was introduced as "the greatest congressman in the United States" or as some reasonable facsimile thereof.

Nothing, however, had prepared me to discover that each member of Congress polishes his or her individual reputation at the expense of the institutional reputation of Congress.[14] In explaining what he was doing in Washington, every one of the eighteen House members took the opportunity to picture himself as different from, and better than, most of his fellow members of Congress. None availed himself of the opportunity to educate his constituents about Congress as an institution — not in any way that would "hurt a little." To the contrary, the members' process of differentiating themselves from the Congress as a whole only served, directly or indirectly, to downgrade the Congress.

At a luncheon of small-town westerners, one member was introduced by the local restaurant owner as "the most fantastic congressman in the United States." In the course of his subsequent "report" on the recent Congress, the member said to the group,

> The biggest failure of the Ninety-fourth Congress was its inability to do anything to encourage conservation. They were incompetent and incapable. They copped out. But I didn't! [Waving index finger in the air.] I was one of only sixty-two votes on one car pollution amendment.

In another district, a church leader fumbled for a way to introduce a member: "How do I introduce this great man? When they introduce the president, they say 'Mr. President.' So I'll just say, 'Mr. Congressman.'" At his next engagement, before a group of college students, "Mr. Congressman" described his job:

> I try to lead my constituency. . . . Too few members of Congress are willing to accept a position of national leadership. They are very opinionated and vote their opinions. But not many try to lead their communities in ideas.

A third congressman began his three major speeches during one of my visits as follows:

I want to tell you a story that symbolizes what people think of Congress. My wife and I went to a Marine Corps dinner in honor of a friend of mine. If you haven't been to a Marine Corps dinner of this sort, you haven't seen anything — several kinds of wine, a band playing, everyone in formal dress. They have an honor guard with crossed swords bring on the beef. [Here, the congressman would cross his arms in front of his chest and strut up and down with mock pomposity to exaggerate the distance between formal Washington and informal home.] We drank a whole bunch of toasts. When we toasted the air force, the band played "Wild Blue Yonder." Then we toasted the navy, and the band played "Anchors Aweigh." We toasted the marines, and the band played the Marine Hymn. And the infantry. As it came my turn to make a toast, I turned to the person next to me and said, "What do you think the band will play for a congressman?" And he said, " 'Here Comes Santa Claus!' " [Laughter]

As a backdrop to his ardent pleas for "fiscal responsibility" and "reduced spending," the transparent implication was that it was "the others," not himself that was the object of the story.

Most of this is quite deliberate. As we listened to a fourth congressman's campaign radio ads, which said in part, "We need fifty more men like Jack Caron in Congress," the congressman commented, "People don't like Congress, but they do like their own man. 'We need fifty more like Caron' plays on that. It's a way of sliding out from under the charges against Congress." The most crucial public event in the campaign of a veteran congressman against a youthful challenger was their one TV debate. The challenger's opening statement was a blistering attack on the Congress and on the senior congressman as the embodiment and perpetrator of its evils. The incumbent immediately retorted,

I do not accept responsibility for any actions of Congress. I do not want to be tarred with the brush being applied to other members of Congress. I want to be judged by how well Sam Smalley has done, what Sam Smalley has said, and what service Sam Smalley has given to the people of the Third District of this state.

This opening comment, "sliding out from under" the criticism of Congress, set the individualistic framework within which all House members wish to explain themselves and to be judged.

A sixth member commented to his campaign strategy group,

> I've been giving some thought to the campaign theme. What
> people want in their public officials today is independence.
> We can't be so vulgar as to use the word "independence"
> in our literature. But we have to differentiate me from the
> rest of those bandits down there in Congress. "They are
> awful, but our guy is wonderful." — that's the message we
> have to get across.

As we moved about his district, he conveyed that message by poking
fun at Congress. After discussing Arab arms purchases, he noted,
"The only place they make more deals is the Congress. [Laughter.]"
Answering a question about the Postal Service — "Isn't there any
sanity up there on the Hill?" — he said, "Not much. No, let me
phrase that positively. There is some sanity on the Hill. [Laughter.]"
To a women's group that announced his 100 percent voting record
on women's issues, he noted, "Congress has a 20 percent approval
rating. That's two points better than 'don't know' and three points
worse than sugar rationing in wartime. [Laughter.]" Shaking hands
with a group of businessmen, he was asked, "How are things in
Congress?" He replied, "Things in Congress are about usual — no,
they are better than usual because we are in recess. [Laughter.]" The
intended message is there: "They are awful, but our guy is wonderful." The message is even stronger than that. If "our guy" is the
exception to the rule, then it becomes almost *imperative* that we
send him back to do battle against "the rest of those bandits down
there in Congress."

Criticizing or ridiculing "the others" comes so naturally to the
congressman at home that some of this explanatory posturing may
not be deliberate at all. How else can we account for the thought-
lessness with which some members, at home in 1974, made public
jokes about the tragic turn of events in the life of Wilbur Mills,
once a respected pillar of their institution: "I've learned one thing
in Washington — to stay away from bodies of water." "You know
what WIN means don't you — Wilbur Is Naughty." Hundreds or
thousands of miles away from Washington, before warmly supportive constituents, such cannibalizing cruelty can seem almost play-
ful. Congress and its other members are remote, cold abstractions.

Collectively and individually they can be attacked at home without fear of constituent disfavor. To the contrary, because most constituents are critical of Congress to begin with, the congressman stands only to increase constituent identification and trust when he joins — and leads — the chorus.

For the individual House member, differentiating himself or herself from the others in Congress, attacking Congress as an institution, and portraying himself or herself as a fighter against its manifest shortcomings is an appealing explanatory strategy because it is without cost. At least it is in the short run, when the member is at home appealing for support within one geographical constituency, in total isolation from all, or most, other geographical constituencies. The performance of Congress is collective; but the responsibility for congressional performance is not. Responsibility is assessed member by member, district by district. It is easy for each congressman to explain to his own supporters why he cannot be blamed for the performance of the collectivity. It is doubly easy to do because the internal diversity and decentralization of the institution provide such a variety of collegial villains to flay before one's supporters at home. There are "the old chairmen," "the inexperienced newcomers," "the tools of organized labor," "the tools of big business," "the fiscally irresponsible liberals," "the short-sighted conservatives," "the ineffective leadership," "the obstructionist minority," "those who put selfish interests before those of country," and so on. The beauty of the strategy is that everybody can use it and nobody will be called to account by those under attack.

It is one more measure of the gulf between the Washington and home contexts that this explanatory pattern violates every syllable of what political scientists (like this author) have long taken to be the overarching norm of the House — institutional loyalty. According to this norm, members are supposed to value the House as an institution and do nothing to diminish its prestige or demean its members. House leaders are supposed to recognize and reward members who follow the norm (i.e., "responsible legislators"). In Washington, one may hear this norm voiced by leaders and see it observed by members. At home, it is breached every day in every way. If members have any institutional loyalty it is kept well hidden on the hustings. It is probably true that in the pursuit of inside power obeisance to the norm helps. But it is a pleasant Capitol Hill hypocrisy. What members will not say in Washington, they will say back home. Institutional loyalty is not something House members take seriously.

In terms of their explanatory behavior, the willingness of House members to stand and defend their own votes or voting record contrasts sharply with their disposition to run and hide when a defense of Congress might be called for. Members of Congress run *for* Congress by running *against* Congress. The strategy is ubiquitous, addictive, cost-free and foolproof. It underlines everything we have said about the individualistic character of home activity. In the short run, everybody plays and nearly everybody wins. Yet the institution bleeds from 435 separate cuts. In the long run, therefore, somebody may lose.

CONCLUSION

The explanatory and presentational aspects of home style are interrelated. A congressman cannot explain without presenting himself, and many presentations will produce explanations of his power pursuits or his policy pursuits in Washington. Still, we have tried to separate them in order to single out and open up the explanatory process to more scholarly scrutiny than it has had. Political scientists, preoccupied with explaining the votes of House members, have neglected to explain the explanations of House members. Yet we would argue that it is impossible to understand the one without understanding the other. The ability to explain and to have his explanation accepted by his supportive constituencies, is the regulator of a congressman's voting leeway in Washington. The search for political support at home is not just a matter of winning reelection. It is also a matter of winning voting leeway. When we combine presentational and explanatory activity at home, it appears that members of Congress are much less constrained by their supportive constituencies and have much more voting leeway on the House floor than they believe or will admit. Washington activity and home activity are interconnected, and the explanatory process provides one important link.

We have speculated about the relationship between presentational and explanatory styles. This subject needs elaboration as we develop knowledge about the full range of member communications practices. We have argued, nonetheless, that acceptable explanations must be compatible with established (or, for new members, developing) presentational styles. In explanation, therefore, as well as in presentation, home style and issue substance are inseparable. "Issues," as one member said, "are not as important as the treatment of issues." Part of that treatment is the way a member explains his Washington voting when he is called on to do so. We have illustrated the relationship with several examples.

The explanatory process helps link Congress and the citizenry, through its legitimating and its educational aspects. Explanation involves legitimation, whereby the acts of representatives are accepted as authoritative by those they represent. Individual House members justify their Washington activity in ways that encourage the acceptance of their activity as legitimate. The familiar "delegate" and "trustee" formulations, we think, should be viewed more as justifications that have explanatory and legitimating usefulness at home, and should be viewed less as formulations describing behavior in Washington. Explanation also involves education, whereby information and evaluation are conveyed by representatives to those they represent. Members of Congress approach their educational activity gingerly because, by definition, any real educational effort means the potential loss of support. The education members do provide is highly individualistic on the informational side and highly critical of the Congress on the evaluative side. Thus members of Congress probably help depress citizen understanding of and respect for the United States Congress. Members get reelected to an institution about which their supporters know less and care less than they otherwise might.

NOTES

1. Richard Fenno, *Congressmen in Committees* (Boston: Little, Brown, 1973), Chap. 1.
2. John Kingdon, *Congressmen's Voting Decisions* (New York: Harper and Row, 1973), pp. 46–53. See also David M. Olson, "The Congressman and His Party," unpublished manuscript, Athens, Georgia, 1970, Chapter 5, pp. 16–26.
3. Kingdon, *Voting Decisions*, pp. 234–40; Roger Davidson, *The Role of the Congressman* (New York: Pegasus, 1969), pp. 115, 199; see also Donald Matthews and James Stimson, *Yeas and Nays: Normal Decision Making in the U.S. House of Representatives* (New York: Wiley, 1975), pp. 169–70.
4. Kingdon, *Voting Decisions*, pp. 41–42.
5. On "position-taking," see David Mayhew, *Congress: The Electoral Connection* (New Haven: Yale University Press, 1974), pp. 61–73.

6. Members may also cast an occasional vote at total variance with their voting record — a "neutralizing vote" we might call it. Like a presentation before one's nonsupporters, it helps cool the intensity of the opposition by proving that the member is not "a wild man" and not irrevocably beyond reach. "Neutralizing votes" help control the explanatory agenda.

7. *Congressional Record*, Daily Edition, July 23, 1974, H6962–H6963.

8. *Ibid.*, August 1, 1974, E5209–E5210.

9. As the "totally independent" member with the "mixed-up district" put it,

> If I were running a campaign against myself, here's how I'd do it. Overall I have a voting record that reasonable people will agree with. But if you start picking out individual votes and attacking each one separately before groups interested in that one vote, it will kill me.

10. By the same reasoning, if we are to understand leadership behavior in the House, we will have to understand the home styles of House leaders. They need leeway in order to lead effectively. See Neil McNeil, "Judging Nixon: The Impeachment Session," *Time*, January 28, 1974; Jamie Rosenthal Wolf, "A Congressman's Day: At the District Office" in *Inside the System*, 3d ed., ed. Charles Peters and James Fallows (New York: Praeger, 1976).

11. A different view, based on data gathered in Washington, will be found in Richard P. Mendelson, "Survival Tactics on Capitol Hill," *Washington Post*, February 1, 1976.

12. His private comment was:

> To me, representative government means you hire a guy to use his own judgment; and if you don't like what he does, you fire him. But you don't keep after him all the time. If it isn't my function to use my judgment, then what the hell is my function? And if that's not my function, I don't want the job. You might as well let a computer make policy. A mongolian idiot could follow the polls if that's all it means to be a representative.

13. Roger Davidson, "Public Perceptions for the Job of Congressman," *Midwest Journal of Political Science* (November 1970), 648–666. A few more members described instances in which they had educated their supportive constituents, but I did not observe them.

14. See also Richard F. Fenno, "If, As Ralph Nader Says, Congress Is 'the Broken Branch,' How Come We Love Our Congressmen So Much?" paper presented to Time, Inc., Symposium, Boston, December 12, 1972, and reprinted in *Congress in Change*, ed. Norman Ornstein (New York: Praeger, 1974), pp. 277–278.

CHAPTER SIX

Constituency Careers and
Stylistic Change

THE STAGES OF A CONSTITUENCY CAREER

Students of Congress are accustomed to thinking about a representative's *career in the House* — early adjustments, rise in seniority, placement on the ladders of committee and party, accumulation of responsibility, the fluctuations of his or her personal "Dow Jones average." Observing and listening to House members at home makes it clear that each one also pursues a *career in the district*. Like House careers, constituency careers have a beginning, a middle, and an end. A person can be just as much a newcomer to the district as he or she is to the House of Representatives. Each individual must gradually work out matters of support, style, and trust in one place as well as in the other. There are successes and failures in both places, too. Indeed, the two careers — one in the House and one at home — affect one another. But we shall have to examine the constituency career — the more neglected of the two — before we can speculate about these interconnections.

In both careers, the controlling variable is *time*, because all careers can be thought of as developing and changing with the passage of time. Firsthand observation over time, however, is difficult, mostly because it requires so much by way of resources — of time, money, stamina, patience. In this study, I shall have to rely on a very short-run perspective. In two cases, my trips to the district covered a six-year span; in four cases they covered a four-year period; in two cases, the visits were three years apart; in six cases they covered two-year intervals; in one case, the trips were a year apart; in four cases I was in the district only once.[1] I have a cross-sectional perspective as well, however, because the members observed had had constituency careers of varying duration at the time I observed them. When I began observing them, two members had yet to be elected, six were in their first term; two each were in their second, third, and fourth terms; and one each was in his sixth, eighth, tenth, and fourteenth terms. We shall piece together these longitudinal and cross-sectional perspectives to explore the idea of the House member's career among his several constituencies.

Constituency careers have two recognizable stages, *expansionist* and *protectionist*. In the expansionist stage, the member of Congress is still building a reliable reelection constituency. The major expansionist thrust occurs before the member's first election. Logically and chronologically, the first step is to solidify a primary constituency, a core of strongest supporters who will carry a primary campaign, if necessary, and who will, in any case, provide the backbone for a general election campaign. The second step is to cultivate the broader reelection constituency by reaching out for additional elements of support. The two activities continue beyond the first election, even though they overlap and intertwine. A congressman described his home activity during his first year in office as follows:

> I got home as often as I could, shook all the hands I could because I wasn't well known. I went home three out of every four weekends and I hit every city and village in the district — every single one. I grasped at every speaking engagement; I worked like a dog at the county fairs; I got to all the TV stations; I dropped in to say hello to the people on all the weekly papers.

The language is unmistakably expansionist.

At some point in most constituency careers, this all-out expansionism ceases to be the major strategic thrust and the member of Congress turns toward protectionism. It is not always obvious just when this change in emphasis occurs, for there is an inevitable telescoping of the two stages. But this comment, by a member nearing the end of his first term, captures the beginning of the change:

> A couple of weeks ago, the staff scheduled me for an evening labor meeting in Franklin. I had had four engagements out in Boone County that day and they wanted me to drive all the way in to Franklin, for Christ's sake. I told them, "Cancel

> it." They said, "We can't." I said, "I'm going to rest this evening. Cancel it." You create a pattern of expectation. For four years we took every opportunity everywhere to meet "two more voters," sixteen hours a day. Margie feels the day is ruined if she leaves fifteen minutes unscheduled. She still wants me to drop in at the fire house between formal scheduled events or tour three more Polish dances. We used to go to six dances in one evening, 300 people each, and shake hands with all of them. Margie will say to me now, "You've never missed the Hampden Policeman's Ball." I'll say, "Stop it. We're going to miss the Hampden Policeman's Ball." I don't have to have every minute scheduled anymore.

Though he is not avowedly protectionist, this member's major expansionist period is clearly behind him.

During the protectionist stage of their constituency careers, House members become less interested in building supportive constituencies and most concerned about keeping the electoral support already attained, about maintaining the existing primary-plus-reelection constituencies. Having worked earlier in their careers to disrupt and rearrange existing patterns of support, they now work to reenforce and stabilize existing patterns of support. Once the members are in the protectionist stage, home activities are dominated by preventive maintenance. The following comment is unmistakably protectionist:

> I'm in a defensive position at this stage and I conduct a defensive operation. There is very little outreach to new groups. . . . Tonight's card party will not be very exciting. They are a bunch of biddies who would no more think of voting Democratic than they would Socialist. . . . But if I don't show up my name will be George G. Mud.

This member believes he has a reliable reelection constituency if only he can hold onto it. This simple idea of a two-stage constituency career is, of course, only a hunch. But there is enough in what House members say and do to make it worth exploring.

No single career timetable is followed by all members of Congress. Each proceeds at his or her own pace. Anyone who wanted to study the expansionist stage of a constituency career would, of course, have to reach back well before the first election. I observed only two individuals prior to their first election. But in neither case was I present at the beginning of the constituency career.

One candidate was expanding his support in a highly organized fashion. He had meticulously "targeted," through the use of a mathematical formula and computerized methods, the election districts most likely to provide political support. He was running a campaign scheduled to the minute all day every day, and reacted with "unspeakable horror" when an hour was left unscheduled. At each stop, he and his staff would canvass for names of people who could help. One day I was there was designated "a trial day, done to determine the usefulness of coffee klatches in the larger communities of the district." The campaign was organized and expansionist. The second preelection campaign I observed was expansionist but unorganized. The candidate was running flat out — everywhere and anywhere. He said,

> We don't have any strategy, I just run. At first we tried to plan a grand strategy . . . but it doesn't work out that way. I'm not that organized; and the campaign isn't predictable either. Things just happen day by day. . . . I speak every chance I get. I've been averaging five churches every Sunday — in and out. . . . You just keep running.

Though their styles differed, both were clearly in the expansionist stage. Indeed, they were well into it. Both had already consolidated a primary constituency by the time I joined them; therefore, they were already in their later rather than their earliest expansionist phase.

Constituency careers, then, begin before a person is elected to Congress. In fact, they may begin long before an individual even decides to run for Congress. Public officials who have already been elected to represent some geographical constituency embedded within the congressional district — state legislators, mayors, district attorneys — will have a head start in their constituency careers. They will bring ready-made supportive constituencies with them to their first race for Congress. For one member, "Forty percent of my congressional district was in my state senatorial district so people knew me." Another said,

> I was a good candidate for the district. It is 75 percent Democratic. The Republicans in the district live up on a hill somewhere; they worry about their ideological purity; they always nominate one of their own, someone who lives

up there; he doesn't have a ghost of a chance of winning, and he always loses. Most of the people live at the bottom of the hill. That's where I lived. I was the [Republican] mayor of the largest, most Democratic city in the district and I had a lot of Democratic friends. So I could get votes that routinely and regularly went to the Democrats.

Some House members will forever delineate their primary constituencies in terms of their precongressional geographical constituencies. One congressman, when confronted with the necessity of redistricting, drew up twenty-six acceptable plans — all of which had but one feature in common, that they included three of the four counties that had comprised the congressman's state legislative district years before. He still perceives these three counties to be "the core counties [out of twenty] of my congressional district" — his primary constituency or, as he puts it, "my tough nut." Theories about the relevance of prior and smaller constituencies for the development of subsequent, larger constituencies are familiar to political scientists.[2] For our purposes here, it is to be expected that House members who have a head start in their precongressional careers will proceed more quickly through the expansionist stage of their careers in the congressional district than will House members whose constituency careers begin with the congressional contest.

Constituency careers develop over time because it takes time to learn about and cultivate a congressional district. Each prospective candidate must take the time to familiarize himself or herself with the district and piece together the two supporting constituencies. How can this be done? One way is to run for and hold an elective office embedded within the district. Another way is for strong political organizations to deliver it to their chosen nominee. Yet another way is for a self-starting individual to make one unsuccessful run for Congress, laying the groundwork for a successful second effort. In effect the candidate undertakes a continuous, three- or four-year effort to find and consolidate support in a strange context.

Among the eighteen representatives in this study, eleven had either run for or held some elective office before their first campaign for Congress. For them, part of the district was familiar territory. Of the eleven, nine captured the congressional seat on their first attempt. For the other seven of the eighteen, however, their first campaign for Congress was their first election campaign. For them, the district was unknown territory, politically. Three of the seven were successful on their first try. They were all from urban areas with Democratic political organizations. One was the anointed organization candidate; one who calls himself "an accident, a fluke" won because the organization was indifferent to the contest; and one beat a weak organization because of his immense personal popularity. As noted earlier, party organizations tend to be weak in congressional districts, as they are in all but one or two of the districts we have studied. So they will not be much help in most cases. Still, the three first-time-out winners were all urban Democrats in areas where political organizations exist.

Four of the seven, however, ran once for Congress unsuccessfully before they captured the seat. For these four, in other words, the first congressional campaign served the same function as running for or holding a noncongressional office had served for the nine who, in the absence of political organization, succeeded on the first try. It enabled them to map the territory, find constituencies, and consolidate their support.

EXPANSIONISM AND PROTECTIONISM

THE EARLIER STAGES: CONGRESSMAN J. Like three of the four second-time winners, Congressman J comes from a heterogeneous district. Even more, it is a segmented district and, therefore, especially hard to digest. "It's in effect four different districts. A guy can concentrate on only one of the four in a campaign, but he can't concentrate on all of them." "I always think of it as pockets in my mind," he says; and he cultivated these pockets one by one. He did it without the organizational help of his party. Individual party members were, however, very helpful.

> The party is no damn good. . . . They can't organize and they can't raise money. . . . I don't have anything to do with the party organization. . . . They have their function. They give you a vehicle to run on. . . . The real function of the party is to have someone to meet the candidate for Congress when he comes into a strange town. You don't know anybody, and you don't walk up to the first person you meet on the street. You look for the party members in town to tell you what you ought to know and introduce you to people.

A primary constituency is built very slowly in his kind of district, by making the right contacts and plugging into local networks in many separate places. It must be done by repeated personal contact. It cannot be done by one concentrated media blitz, because there are no districtwide media.

> There is no way you can get total coverage across the district, not unless it's something very, very big. It can't be a PR campaign. I don't like that kind of campaign anyway. I'm no good at it and I don't do it.

His preferred presentational style was (and is) person to person. "It doesn't fit my temperament to handshake without stopping to talk with each person. Then I feel like I can understand them and they understand me." So he made piecemeal progress, handshaking and visiting his way around the district for several years. He ran one unsuccessful campaign before he was victorious. The first campaign, as he put it, "served as the primary for my second campaign."

As we drove into one of the largest cities in the district on his first reelection try (his third campaign there) he called it "a great town," but remembered how different it had been during his earliest efforts. He had met indifference ("Nobody knew my name"), and hostility ("Three times I sat for forty-five minutes in the waiting room of the newspaper, and the editor never would speak to me"). His wife added, "I would rather have lost than come back here." The day we drove into the Holiday Inn, the signboard read "Welcome Helen and Dan Fillmore." He recalled that a "Welcome Dan Fillmore" sign had first appeared during his second campaign. Symbolically, he says, "that was the turning point." He later described his fourth campaign effort in that area as "a triumphal tour." His electoral support there in his first four election efforts was 27 percent, 44 percent, 56 percent and 63 percent, respectively.

On that same trip, he described his early expansionist phase by commiserating with his opponent:

> That poor devil. He's out there running around the district and he doesn't know where he's going. When he gets there, nobody will be there to meet him. Can you imagine how hard it would be to come into these communities without knowing people to begin with? I know; I've been there.

During his second reelection bid, he spoke similarly about his new opponent:

> The same thing is beginning to happen to him as happened to all of us when we ran the first time. You start in April or May and you work your tail off for six months bouncing around the district, going to every meeting. You don't set your own schedule; you accommodate to everyone else's schedule. Come September, you ask yourself how you're doing. And you find that you are worn out, broke, and losing — after all that effort. . . . This district will kill you. It's killing him just like it did me. He would have to run twice before he would get any profit out of it.

Now, of course, Congressman J is the incumbent. And the segmented district he swallowed in small, sequential bites now protects him. No one can swallow it whole. "The first term is the hardest. If you win election a second time," he believes, "you're in for quite a while." He added,

> Each area is interested only in its own problems. That's what makes it so easy for an incumbent. He can provide services for each of the towns. If something disastrous happens to him in one town, it won't hurt him elsewhere. . . . That's how my predecessor did it. He never came home. He didn't have to. Once you get by the first election, I don't see how they can beat you.

> In a [totally] suburban district, someone can move in and take over. You can't do that with mine. It's too big and diverse. I may lose my district if people get mad at me for something I've done. But no one can come in here and take it away from me.

The prize is easy to hold for the same reasons it was so hard to capture in the first place. "It takes a long time before you have a district in the palm of your hand, so that you really know it," he says. But now he does. "I'm the only one who knows the district. I'm the only one who can know it."

When I rejoined him during his second reelection campaign, Congressman J's stance was distinctly more protectionist. On the long nighttime drive home from a day of farflung campaigning, he reflected,

> We didn't gain anything we didn't already have, but we reenforced some strength. It was an average day on the road. . . . I have to make an adjustment now that I'm the incumbent. People come to me and want to help. They came to the cocktail party tonight to see me. When I first ran, no one came to help. I was all alone. I'd walk down the street in Granger by myself. Everyone was too busy. Today I could have had an entourage so big that they couldn't all fit in the stores. But the people who came to see me are the same ones.

He is "reenforcing" his strength by dealing with the "same" people. He is not meeting new ones. During the day, moreover, he had regularly passed up expansionist opportunities. In the afternoon, his staff had scheduled him to "hit the bricks" in the downtown business district; but he had visited only two of the hundred or so stores there. He had refused, also, to retape a radio interview that failed to record properly. His operation has become strongly protectionist.

Between my two visits, another element had crept into his thinking, a new phrase had been added to his conversation: "my career in Washington." A new committee assignment had led to "the most important, the most interesting thing I ever did in my whole life. . . . All the staff guys said I worked harder than anyone else on the committee. . . . The others learned from me." And at his home town Rotary Club luncheon he opened by saying,

> It's been a fruitful two years for this state and for my ambitions in Washington. We all worry about how we will do there. It's like Harry Truman said, "At first you stand in awe of the place and you look at the others and ask yourself 'How did I ever get here?' Then after a while, you look at the others and ask 'How did they get here?' "

Later, he discussed his legislative life briefly:

> It's a matter of learning how to get things done, knowing the people, and working without raising hackles. Guys like Schuler and Wiley, I work with them even though I disagree with them on most things and even though I don't even like

the two of them. . . . Then when I want something, it's easier for me than some of my colleagues. . . . I'm nothing special. I've just gotten better at working the legislative process. Mostly people know I'm not a political bullshitter. In Congress, people are wary and scared of guys who are ambitious. . . . I have no illusions that I will ever be part of the leadership.

These are the first stirrings of a Washington career. The early onset of a House career may propel members toward a more protectionist attitude at home. We shall address this question later.

THE EARLIER STAGES: CONGRESSMAN K. Congressman K had been in office a year and a half when I first went to his district. Very nearly the first thing he said to me was,

I'm still caught up with reelection, with my survival. I've been in office nearly two years and I'm still campaigning. I'm still trying to please everyone, still running. I don't feel like an incumbent and I haven't started acting like an incumbent.

It was an expansionist-stage comment. Congressman K was elected to Congress on his first try, doubtless helped by two earlier election campaigns, one of which encompassed part of the district and the other of which encompassed all of it. "I've been running continuously for five years," he said, "and all up hill." But he had not yet developed any sense of identification with the district. He had moved over the district line shortly before his congressional primary campaign. "I wasn't a member of the community when I ran for Congress," he said. "Traditionally, incumbents grow up in this district like the trees. But I was an outsider." Even after a year and a half, he evinced no sense of fit with the district and spoke of the "ideal candidate" there as someone with all the identification he lacked — someone, he said, "who grew up in the district, knows the district well, has worked in the mills, hunts and fishes, has connections all over and can talk the language of the Jaycees." Like Congressman J, he remained close enough to his earliest expansionist phase to recall its difficulties:

Phyllis kept a diary, and the other day we took it out to see where we were exactly two years before. It was a day we had

> a spaghetti dinner cooked for 2000, and 40 showed up. It was
> so painful to read, we put the diary back in the drawer.

Nonetheless, he won a difficult congressional primary shortly thereafter.

He describes that primary victory as "luck." It was "a case of the
right person campaigning in the right way on the right issues at the
right time." His primary constituency had to be created almost
from scratch. "Every business, every labor union except one, every
newspaper, and every state legislator — the entire establishment of
the district" supported his primary opponent. "We had to form our
own organization and find our own support," he says. And he did —
with a nucleus of "25 core supporters" and "400 or maybe 500 or
600" others recruited by them from outside "the establishment."

A crucial expansion of primary support came in the middle of the
primary campaign when he "just stumbled on" an issue with intense
appeal to a group of small businesses — an issue without which "I
never would have been able to raise enough money to finance my
campaign." Beyond that, he conducted a person-to-person campaign
among ordinary voters. It was this kind of campaign, he thinks, that
gave him the rest of his supportive constituencies:

> My opponents in both the primary and the general election
> were aloof and arrogant. My primary opponent was a big shot
> and had trouble talking face to face with ordinary people.
> My general election opponent had a very abrupt way with
> people. He carried a little counter in his hand and would click
> people off as he talked to them. He went for quantity. I went
> for quality. I took time to listen to people and made their
> problems part of my ideas.

"It was not charisma," he said, in summing up his early career in
the district. "Mostly, I just sensed the mood, that people wanted a
fresh face, honest and open government."

Once elected, Congressman K sought to incorporate his person-
to-person strength into an appropriate home style. He inaugurated
"open office hours," in which he regularly meets anyone who wants
to see him in the various public meeting places around the district.
He mails announcements of his visits to the people in each area. In
the city hall or library or union hall he sets up two or three chairs
and a table in the corner of the room, and everyone who comes gets

five minutes (first come, first served) of personal conversation with the congressman. The congressman sits beside the table, not behind it; and a staff aide sits nearby should follow-up casework be necessary. Congressman K eschews the town meeting idea because "two or three people always tend to dominate the discussion and people with real problems will not speak up." Of all the things he does at home he feels personally most comfortable at his open office hours. In such a context, he plays to certain personal strengths — an openness, a lack of pretension, an ability to empathize. It is his major expansionist device. "It's a way of making myself accessible to the average citizen. It's my only chance to meet people other than the local political leaders of the establishment."

During that first term, Congressman K was not reaching out to the people who had opposed him. "After a congressman has been in a while," he commented, "he gets into a close relationship with the establishment. I don't have that. I'm still new. They don't know me. And I don't owe them anything." But the local establishment had been neutralized, nonetheless:

> Business people saw me as a radical, unpredictable, young, ambitious politician, when I first ran. Now they say, "he's not so bad," because I haven't been as wild as they thought and have even supported their position on regulation. They don't like me — but they know they can't beat me.

He won a second term with about two-thirds of the vote. In two years he had expanded about as far as he could go — or wanted to.

When I returned to the district, six months after his reelection, the signs of protectionism were everywhere. Open office hours remained the centerpiece of his home style, but I heard about one-quarter of the individuals on each of two afternoons say they were repeaters. "Do you feel like an incumbent now?" I asked. "Yes. We still do the things we did during the campaign, getting around and seeing people. But I feel more confident now." Not once did he mention anything that suggested a lack of fit with the district. Nor was he reaching hard for new support. On the way to a privately arranged discussion group in one of his largest communities, he commented, "We're actually going to meet some new people — maybe five or six! You do keep growing, but we've pretty well saturated the area." The major problem of his incumbency, he felt, was the temptation to expand beyond his original reelection constituency, thereby losing touch with those constituents who had been supportive from the start. He worried, therefore, about keeping in contact with his constant supporters — a protectionist worry.

Because of the safety concerns of a union — the one union that had supported him in his primary — he toured a small factory. As we walked away, he said,

> During my first campaign, I stood over there at the check-in gate handing out literature, and Dave St. James [the union leader] stayed with me to the end. The management people stood over here looking out these windows and glaring at me. Honest to God, they think I'm some kind of communist or socialist — that I'm evil. I felt intimidated. . . . Now, I want to keep them at arms distance. You know there's a tendency after you've been in office to get in bed with the Chamber of Commerce and the local businessmen. I don't ever want Dave St. James to think I've done that. He's the kind of person I represent, by and large. . . . My visit to the plant today is highly symbolic. Tomorrow the word will get around among the union members that I was here and that I stood up for them.

Later that evening, he recalled how helpful that union had been in his primary and said this was the first time he had been back to the factory since that time.

"Once you're in office, it's so hard to stay in touch with the people who elected you," he said.

> It's the establishment that comes around and wants things from you. They ask you to their meetings. They seduce you over and over and over. The easy thing is to go along and forget the people who elected you. Laurie, with the exception of the coffees you hold, who else have I seen recently in your town except the Rotary, the Kiwanis, the industry people, and the local officials?

Congressman K uses "coffees" to help countervail against these temptations and to shore up his existing support. He says,

> Coffees played a large part in our primary campaign. We held about 100 of them. We have tried to keep up by asking the

same people back again to coffee. We schedule them whenever there's a free evening when I'm home. We'll call someone who gave a coffee before and ask them to get their same
neighbors back again. You get stronger support that way.
Those people will stay with you.

The coffees reflect his protectionist instincts. The one I attended
placed second to his open office hours on his own at-homeness rankings.

Speaking to "my earliest supporters" at the coffee hour, Congressman K talked not only like incumbent, but like one who already
saw a Washington career worth protecting. He had become a House
spokesman in a national policy controversy that had brought him
notice beyond the district. And he told the group, "I'm expecting a
telephone call from the Secretary of _____ anytime now. So we
may have an exciting telephone call here this evening." When the
call did come the next morning, he emerged smiling from his office,
"That's the first time I've ever been called by a high-level person in
the government." And later, he reflected on this earliest taste of a
long-term career.

Congress is more than a job. It's a way of life. You don't see
many people retire after one or two terms, do you? If it's
unthinkable to do that, there must be something pretty
absorbing and exciting about the job. You begin to settle in
and you begin to look down the road a few years to that subcommittee chairmanship. I don't feel like [the senior members
of my delegation]. I don't have the influence they do. But
you begin to have some effect, like the Secretary of _____
touching base with me. That was exciting. It was the first
time anything like that ever happened to me.

How long can a member of Congress continue to think in expansionist terms at home when he sees a Washington career beckoning?
Congressman K already worries about that question out loud:

It would be interesting to do a study four years from now and
ten years from now to see if people like me have turned the
corner and become more interested in national problems and
legislative problems than in the district. "How often do you
come back to your district, Mr. Congressman?" "Oh, twice a
year!" Our class works their districts much harder than the

older members. We're back here all the time. We're crazy to come back here and work as hard as we do. But we feel it's an important part of the job. Will we turn that corner?

As in the case of Congressman *J,* there is probably a connection between the career at home and the career in the House. But for the moment, the case of Congressman *K* illustrates the startling speed with which a constituency career can move from its expansionist to its protectionist stage. Judging from his comments, his earlier races had given him a very modest head start. Yet six months into his second term, the balance of his attitudes and actions had clearly swung from expansionist to protectionist.

Representatives *J* and *K* have each had fairly short constituency careers. When I first visited, each was close enough in time to his constituency beginnings to recall the difficulties of his earliest, pre-election expansionist efforts. In each instance, I made two trips to the district — to observe Congressman *J* during his first and second reelection campaigns, and to observe Congressman *K* six months before and six months after his first reelection campaign. In both cases the change was the same — the swing from a dominantly expansionist phase to a dominantly protectionist phase of the constituency career. Each spends more time now reenforcing old support than reaching out for new support. Each seems more comfortable and confident now about his relationships with his supportive constituencies and about his home style. Each feels the first competing tugs of a Washington career. Both began their constituency careers well before their election to Congress. But, once in office, their careers moved very quickly from the expansionist into the protectionist stage.

We would not want to generalize on the basis of two cases, but it is common for first-term House members to make their greatest leaps forward in electoral percentages the second time around.[3] Along with their first successful election, this first reelection campaign is often a "testing election," of which we spoke in Chapter One. The early transition from expansionism to protectionism by Representatives *J* and *K* is probably not unusual. In any case, the constituency careers of Representatives *J* and *K* are still near the beginning and a long way from the end. Both are ambitious. We can think of them then as only recently embarked on long constituency careers.

THE LATER STAGES: CONGRESSMAN L. Other members with whom I traveled were obviously closer to the termination of their constituency careers. Of the ill-defined "middle" of such careers, we shall say little. But in looking at the middle or the end of the constituency career, we must observe one caveat. Constituency careers may not always develop in a linear progression from expansionist to protectionist. Events may occur after the member has reached the protectionist stage to propel him or her once again into the expansionist stage. Constituency careers, that is, may be cyclical. Two circumstances come to mind. One is the deterioration of the original primary constituency and the necessity for building a new one. For example, an issue-oriented primary constituency may drift away when the coalescing issue is gone; or, a volunteer organization may atrophy if it is not called on to do anything for a number of elections. A second problem is a redistricting, where redrawn boundaries force the member to rebuild political support in a new context.

I traveled with one House veteran, Congressman L, in the midst of his most difficult electoral challenge. Within five minutes of our first meeting, he ran quickly through the three-day schedule, largely filled with "candidates' nights," and commented,

> Candidates' nights are an old tradition here — a tradition begot of the devil. But it's destined to go on forever. Every group in the city feels it must have one. Each one draws only a corporals' guard. So you can't make any positive gains. But each group will be insulted if you don't show up.

He showed up at five in two days — a protectionist performance befitting his protectionist perspective. He would pass up chances to try something new. When asked to meet with the editorial board of the newspaper to discuss constitutional amendments, as his opponent had done, he answered, "I'm not going to change a policy of twenty years. I'm just not going to do it. Life is too short." When asked to debate his opponent, he said, "I have never paid any attention to my opponent since I've been in office; but I'll give that one some thought." And the sense of having gotten out of touch was present. "Have I spoken there recently?" he inquired of a campaign invitation. "Can't tell," replied his district aide. And Congressman L said, "We ought to keep a running record on these things. It's the squeaky wheel that gets the grease. I speak before some of these same groups over and over, while I neglect some of my old buddies."

As a House member with an urban district whose city had lost population, Congressman L had been given some compensating suburban territory in the recent redistricting. And that change, after many years, had made him uneasy about constituency relationships. He did not feel at home in the suburbs.

> My old district was easier to run in. I don't feel comfortable
> in suburbia. They have so many local jealousies and rivalries.
> I wasn't prepared for their pettiness and petulance, for the
> dozen different city councils and all those government districts
> of one kind or another. I'm used to dealing with a city. It
> has problems, but if you have a reasonable solution to those
> problems, people listen to you and you can accomplish some-
> thing. Not in suburbia.

His constituency relations became even more tenuous as he sensed that their issue orientations had changed. "I came in as a strong liberal and have ended being more conservative. I didn't change. My reference points remained the same. But the world has changed." He was uncomfortable, out of touch, and worried. "I used to be representative of the district," he said, "I don't know if I am now." But he was not working to accommodate himself to the changed situation. In the year following the redistricting, he made five trips home and spent sixty-two days in his new district.

Furthermore, Congressman L's ambition had clearly waned — or perhaps peaked. Fatalism had replaced that intense concern about reelection that animates so many members of Congress.

> We'll see. I don't care if I lose. I seriously considered not
> running at this time. . . . I've been pretty damn successful,
> so I don't have anything to prove. My ego is not involved in
> this election. I like the job. I like to work the system. But I
> want it only on my own terms. I want it the way I want it.
> If I can't, I don't. . . . Gordon Steinfeldt has already talked
> to me about the job he wants me to have.

As for a career in the House, he wanted nothing more.

> I've been asked to run for various leadership positions many
> times. But I have absolutely no ambitions for the leadership.

> I don't want it. When I tell people, they don't believe me.
> They think there's something wrong if you aren't ambitious
> for higher office. I'm not.

Besides that, a tinge of personal weariness crept through in private,
as he admitted, "I'm an introvert. I'm terribly, terribly shy. I'm a
misfit in this business of politics. Somehow, I've blended it all in.
But I don't know how much longer I can take it." These are the
sentiments of a man who is hanging on to the last years of his constituency career — a protectionist who has long since put any expansionist enthusiasms behind him.

He won the election. And he might well have won more elections
had he not been visited with a second, massive redistricting, which
replaced a large number of people in his district. This event would
have required a return to his expansionist phase, a cyclical career
adjustment he was unprepared to make. So he retired.

> There was a crazy, outrageous redistricting. . . . That was
> the last straw. It had been getting rougher and rougher and
> rougher. . . . I could have won, because I have won in areas
> like that before. But it would have meant shoe leathering the
> new part of the district, block by block. And I just didn't
> want to do that. . . . Even if I had won I would have to be
> right back at it next year. I would have had to work for six
> years to digest that new area and solidify that district.

It is a perfect description of the expansionist stage of a constituency
career. But such a wholesale reversion to the stage he had left many
years before was beyond contemplation, teetering, as he was, at the
end of his career. Besides, it would have cost him the benefits of
his established House career — a career he wanted, as he said, on
his own terms. "What's the use of having high seniority with the
opportunity of being influential in Congress if you have to spend
all your time in your district? You can't be a senior congressman
with an insecure district. They are incompatible."

The contrast between Representatives *J* and *K* and Representative *L* is considerable — in the latter case the purely protectionist
perspective, the lack of concern for reelection, the stabilizing of
ambition, the inattentiveness to supporting constituencies, the
steady worsening of fit in terms of "me-in-the-district" — signs of
the latter stages of the constituency career. Then, the decision to

retire. There was another difference, too. Congressman *L* had clearly appropriated the language of trust:

> They trust me. That is proven by letters I've gotten since I announced my retirement. Many people have written and said, "We never have written you, but we trusted you. Who are we going to trust now?" They had built up a familiarity with me slowly and over a long period of time.

As their constituency careers continue, Representatives *J* and *K* will win and talk about trust, too. It is a word that does not creep into their vocabulary much now. But, as Congressman *L* says, it takes time.

STYLISTIC CONSTRAINTS

As constituency careers move through the expansionist stage and toward the protectionist stage, home styles tend to become more firmly established and less likely to change. The expansionist stage, during which the congressman cultivates first a primary constituency, then a reelection constituency and during which he works out a viable, comfortable home style, has a largely experimental impulse to it. Once in the protectionist stage, however, the dominant impulse is conservative. Whereas, in the beginning, prospective House members are uncertain as to what kinds of home activities will work, once they have one or two testing elections behind them, they become more confident. They probably have no clear idea, as we noted earlier, of which element of home activity was responsible for how much of their support. But they do know that the sum of the elements contributed to victory. So the temptation is to keep the support they had "last time." Maintaining an established home style becomes part of the protectionist perspective.

As a congressman's home style solidifies, so do the expectations of his supporters. Whether he imposes a style on them or they impose one on him, constituents eventually come to expect the style they are accustomed to. And these constituent expectations in turn become a constraint on the congressman, keeping him in his mold whether he wishes it or not. Political scientists, researching congressman-constituency relationships from the Washington vantage point, have become accustomed to thinking of House members as constrained in their voting behavior by the policy attitudes of their constituents. The central idea has been that House members must vote in certain ways or risk losing constituent support. Watching members of Congress at home introduced me, however, to quite a different set of constraints — *stylistic constraints*. A congressman may feel every bit as constrained by constituent expectations concerning his home style as by constituent expectations concerning his policy positions. Perhaps more.

Late one afternoon, as Congressman A (see Chapter Three) was driving home for dinner after a day of person-to-person visiting, we came to a fork in the road, and he said,

> I should turn right here and go on down to Maple Grove. But I haven't the time. If I went, there are about a dozen people I'd have to see. Two of them are very close to me, much closer than the others. But if I went to see those two and didn't get around to see the other ten, word would get around and I'd lose Maple Grove in the next election. That's how it is.

Sitting at his dining room table one morning with his two top campaign aides planning campaign strategy and literature, Congressman D, the issue articulator (see Chapter Three) was asked, "Do you want to make a campaign pledge to continue the 'open meetings' twice a year in each town for the next two years?" Congressman D answered yes. Then he rolled his eyes, heaved a long sigh of resignation and added, "Ohhh Jeeesus!"

Congressman F, the community leader (see Chapter Four) thinks about yielding, but cannot yield, leadership of the South Side Community Caucus.

> After I showed so much strength in the primary, I toyed with the idea of giving up my leadership of the caucus. . . . But I decided that if I disbanded the caucus, a lot of people would think I'd weakened myself and might decide to run against me. I'd look just like everybody else in the black community, without any district-wide organization. . . . I'm the leader; and when you are the leader people expect you to lead. As the highest elected official in the district I can't let anyone lower in the hierarchy get the idea that I'm not the leader.

After spending all afternoon at a community clambake, Congressman J, successful cultivator of his segmented district, went to spend the evening with the clambake organizers — his strongest supporters in the area. As we drove, he and his wife explained why they were doing it:

> *Congressman J:* You have to walk a very thin line. You don't want people to say the congressman is always out drinking and partying. But you can't just leave these people and not go to their homes and talk with them personally. You can't come to their meetings, stay from two till four and then leave. They want to know you as a human being. They want to feel they are your friend.

> *Wife:* They not only want to party with you, they want you to stay in their houses, sleep in their beds, and use their bathrooms. I don't want to let them hear my toilet flush, but they will feel hurt if you don't. After they have done all that work on the clambake, they will be discouraged if you say, "So long kids." They want to be your friend. They want to say, "The congressman is my friend." "The congressman and his wife slept in my house." We don't want to do it always, but we have to.

The expectations that supportive constituents have about home style can feel just as constraining as their issue preferences. Representatives A, D, E, and J, just discussed, are facing support calculations of the same sort as they face in constituency-related roll call votes in Washington. But home constraints are matters of style — of allocation, presentation, and explanation — not policy. If these House members failed to see ten people in Maple Grove or canceled the open meetings or relinquished caucus leadership or left immediately after the clambake, they believe it would cost them dearly in electoral support. They might lose support they had "last time," because they believe that their present home style helped them to victory last time. Though they might, on other grounds, be tempted not to follow their established patterns, they do not deem it worth the risk. So they follow a conservative, reenforcing, protectionist home strategy.

As suggested at the end of Chapter Four, and the illustrations here indicate, the dominant constituent expectation — in nearly every district and among all groups of constituents — is *access*. The congressman feels constrained because the people to whom he has granted access want the relationship to be a continuing one. They want to see him, talk with him, meet with him "lately." And he,

mindful that his established patterns of access have served him well
in the past, complies. But then the question arises as to whether
patterns established early in his constituency career will continue to
serve him well in the later stages of that career. Congressman H, the
"nice guy" who is "accessible and available" (see Chapter 5) put
his finger on the problem:

> I don't have time to speak to constituents who are un-
> committed. I'm so badgered by people to whom I'm obli-
> gated politically that I spend most of my time performing
> ceremonially before the people who agree with me. . . .
> The most important thing is that you don't seem too big for
> your britches. You don't want people to say, "What's the
> matter with George? Why doesn't he come around any-
> more?" So I have got to keep talking to my supporters to
> prove to them I haven't gotten too big for my britches. I hope
> it's not an ever-narrowing group.

It doubtless worsens as careers lengthen. One member summed up
the problem:

> The thing that intrigues me about George Mahon, Chet
> Holifield, and Manny Celler is that all their contemporaries
> have died or are too old. Where are their friends now? What
> can they use as the base of their support? There just isn't
> anyone left, and they have completely lost touch with the
> district. Manny Celler didn't even have a district office. It
> wasn't that he didn't care about people. It's just that no one
> was there to tell him to do it. He and his friends come from
> another generation.

In one district I saw evidence of this problem. I accompanied a
veteran representative, facing his stiffest electoral challenge, on a visit
to one of his towns, one that he always considered among his own
strongest and most crucial. He touched base there with his long-time,
hard-core supporters — a doctor, a barber, a hardware store owner, a
furniture store owner, a banker, and a lawyer. Everyone told him that
"things look good," "you'll carry Fieldston all right," "I hope things
are in as good shape elsewhere as they are here." Driving from the
bank to the lawyer's house, I asked him, "Would these people tell
you if there were any soft spots here?" He said, "The last man we

saw at the bank would tell me. If there were any trouble, he'd draw me aside, take me into his office, close the door and tell me who was falling off." Then the congressman reminisced for an hour in the Victorian drawing room of the lawyer — a lifelong friend and political ally, once one of his state's most renowned attorneys, now a man of eighty-two. At one point, the lawyer wheezed, "Everything I hear is good. Everybody I know says you're going to be all right, Ed." To which the congressman added cautiously, "The trouble is that there are too many people moving in that you and I don't know."

Two days before election the congressman predicted (in writing) that he would carry that town by 55 to 45 percent. He lost it by 42 to 48 percent. And it nearly cost him the election. "It was a disaster," he said later. But he had no explanation — only that his campaign manager there had failed him. My guess is that his established patterns of access were no longer adequate. He remained in touch with his primary constituents, but they (and hence he) had gradually grown out of touch with the voters of the town. The congressman will have to alter his patterns of access, his home style, or he will soon move from the protectionist stage of his constituency career to its end.

Home styles, we conclude, tend to harden in the course of a constituency career, as careers move from their expansionist to their protectionist stages. Table 6.1 provides some supportive evidence for this conclusion. From a questionnaire administered to staff aides in 253 House offices in January 1968 (about their 1967 practices), we can compare the allocation of resources for those 149 House members whose offices were contacted both in 1968 and 1974.[4] The data in Table 10 compare, for all 149 House members, the number of trips home taken in 1967 with the number taken in 1973, using the three categories established in Chapter Two. The great majority of members — 103 out of 149, or 69 percent — remain in the same category in both years. Using this one indicator, it appears that home styles do become resistant to change in the course of a constituency career.

The figures in parentheses indicate the numbers of 1967 freshmen who appear in the various categories. Though the number is small (twenty-five in all), the evidence complements the case studies of Representatives *J* and *K* in suggesting that home styles tend to be established very early in a member's constituency career. Freshmen show as little change over the six-year span as nonfreshmen, with

Table 6.1
Trips Home: 1967 and 1973

1967 Frequency of Trips Home	1973 Frequency of Trips Home			
	Low (0–23)	Medium (24–42)	High (43+)	Total
Low (0–23)	42 (67%) (5)*	17 (27%) (1)	4 (6%) (1)	63 (100%) (7)
Medium (24–42)	8 (21%) (4)	22 (56%) (6)	9 (23%) (1)	39 (100%) (11)
High (43+)	3 (6%) (1)	5 (11%) (0)	39 (83%) (6)	47 (100%) (7)
Total	53 (10)	44 (7)	52 (8)	149 (25)

Gamma = .831 (Gamma for freshmen = .703.)
* Figures in parentheses are for 1967 freshmen.

seventeen of the twenty-five, or 72 percent, appearing in the same category in both years. Of course, in both cases, there could be fluctuations in between those dates; but everything we have observed leads us to doubt it.

STYLISTIC CHANGE: INDIVIDUAL

Although Table 6.1 indicates that most House members do not change their home styles over time, it also indicates that some members do. This question arises, then: When and under what circumstances do home styles change? The question can be asked on the individual level and on the aggregate level. That is, do individual members alter their particular home styles over time? And, does the overall distribution of home styles within the House of Representatives change over time? It may well be that although individual members might not alter their home styles, the gradual replacement of members over time could produce an overall change in the kinds of home styles most prominent in the House as a whole. The data of this study are, of course, almost wholly about individuals, not aggregates. And our "sample" is such that no statistical inferences can be drawn about the aggregate. So we shall devote most of our energy, here, to addressing the question of change on an individual level. But, as elsewhere, we shall not hesitate to make speculative generalizations about behavior in the aggregate.

Observing eighteen cases suggests, along with Table 6.1, that a few members do change their established home styles. The proximate causes, we would guess, will be of three types: contextual, strategic, and personal. The most common contextual causes would be a redrawing of district boundaries and a marked population shift within old boundaries. The most common strategic cause would be a substantial decline in support among primary or reelection constituencies. The most common personal cause would be a shift in personal circumstances or goals. Singly or in combination, these factors probably produce home style change. But we have not observed enough cases to do more than confirm the presence of such factors.

FROM SMALL TOWNS TO SUBURBIA: CONGRESSMAN M. In no case did I observe an actual change in home style brought about by redistricting. But I did travel with Congressman M to "the new part of the district" shortly after he had been redistricted; and I observed the stylistic bewilderment such an event can produce. Congressman M had established a person-to-person home style in his rural, small-town district when he was redistricted into unknown territory — suburbia. For three and a half hours, we drove around, "exploring" the new suburban segment. A primary opponent had emerged from the area; and we set out first to find his home. We drove up and down his street several times looking for telltale signs — "a Cadillac and a boat" — before the congressman satisfied himself that we had probably found it. For a man who campaigned comfortably along the main streets of little towns, the amorphous suburban area was puzzling.

> How would you campaign in this kind of district? It's going to be an entirely different kind of campaign for me. It's going to be hard to reach. You can't do it by TV, because you reach such a small part of the market you pay for. So economics rules that out. And there's no focal point of interest, no incorporated areas.

Reference points were hard to find. As we wandered about the busy area, he grew frustrated. "We've been exploring the new district for one hour and we haven't seen one person yet." We had "seen" thousands of people. But he had no idea how to make contact with them. He had not stopped to shake hands and chat with them as he would have done in "the old part of the district."

We drove into the parking lot of a large, modern shopping mall and rode up and down along the store fronts, sizing up this strange terrain. Again, Congressman M was baffled by its stylistic implications.

> To my way of thinking, campaigning in shopping centers is a complete and total waste of time. I may be wrong, but I believe that when people are shopping, they don't want to be interrupted by someone handing out political literature.

A suburban friend of his had wanted a brochure to hand out in the suburbs during the primary. But the congressman had refused. Why?

> I thought they knew me; and if they didn't, I didn't want their support anyway. It's like the story of Paul Huckins over in Harrison Corners, when the new highway came through and people suggested he build a hotel. He said he didn't want a hotel. And people said, "What about the people coming to Harrison on the new highway?" He told them "If they're good people, I'll invite them to stay in my house. If they aren't good people, I don't want them stopping in Harrison Corners."

It was a rural, not a suburban analogy. And it did not augur well for a prosperous constituency career in the suburbs.

Clearly, Congressman M was not at home — not, that is, until we chanced upon a small country church left standing amid the suburban sprawl. There, near the end of our exploration, we made our first stop (except at a gas station, where we had had our only conversation of the morning, with the attendant). The congressman got out, and went into the small cemetery adjacent to the Eagle Rock Church. He roamed excitedly among the headstones, checking for the deceased relatives of people he knew. "Well, I never knew that Hamilton Beard's family was buried here in this area. . . . I wonder if Mary Hofstetter was any kin of Sarah and John Hofstetter? The dates are about right. Sarah and John moved to Carleton in 1921." Finally, he had found some people he knew and could relate to. And he campaigned among them, there in the graveyard, much as he campaigned in "the old part of the district" — with a person-to-person home style. But it was symbolic as well as poignant that they could not help him carry the suburbs. An observer could not help feeling that if Congressman M did not adopt a home style more appropriate to the suburban context — which seemed highly unlikely — he would have a shortened constituency career.

FROM ISSUES TO HANDSHAKES: CONGRESSMAN N. A second congress-man did make a midcourse adjustment in his home style — for strategic more than contextual reasons. Congressman N nearly lost an election. "There's something very good about almost losing," he says, "you learn a lot." A strongly issue-oriented person, especially in civil rights, he "learned" that an issue-oriented home style was not best suited to his more conservative "typical middle-income suburban" district. "Issues nearly killed me in 1968." He explained,

> Through the 1968 campaign, I played the role of teacher and preacher, persuading people of what I thought was right. . . . I went to lots of political meetings. When I almost lost, we realized that this was not going to be a successful way of campaigning. I decided then to shake hands as much as I could. And we got better at casework, which I certainly be-lieve is an important way that a congressman can help people.

> Up to 1968 we did a lot of coffee hours. After I did so miserably in 1968, we changed our entire campaign operation. It's pretty hard campaigning in people's living rooms by tell-ing them they ought to have a black person living next door to them. We realized that our coffee hours were counter-productive. When the issues are against you, you lose more friends than you make. So we started handing out pens — at plant gates in the morning, shopping centers during the day, and bowling alleys and theatres in the evening.

Now, he campaigns impersonally, pumping out his autographed ball-point pens hand over hand, wherever there is a heavy volume of traffic or wherever people congregate in unorganized contexts. "Hi folks, may I give you a pen?" "I'm Congressman N; I hope you'll vote for me on election day." "I'm Congressman N, I'd appreciate your vote."

After handing out 900 pens in front of a large K Mart, he exclaimed,

> That's the most effective campaign technique we have. It's a whole lot better than sitting around someone's living room arguing about whether or not we ought to get out of the UN. . . . You catch people with pens that you don't catch any other way; and they talk about it later with other people.

It also gives him "a reputation as being a hard worker. Part of that comes from my service to the district and part of it comes from the nature of my campaign. If you see a guy at 6 o'clock [handing out pens] at a plant gate you think to yourself, 'that son of a bitch works hard all the time.'" Congressman N's new home style represents a retreat from "the issues" and a retreat from close personal contact. Although he has been redistricted more than once and although he admits "my district has drifted around a lot," he makes no connection between a change in district and a change in style. "Pens," he says, "are useful everywhere — except where you have to use television." He wants to be reelected, and he thinks he has found a more effective method for cultivating a reelection constituency.

Related to Congressman N's altered home style is his heavy reliance on newsletters. It is another all-purpose technique — "Any congressman who doesn't send out all the newsletters he can has to be crazy." Here, too, he has beat a retreat from his earlier issue-orientation.

> My political strength is my newsletters. I've learned to improve them. We used to have a small, four-page, offset-printed letter. When you are more liberal than your district, you try to reach to them a little. So we used to take one issue each letter and talk about it. . . . [But] most people just didn't read it at all. . . . So we changed the format to have about a dozen news items, at least one picture and a graph in each issue. . . . We send it to postal patrons, about once a month. And you can see the results.

The newsletters reflect the same impersonal style the pens do.

> It's not so much the content that matters with my newsletters. . . . The name identification is the thing. It's like

> selling a bar of soap. People won't buy it if they hear it only once. They have to hear it over and over. . . . Most people don't know who their congressman is; but when they see your name on the ballot, you want them to see it favorably.

In 1972 he took a poll. The poll showed that, though he was still more liberal than his district, his constituents *trusted* him more than any other figure in American politics — more even than Walter Cronkite. Twice again as many voters — 38 percent in all — praised his newsletter as praised any other personal characteristic. His revamped home style — less issue-oriented, less personal — has given him a highly supportive, trusting reelection constituency. And he has not been in electoral difficulty since 1968. "Now I know how the old dean of our delegation used to feel. I used to scramble and scratch; and I'd look at him and he was so relaxed. If an incumbent has any brains at all, I don't see how he can be beaten."

Is Congressman N personally comfortable with his new style? Not entirely. "The pens are a great prop. I'm really shy. I couldn't go through those bowling alleys just shaking hands with people. . . . I didn't come by this naturally. Walt and Warren [two intimates] pressured me into it." But his rationale underlies a major theme of the previous chapter. Congressman N has been a leading opponent of the oil depletion allowance in Congress. Near the end of a long day spent handing out pens and asking for votes, as we heaved ourselves into the car to "hit" one last shopping plaza, he asked whimsically, "Do you think Standard Oil of New Jersey would be scared if they could see me now?" And I said, "Sometimes it must be hard to connect what you do here with what you do in Washington." "Oh, no," he replied, "I do what I do here so I can do what I want to do there."

CHANGING WITH THE TIMES: CONGRESSMAN O. Congressman O returned to his urban district every week in 1967. In 1973 he returned only twenty-five times and spent only fifty-one working days there. The change is indicative of a series of adaptations Congressman O has made in his home style, about which he is unusually analytical, self-critical, and experimental.

> I'm very interested in the subject. I spend a lot of time scrutinizing my operation to make it work better for me. I

keep trying to improve. I talk to other people about it a lot. You've got to change with the times.

The first of such changes — one that probably accounts most for the precipitous drop in trips home — came when he broke the precedent of his predecessors by moving his family to Washington. It was a step taken after he had been in office for a while.

> When I was first elected, my family was back in the district and I was back there all the time. At the same time, the job of congressman was changing. . . . At first, I saw it not as a full-time, year-round job. I thought I would keep my business. But because of the change in the nature of the job, I moved my family to Washington. I was enormously frightened of the political effect of that move. . . . Many people in the district were upset.

When I first visited his district, Congressman O's family was in Washington; but he was allaying the doubts of his constituents by returning home just as often as before.

> I can relax and have a more normal family life, and tend to legislation in Washington. But it increases the distance between me and my constituents; and I feel all the more strongly that I have to come back and be seen. I come back at least once a week.

But he added, "I really don't like it that much." It was a transition period for him. By the time I returned to the district, four years later, this reluctance to return home would be a dominant theme.

Congressman O is aggressively issue-oriented. "I never duck controversies. I turn controversies into a political plus for me." From the beginning, his home style has reflected that predisposition. In his urban, Democratic district, his electoral worries focus on the primary. He has had to adopt a home style that would appeal to the two elements of his primary constituency — the Democratic party regulars and the issue-oriented liberals. To the party regulars he stresses accessibility and service. As we toured the ward organizations at election time he commented in protectionist terms,

> This is pro forma campaigning. It's necessary. I'm not breaking new ground; I'm just making routine stops and massaging

> the organization members. . . . These people are — I can't
> think of the word for it — not mummies, but party auto-
> matons. They aren't the thinking man's filter — let's put it
> that way. It's not like the League of Women Voters or some
> objective organization like that. These people vote for me
> because I come by and say hello to them or do them a service
> or just smile. I stop by just to show them I'm alive and
> breathing. Some of these old ladies have been doing this for
> twenty years, forty years. You don't need them in the general
> election. But they are the foot soldiers of the organization —
> circulating the petitions to get you on the ballot.

To the issue-oriented liberals, he emphasizes his issue positions —
even his issue leadership. Throughout the early part of his tenure,
the central issue was the Vietnam War, of which he was a leading
opponent.

> The people in the peace movement are probably my very
> strongest supporters. Don't forget, I was one of the first
> congressmen to come out against the war. To the peace
> people, I'm a semihero. We went through hard times to-
> gether when being against the war wasn't popular, and they
> worked very hard for me. . . . There probably aren't more
> than 100 of them in all, scattered around the district. But
> 100 activists can do a lot. On Moratorium Day, they had
> 15,000 people marching up Riverside Boulevard.

To the party regulars Congressman O gives routine attention; and
he receives routine support in return. To the issue-oriented people
he gives enthusiastic leadership; and he receives enthusiastic support in return. But within this fairly constant set of strategic constraints he has made substantial adaptations in his home style.

At the time of my initial visit, the war had not yet ended, but its
emotional divisiveness had declined sufficiently to cause Congressman O to ponder the future shape of his political support. Of "the
peace people," he wondered, "I guess they're still with me now,
maybe not. They want 'more' and there is no 'more.'" As the Vietnam issue faded, he continued to present himself by discussing
national issues — education, medical care, transportation, housing.
But, he said later, "I didn't see any clearly coalesced large constituency that needed massaging or any large issue I wanted to push."
He was receptive, therefore, to seeking solid support on other bases.

It was at this juncture that a number of local grievances forced themselves upon him. Of timely importance was the case where a number of families in a neighborhood of party regulars were being dispossessed to make room for a freeway. They had protested. Congressman O had worked to help behind the scenes but had not intervened publicly on their behalf. "They are mad at me," he said during my first trip.

> I could have done better. I should have gone to their meetings and been more visible. These people are mad. I don't blame them. . . . I'll just have to suffer. What do these people care about the war or "new priorities"? They've lost their homes. This local thing will cost me 500 to 1000 votes — maybe more. It will cost me more votes than any vote I could ever cast in Congress would cost me.

In Washington, several months later, he said the case of the dispossessed families had "caused me a lot of worry." It was a worry about the adequacy of his home style. "I didn't do enough," he said.

> How involved should the congressman get in community affairs? I'm tending toward the view that whenever anyone is being screwed by the system that the congressman should use the prestige of his office to interpose himself between the people being screwed and the system.

After election, his estimate was that "the whole thing cost me 500 to 700 votes." But he was contemplating a larger significance.

> I'm not excited about the election. But you do have to take stock and make changes. You grow flabby down here. The McNally [a member recently defeated in a primary] syndrome sets in. You can't be content with what you did before.

"I have some ideas," he concluded, "maybe including personnel. We're always concerned about the next primary."

Two years later, these tentative thoughts had crystallized into a new element of Congressman O's home style.

> I've changed my thinking about the congressman's involvement in constituency projects — partly for political reasons and partly because the public wants us to be involved in their

concerns – the problem of alienation: no one cares. In the antiwar period, I had a 5000 to 25,000 floating constituency. I was a hero. Now that has cooled down and although these people still support me there isn't the glue there used to be. There isn't the fervor. So, partly to make up for the politics and partly because the concern is legitimate, I've begun to emphasize my interest in community projects.

The change would clearly help to shore up the support of the rank-and-file Democrats at a time when his liberal activist support had lost some of its intensity.

The most important manifestation of the change has been — as he had contemplated earlier — a change in staff personnel.

I have added two full-time people working on community projects. One goes to every little two-bit community meeting in the district. The other spends one week in four in the district getting the smell and the feel of the problems and three weeks in Washington working on them.

A related change in the congressman's own home activity has been the simultaneous inauguration of town meetings. Through these meetings in thirteen neighborhoods, "I try to make myself available . . . [and] I try to identify with each community. . . . The town meetings are the most successful things we do. We send out 10,000 invitations. Only about 150 come, but the others know I'm there." Thus he demonstrates and publicizes his increased attentiveness to local concerns. Furthermore, he uses the town meetings to advertise the availability of his staff.

My district office is as strong a service-oriented office as possible. In fact, we have solicited clients. I have been holding town meetings around the district. In order to get people to come, I send six to seven thousand letters to postal patrons. I tell them in that letter that if they can't come to the meeting and they have a problem, to get in touch with my office. So, I've tried to create business.

A heightened sense for local communities and their special problems has added a substantially larger constituency service component than ever before to Congressman O's home style.

The change has not, however, resulted in major shifts in the allo-

cation of the congressman's own time. Of "constituency projects"
he says, "At some point, I may have to get involved in some project;
but I can pick and choose. Most of the time, the operation will run
without me." And of individual problems he says,

> We have as good a casework operation as anyone in the
> business. As a result I'm probably in the bottom one-tenth
> of the Congress in the amount of time I have to spend on
> casework. I won't touch it unless it's something unusual or
> dramatic or a personal friend of mine.

The impulse for the stylistic change was his. But the implementa-
tion is mostly left to the staff. "They make my job incredibly easier
and let me do what I want to do." Just what is it that he wants to
do? Concentrate on national issues — in Washington and at home.
When he is home he would prefer to make speeches on the issues,
if not to the "rallies of 2000 and 3000 people" of the Vietnam days,
then at least to as large a group as he can now find.

Despite his new attentiveness to local problems and his town
meetings, he does not come home more than he did — but exactly
the opposite, as we noted earlier. Nor do his town meetings entail
the kind of rugged home schedule of, say, Congressman D (see
Chapter Three) who does the same thing. In 1973 Congressman D
held a total of sixty-seven town meetings; Congressman O held
thirteen. Mostly, he emphasizes, he does what he likes to do. "I
want to put it all into perspective," he comments. "First of all I'm
lazy. Second, I want to have a personal life. . . . No matter how
you look at it, being a congressman is disastrous for your family
life." He will no longer go home for one meeting; nor will he go
home two weeks in a row. "I have to calculate the benefits of everything I do against the dangers to my sanity and life style. . . .
When you get these invitations, you have to computerize the cost
benefit ratio." Whatever might be the benefits, the costs of "playing the groups" and "attending every American legion meeting" are
too high to be staples of his home style.

> I want to save myself for meetings where I can make a speech
> on an issue. If there are twenty people meeting in a morning
> and I have a chance to play tennis, I'll play tennis. I'll accept
> the penalty and try to compensate for it in another way. But

> if 400 people ask me to make a speech — or 150 people —
> I'll come. I've tried consciously to draw the line.

The change from fifty-two yearly trips to twenty-five yearly trips to the district, and the reduced number of personal appearances this entails, has not been cost-free. "I don't go to every meeting and I don't think I should have to. . . . A lot of people differ with me. The people of this city think you ought to be there. [But] I think I'm educating them."

Congressman O is too much a student of home style to have left his fate to the education of his constituents. He has compensated for his decreased availability in the district with a new emphasis on the mass media. When I returned to the district, four years after my first trip, his preoccupation with the media presented the most striking change. The day I arrived, he had just broken a personal record — five straight days of coverage in the *Sentinel*, the major metropolitan newspaper. It was a central topic of congratulatory conversation. Several times a day we stopped to pick up newly available editions of all papers to see if our activities were being covered. Congressman N was exultant when he saw reporters covering an event — "The *Sentinel* and the *Standard* are here!" "The *Standard* guy sat through the whole thing!" "If we get coverage in the *Sentinel*, that meeting will have been today's most profitable thing politically." Privately, there was talk about improving press relations, about variations among reporters, about the value of local versus Washington press releases. At dinner, Congressman O expatiated at length:

> I'm a student of the press — of the mechanics of the press. One-half of the stories I get happen because we make them happen. It's the mechanics — who you call, when the deadlines are. . . . The *Sentinel* sets up a preliminary front page in the early afternoon and a final page at 5:30. Unless the president shoots the president's wife, you can't get a story in after 3:30. But you stand a chance of getting only a pretty good story in if you get it in by 10:00 A.M. Another thing, certain reporters are lazy. You have to help them with their job if you want a story. I'll give you another example. The other day, the Walter Cronkite show called and wanted to do an interview on my reaction to the president's veto. They said they'd come over to the district. I knew that if they came

here the crew might not get back in time, so I said, "No, we'll come right over." My staff and I hopped in the car and drove to the studio. At the same time they interviewed me, they interviewed Congressman Brevard in a downtown restaurant. He's more articulate than I am. But I told my staff, "They won't use his interview; they'll use mine." I knew the technical quality of my interview would be better than that of his — the lighting and the sound. They used mine; and I was on the Walter Cronkite Show.

After two days of conversation devoted to this subject I asked Congressman O if this new emphasis on the media was not a deliberate substitute for his reduced personal availability at home. He answered,

Yes. I have willfully and consciously done that. Some congressmen tell me they can't get their name in the paper. . . . I don't have that trouble. *The Daily Press*, the *Standard*, the *Sentinel* — I'm in the papers all the time. American society is a society of name recognition. . . . But I like to do the things that produce news. I like to deal with the issues. My practice does not go against my instincts. It follows my instincts.

These instincts are, as ever, issue-related.

In his attitude toward media relations, Congressman O remains as aggressive on the issues as he once was in the Vietnam era. "I want to engage in substantive public relations," he says, "not horseshit public relations." Probably, his media coverage helps keep the support of the district's liberal activists. "People think I'm a fighting congressman, and that helps," he says. If so, his stylistic alterations — toward constituency service on the one hand and toward mass media manipulation on the other — will have been directed toward the constant elements of his primary constituency. And he will not have sacrificed his ability to concentrate his own energies on the issues. He may even have enhanced it.

STYLISTIC CHANGE: AGGREGATE

Among the eighteen House members studied, there is, then, evidence that two have measurably altered their home styles in the course of their constituency careers. There is evidence that a third faces the necessity of doing so. The other fifteen, so far as I can tell, have remained fairly stable. If they have changed, they have not communicated it to me and I have not observed it. From what we have observed, it seems likely that contextual, strategic, and personal factors will be the major producers of stylistic change, just as they are the major determinants of home style in the first place. But from this small sample we can draw no conclusions about changing home styles in Congress as a whole.

The question of aggregate change is interesting, however, because it has an analogue in the political science study of roll call voting in Congress. In this literature, the question is often put: How is policy change most likely to come about in Congress — through the conversion of members already elected or through the replacement of these members with new members? We can ask the same question with regard to stylistic change: Are home styles more likely to be changed by the conversion of House members or by the replacement of House members? To date, evidence in the policy area seems to favor the replacement alternative. House members are found to adhere to established voting patterns over time; and major policy change is held to come about primarily through the infusion of new members who will establish new voting patterns.[5]

With regard to home style, the weight of the evidence in Table 6.1 supports the same conclusion. If most members adhere to established styles, any sea change in home styles will have to come through the electoral replacement of sitting members with new members. Still, Table 6.1 reveals some conversion — at least in terms of trips home. Because the bulk of such conversion runs toward more trips home (thirty cases) rather than less (sixteen cases), there is at least a hint that an aggregate change toward increased attentiveness to home may be occurring — some of it through conversion. There is every reason to expect that some conversion in this direction should have occurred, because House members have steadily increased the allowances available to themselves for the reimbursement of trips to the district. Between 1967 and 1973, for example, reimbursement increased from one each month Congress was in session to thirty-six for the two-year period.

The question arises whether the same increased attentiveness to home may not also be occurring through replacement. The answer is yes. Regardless of changing incentives, freshmen House members are more attentive to home than nonfreshmen. From our two sets of interviews focusing on 1967 and 1973, there is evidence that freshman House members took more trips home than nonfreshmen in both years. And, further, there is evidence that these 1967 freshmen who were still in the House in 1973 continued to go home more than the 1967 nonfreshmen who remained in the House six years later.[6] These results are displayed in Table 6.2.

Table 6.2
Attentiveness to Home: Freshmen and Nonfreshmen, 1967 and 1973

	Number of Trips Home	Percentage of Staff Personnel in District
Freshmen 1967	32.3 (N = 25)	31.9 (N = 26)
Nonfreshmen 1967	29.5 (N = 128)	27.5 (N = 131)
Freshmen 1973	38.0 (N = 69)	36.5 (N = 69)
Nonfreshmen 1973	33.8 (N = 350)	33.5 (N = 347)
1967 Freshmen 1973	34.0 (N = 25)	34.3 (N = 26)
1967 Nonfreshmen 1973	32.3 (N = 124)	32.9 (N = 123)

As Table 6.2 indicates, freshmen returned home more than nonfreshmen both in 1967 and 1973. And, when they were in their third terms, the members of the freshman class of 1967 were still returning to the district more often than their 1967 senior colleagues. Table 6.2 also indicates that between 1967 and 1973 the absolute number of trips home steadily increased for both groups. Freshmen go home more than nonfreshmen, but both groups go home more often now than they used to.

Table 6.2 also describes the difference in staff allocation practices for the freshmen and the nonfreshmen among the interviewees in 1967 and 1973. We might expect a general increase here, too, because House members have been voting themselves larger staff allotments, larger staff budgets and reimbursement for more district offices. Between 1967 and 1973, staff allotments were increased from eleven to sixteen. The freshmen of both groups allocated a greater percentage of their office staff personnel to the district than did nonfreshmen. And, six years later, the 1967 freshmen continued to allocate a greater proportion of their staff to home than did the 1967 nonfreshmen six years later. Staff personnel, like trips home, increased — on the average — for all members of Congress between 1967 and 1973 — a conversion doubtless fueled by the availability of more staff. Still, the increase could have been absorbed in the Washington office. Changes taking place among individual members confirm this overall trend. Of the 149 House members for whom we have data in both years, 32 reduced the percentage of staff personnel in the district during the period, 42 kept it the same (in the ± 5 percent range), and 75, or 50 percent, increased the percentage of staff in the district.[7]

Such data as we have, therefore, indicate that freshmen are more attentive to home than nonfreshmen and that House members on the whole are becoming increasingly attentive to home. Increased allowance and allotments have given veteran members an incentive to change home styles. So, both conversion and replacement seem to account for the increase in home attentiveness — whether measured by allocations for trips or staff. But, given the tendency of home styles to be established quickly and to persist over time, it is our guess that replacement — the infusion of more home-oriented freshmen — is the more important factor in producing aggregate stylistic change.

The subject of long-term change in home style needs much more study. Our aggregate findings do, however, lend support to the speculation of others, like Morris Fiorina, that House members — especially the newer generations — have become increasingly attentive to home.[8] In offering such tentative generalizations about change, however, we must be careful not to explain too much. First, we are still talking about a distinctly short-run change. In terms of overall attentiveness, the House member of fifty years ago was probably more attentive than the House member of today. After all, he spent a much larger proportion of his working year at home than he did in Washington. Or so, at least, we would surmise. But he did not have a large staff to establish a district presence for him when he was not in the district. Just how these ingredients ought to be balanced in any overall estimate is not yet clear.[9] But the complexity inspires caution.

Second, even if we could calculate the change in home attentiveness over time, we would still not be able to conclude much about stylistic change in general. The allocation of resources to home is but one aspect of a congressman's home style. Presentational practices are equally, if not more, important in the final analysis. Studies in the allocation of resources provide important clues, but only clues, as to just what is going on at home between a congressman and his supportive constituencies. If home style encompasses a complex set of behaviors, secular change in home style is likely to be a complicated matter.

CONSTITUENCY CAREERS: SUMMARY SPECULATION. The home relationship — between the member of Congress and his or her several constituencies — must be viewed as something that develops over time. Every congressman has a career in his district, during which he works out a set of allocative, presentational, and explanatory practices designed to bring him the votes and the trust of supportive constituents. His constituency career typically goes through an expansionist and then a protectionist stage. Once a member is in the protectionist stage, established practices — and particularly their associated patterns of access — become constraining; and home styles tend to be resistant to change. Under some circumstances, however, home styles do change, both individually and in the House as a whole.

The idea of a member's career in the district highlights an important fact about the congressman as an elected politician. As any textbook treatment of incumbency tells us, the congressman is a particularly long-lived political species. He has been (or will be) allocating, presenting, and explaining at home for a long time. People in various constituencies have been (or will be) looking at him and evaluating him "as a person" for a long time. Compared to elective politicians with much briefer constituency careers — like the president of the United States — a congressman depends for political support especially on those long-term relationships he has developed with supportive constituents. This, of course, is precisely what House members themselves tell political scientists whenever we have inquired.

They tell us that their "records and personal standing" or their "personalities" are more important in explaining their election than "issues" or "party identification." [10] They tell us, in other words, that their home style is the most important determinant of their political support. When Miller and Stokes discovered that four-fifths of the incumbent House members ranked "records and personal standing" highest in explaining their reelection, the two political scientists interpreted that finding by concluding, "Congressmen feel that their individual *legislative actions* may have a considerable impact on the electorate [Italics added]." [11] But our guess is that what House members meant may have had little or nothing to do with "legislative actions" and mostly or everything to do with actions at home. Miller and Stokes, with a presidential model in mind, were not thinking of a long-term constituency career and, hence, could not have recognized the relevance of home style.

The idea of a long constituency career helps us understand what the 1958 respondents probably meant. We can now view home style as a durable, consistent, persistent, "long-term force" in congressional electoral politics. As such, we would expect it to be more important in the study of congressional elections than it has been in the study of presidential elections.[12] In any congressional electoral analyses patterned after our presidential electoral analyses, therefore, home style may have to be elevated to a scholarly status heretofore reserved only for party identification and issue voting.

If the fact of lengthy congressional incumbencies underlies the importance of home style, the striking variety of home styles helps illuminate the idea of incumbency itself. A focus on home style makes it clear that incumbency is not an automatic entitlement to a fixed number of votes or percentage points toward reelection. Nor is "the power of incumbency" something each member finds waiting to be picked up and put on like a new suit. Incumbency should be seen as a resource to be employed, an opportunity to be exploited; and the power of incumbency is whatever each member makes of the resource and the opportunity. The variety of home styles we have found indicates that House members take advantage of their incumbency in very different ways. Incumbency is what you make of it; and the power of incumbency is conditional. It will be helpful to keep this perspective as we explore the effects of incumbency on electoral outcomes. We should expect to find "incumbency effects" varying considerably from member to member, from constituency to constituency and, it may yet be discovered, from home style to home style.

NOTES

1. See Appendix, Figure A. In one of the five cases, I traveled with the congressman twice, but only once in his district.
2. For example, Joseph Schlesinger, *Ambition and Politics* (Chicago: Rand McNally, 1966); David Rohde, "Risk Bearing and Progressive Ambition:

The Case of Members of the United States House of Representatives," paper delivered at Conference on Mathematical Models of Congress, Aspen, Colorado, 1974; Roger H., Marz and William D. Morris, "Treadmill to Oblivion: The Fate of Appointed Senators," paper presented at American Political Science Association Convention, San Francisco, 1975.

3. See Albert D. Cover and David R. Mayhew, "Congressional Dynamics and the Decline of Competitive Congressional Elections" in *Congress Reconsidered*, ed. Lawrence Dodd and Bruce Oppenheimer (New York: Praeger, 1977), pp. 54–72.

4. The 1968 interviews were conducted by three University of Rochester undergraduates who spent January 1968 in Washington interviewing in 253 congressional offices about office organization and the congressman's work habits. The 253 do not constitute a random sample, because the students divided up the office buildings and interviewed up and down corridors until time ran out. But they do approximate the whole House in terms of region, seniority, and party. And 149 represents over half, 55 percent, of the 270 members who were in Congress in 1967, 1968, and 1974.

5. Herbert Asher and Herbert Weisberg, "Congressional Voting Change: A Longitudinal Study of Voting on Selected Issues," paper delivered at American Political Science Association Convention, San Francisco, 1975; Aage R. Clausen, *How Congressmen Decide: A Policy Focus* (New York: St. Martin, 1973); Gary Orfield, *Congressional Power and Social Change* (New York: Harcourt Brace Jovanovich, 1975).

6. We ought to note, however, from Table 6.1, that more freshmen decreased than increased their trips home. But the numbers are probably too small to make anything of it.

7. Between 1967 and 1973 the number of allowable district offices increased from two to three, the number of allowable staff personnel increased from eleven to sixteen, and the maximum salary allowance increased from about $120,000 to $173,000.

8. Morris Fiorina, *Congress: Keystone of the Washington Establishment* (New Haven: Yale University Press, 1977). Fiorina argues that the secular decline in statistically marginal districts is explainable primarily by a corresponding secular increase in member attention to constituency service. Our study supports his decision to look at the home relationship to explain electoral change; and it supports his idea that change in attentiveness to home has been a major stylistic change. His further, more specific, argument – that the change in attentiveness is mostly a matter of increased attention to constituent service – is one that needs to be researched. My inclination would be to think of constituency service activity as one element in the more encompassing set of home activities we have examined under the rubric of home style – and to broaden the research focus accordingly.

9. Cronheim inquired of senatorial assistants how often senators went home in 1956. Of the fifty-two interview replies, thirty-nine senators went home ten times a year or less, and thirteen went home more than ten times a year. Dorothy Cronheim, "Congressmen and Their Communication Practices," unpublished manuscript, Ann Arbor, Michigan, 1957, p. 129. It is hard to know whether this lack of attentiveness to "home" twenty years ago is senatorial or further evidence in support of the more recent trend. Senator Paul Douglas noted, "I never spent less than 100 days a year in Illinois" and says he went home "at least two weekends a month" during his eighteen years of service from 1949 to 1966. His discussion of "trips home" sounds

very familiar. Paul Douglas, *In the Fullness of Time* (New York: Harcourt Brace Jovanovich, 1971), pp. 156–61.

10. Stokes and Miller, "Party Government and the Saliency of Congress," *Public Opinion Quarterly* 26, (winter 1962), 531–546; Charles S. Bullock, III, "Explaining Congressional Elections," *Legislative Studies Quarterly* 2 (August 1977) 295–308.

11. Stokes and Miller, "Party Government and the Saliency of Congress," p. 54.

12. The first people to view congressional incumbency as a long-term force, in the light of SRC analyses, were Robert Arseneau and Raymond Wolfinger, "Voting Behavior in Congressional Elections," paper delivered at American Political Science Association Convention, New Orleans, 1973. Observations consistent with those here, made in different contexts, are David Mayhew's emphasis on "the expected incumbent differential" and Charles Jones' conclusion that House campaigns are less likely to be "issue-oriented" than "image-oriented" and "issue-involved." Home style contributes to the congressman's "incumbent differential" and to his "image." Mayhew, *The Electoral Connection* (New Haven, Conn.: Yale University Press, 1974); Jones, "The Role of the Campaign in Congressional Politics" in *The Electoral Process*, ed. Harmon Zeigler and Kent Jennings (New York: Prentice-Hall, 1966). From an election analysis perspective, Walter Dean Burnham has recently emphasized the "office specific" nature of elections and the need to develop ways of looking at congressional elections that do not simply imitate what we have done for presidential elections. Walter Dean Burnham, "Insulation and Responsiveness in Congressional Elections," *Political Science Quarterly* 90 (Fall 1975): 411–35.

CHAPTER SEVEN

Home and Washington:
Linkage and Representation

We have examined the perceptions and attitudes of United States Representatives concerning their several constituencies, and we have examined their activities in those constituencies. We have, of course, remained aware of the existence of Washington, D.C., throughout the book. But it has been a dim awareness, and intentionally so. We have been able to learn a great deal about House members at home without knowing much about them in Washington. And, it appears that we cannot know all we need to know about House members in Washington unless we do move out beyond the capitol city into the country and into its congressional districts. Washington and home are different milieus, different worlds. But they are not unconnected worlds. The theory and the practice of a representative form of government links them one to the other. Though a congressman be immersed in one, he remains mindful of the other. So a book about home cannot conclude without some attention to the subject of linkage and, more broadly, of representation.

Unfortunately, our treatment of these large subjects must be brief and speculative. We have paid insufficient attention to the Washington scene to do otherwise. In this chapter we pay the price for our lopsidedly local perspective. Because, however, it is a fairly uncommon perspective, even some brief speculation may be worthwhile. We shall speculate about two possible linkages, and then move to some thoughts on representation.

LINKAGE: CONSTITUENCY CAREER AND WASHINGTON CAREER

In Chapter Six, we noted the interaction between constituency careers and Washington careers. Of all the links between home style and House performance, this is the most apparent. When we speak of constituency careers, we speak primarily of the pursuit of the goal of reelection. When we speak of Washington careers, we speak primarily of the pursuit of the goals of influence in the House and the making of good public policy. Thus the intertwining of careers is, at bottom, an intertwining of member goals.

So long as they are in the expansionist stage of their constituency careers, House members will be especially attentive to their home base. They will pursue the goal of reelection with single-minded intensity and will allocate their resources disproportionately to that end. As noted in Chapters Two and Six, first-term members go home more frequently, place a larger proportion of their staff in the district, and more often leave their families at home than do their senior colleagues. Building a reelection constituency at home and providing continuous access to as much of that constituency as possible requires time and energy. Inevitably, these are resources that might otherwise be allocated to efforts in Washington. "The trouble is," said one member near the end of his second term,

> I haven't been a congressman yet. The first two years, I spent all of my time getting myself reelected. That last two years, I spent getting myself a district so that I could get reelected. So I won't be a congressman until next year.

By being "a congressman" he means pursuing goals above and beyond that of reelection (i.e., power in the House and good public policy).

In a House member's first years, the opportunities for gaining inside power and policy influence are limited. Time and energy and staff can be allocated to home without an acute sense of conflict. At rates that vary from congressman to congressman, however, the chances to have some institutional or legislative effect improve. As members stretch to avail themselves of the opportunity, they may begin to experience some allocative strain. It requires time and

energy to develop a successful career in Washington just as it does
to develop a successful career in the district. Because it may not be
possible to allocate these resources to House and home, each to an
optimal degree, members may have to make allocative and goal
choices.

A four-term congressman with a person-to-person home style described the dilemma of choice:

> I'm beginning to be a little concerned about my political
> future. I can feel myself getting into what I guess is a natural
> and inevitable condition — the gradual erosion of my local
> orientation. I'm not as enthused about tending my constit-
> uency relations as I used to be and I'm not paying them the
> attention I should be. There's a natural tension between
> being a good representative and taking an interest in govern-
> ment. I'm getting into some heady things in Washington,
> and I want to make an input into the government. It's making
> me a poorer representative than I was. I find myself avoiding
> the personal collisions that arise in the constituency — turn-
> ing away from that one last handshake, not bothering to go
> to that one last meeting. I find myself forgetting people's
> names. And I find myself caring less about it than I used to.
> Right now, it's just a feeling I have. In eight years I have
> still to come home less than forty weekends a year. This is
> my thirty-sixth trip this year. What was it Arthur Rubinstein
> said? "If I miss one practice, I notice it. If I miss two prac-
> tices, my teacher notices it. If I miss a week of practice, my
> audience notices it." I'm at stage one right now — or maybe
> stage one and stage two. But I'm beginning to feel that I
> could be defeated before long. And I'm not going to change.
> I don't want the status. I want to contribute to government.

The onset of a Washington career is altering his personal goals and
his established home style. He is worried about the costs of the
change; but he is willing to accept some loss of reelection support in
exchange for his increased influence in Congress.

This dilemma faces every member of Congress. It is built into the
twin requirements that Congress be a representative and a legislative institution. Some members believe they can achieve reelection
at home together with influence or policy in Washington without
sacrificing either. During Congressman O's first year as a subcommittee chairman (see Chapter Six), I asked him whether his new

position would make it more difficult to tend to district matters. He replied,

> If you mean, am I getting Potomac fever, the answer is, no. If you mean, has the change in my official duties here made me a better congressman, the answer is, yes. If you mean has it taken away from my activity in the constituency, the answer is no.

Congressman O, we recall, has been going home less; but he has been increasing the number and the activity of his district staff. Although he speaks confidently of his allocative solution, he is not unaware of potential problems. "My staff operation runs by itself. They don't need me. Maybe I should worry about that. You aren't going back and say I'm ripe for the plucking are you? I don't think I am."

A three-term member responded very positively when I paraphrased the worries of the congressman friend of his who had quoted Arthur Rubinstein:

> You can do your job in Washington and in your district if you know how. My quarrel with [the people like him] of this world is that they don't learn to be good politicians before they get to Congress. They get there because some people are sitting around the table one day and ask them to do it. They're smart, but they don't learn to organize a district. Once you learn to do that, it's much easier to do your job in Washington.

This member, however, has not yet tasted the inside influence of his friend. Moreover, he does not always talk with such assurance. His district is not so well organized that he has reduced his personal attentiveness to it.

> Ralph Krug [the congressman in the adjacent district] tells me I spoil my constituents. He says, "You've been elected twice; you know your district; once a month is enough to come home." But that's not my philosophy. Maybe it will be someday. . . . My lack of confidence is still a pressure which brings me home. This is my political base. Washington is not my political base. I feel I have to come home to get nour-

ished, to see for myself what's going on. It's my security
blanket — coming home.

For now, he feels no competing pulls; but he is not unaware of his
friend's dilemma.

Members pose the dilemma with varying degrees of immediacy.
No matter how confident members may be of their ability to pursue
their Washington and their constituency careers simultaneously,
however, they all recognize the potentiality of conflict and worry
about coping with it. It is our guess that the conflict between the
reelection goal on the one hand and the power or policy goals on
the other hand becomes most acute for members as they near the
peak of influence internally. For, at this stage of their Washington
career, the resource requirements of the Washington job make it
nearly impossible to meet established expectations of attentiveness
at home. Individuals who want nothing from their Washington
careers except the status of being a member of Congress will never
pursue any other goal except reelection. For these people, the dilemma of which we speak is minimal. Our concern is with those
individuals who find, sooner or later, that they wish to pursue a mix
of goals in which reelection must be weighted along with power or
policy.

One formula for managing a mix of goals that gives heavy weight
to a Washington career is to make one's influence in Washington
the centerpiece of home style. The member says, in effect, "I can't
come home to present myself in person as much as I once did, because I'm so busy tending to the nation's business; but my seniority,
my influence, my effectiveness in Washington is of great benefit to
you." He asks his supportive constituents to adopt a new set of
expectations, one that would put less of a premium on access.
Furthermore, he asks these constituents to remain sufficiently intense in their support to discourage challengers — especially those
who will promise access. All members do some of this when they
explain their Washington activity — especially in connection with
"explaining power." And, where possible, they quote from favorable
national commentary in their campaign literature. But, though Congressman L (Chapter Five) comes close, none of the eighteen has
made Washington influence the central element of his home style.

One difficulty of completely adopting such a home style is that
the powerful Washington legislator can actually get pretty far out

of touch with his supportive constituents back home. One of the more senior members of my group, and a leader of his committee, recounted the case when his preoccupation with an internal legislative impasse affecting Israel caused him to neglect the crucial Jewish element of his primary constituency — a group "who contribute two-thirds of my money." A member of the committee staff had devised an amendment to break the deadlock.

> Peter Tompkins looked at it and said to me, "Why don't we sponsor it?" So we put it forward, and it became known as the Crowder-Tompkins Amendment. I did it because I respected the staff man who suggested it and because I wanted to get something through that was reasonable. Well, a member of the committee called people back home and said, "Crowder is selling out." All hell broke loose. I started getting calls at two and three in the morning from my friends asking me what I was doing. So I went back home and discussed the issue with them. When I walked into the room, it made me feel sad and shocked to feel their hostility. They wanted me to know that they would clobber me if they thought I was selling out. Two hours later, we walked out friends again. I dropped the Crowder-Tompkins Amendment. That's the only little flare up I've ever had with the Jewish community. But it reminded me of their sensitivity to anything that smacks of discrimination.

The congressman survived. But he would not have needed so forceful a reminder of his strongest supporters' concerns were he nearer the beginning of his constituency career. But, of course, neither would he have been a committee leader, and neither would the imperatives of a House career bulked so large in his mix of goals.

Another way to manage conflicting reelection and Washington career goals might be to use one's Washington influence to alter support patterns at home. That is, instead of acting — as is the normal case — to reenforce home support, to keep what he had "last time," the congressman might act to displace that old support with compensating new support. He might even accomplish this inadvertently, should his pursuit of power or policy attract, willy-nilly, constituents who welcomed his new mix of goals. The very Washington activity that left him out of touch with previously supportive constituents might put him in touch with newly supportive ones.

A newly acquired position of influence in a particular policy area or a new reputation as an effective legislator might produce such a feedback effect. We describe the pattern in conditional terms, because we have not observed such an effect. It would probably take a longer period of observation, with more of a focus on Washington to do so. In theory, however, the Washington and the constituency careers should influence one another reciprocally.

In Chapter Six, we noted a tendency for successful home styles to harden over time and to place stylistic constraints on the congressman's subsequent behavior. The pursuit of a Washington career helps us explain this constituency phenomenon. That is, to the degree that a congressman pursues power or policy goals in the House, he will have that much less time or energy to devote to the consideration of alternative home styles. His predisposition to "do what we did last time" at home will be further strengthened by his growing preoccupation with Washington matters. Indeed, the speed with which a congressman begins to develop a Washington career will affect the speed with which his home style solidifies. We noted in Chapter Six that the home styles of Representatives J and K seemed to take permanent shape very quickly. We also noted that their first taste of a Washington career came very quickly. It is our guess, then, that the sooner the Washington career begins, the sooner the home style will harden.

A broader statement of this feedback effect would be that the sooner a congressman's Washington career begins, the sooner will his constituency career move from its expansionist stage to the protectionist stage. For most House members, we believe, constituency careers move fairly naturally from their expansionist to their protectionist stage at about the same time that the opportunities for a Washingon career begin to improve. The two career rhythms complement one another. But the tempo can change. And we may be witnessing just such a sea change in the 1970s. With the obsolescence of the old apprenticeship norms in the House, and with the reform-induced decentralization of influence in the House, the opportunities for pursuing power or policy goals are coming sooner than they have for a long time. This change will tend to shorten the period of experimentation with home styles, hasten the onset of stylistic constraints, and propel House members more quickly into a protectionist stance at home. Such changes will not necessarily affect the ability of House members to manage a mix of personal goals. But present-day House members will probably have to start concerning themselves with the problem earlier in their legislative lives than their predecessors ever did.

In all of this speculation about career linkages, we have assumed that most members of Congress develop, over time, a mix of personal goals. We particularly assume that most members will trade off some of their personal commitment to reelection in order to satisfy a personal desire for institutional or policy influence. It is our observation, based on only eighteen cases, that House members do, in fact, exhibit varying degrees of commitment to reelection. All want reelection in the abstract, but not all will pay any price to achieve it; nor will all pay the same price. This complex view of House member goals is, we think, a realistic view. And it is the job of an empirical political science to describe and explain the various mixes of goals, and the conditions under which they are adopted or altered.

One senior member contemplated retirement in the face of an adverse redistricting but, because he had the prospect of a committee chairmanship, he decided to run and hope for the best. He wanted reelection because he wanted continued influence; but he was unwilling to put his present influence in jeopardy by pursuing reelection with the same intensity that marked his earlier constituency career. As he put it,

> Ten years ago, I whipped another redistricting. And I did it by neglecting my congressional duties. . . . Today I don't have the time, and I'm not going to neglect my duties. . . . If I do what is necessary to get reelected and thus become chairman of the committee, I will lose the respect and confidence of my fellow committee members because of being absent from the hearings and, occasionally, the votes.

He did not work hard at reelection, and he won by his narrowest margin ever. But he succeeded in sustaining a mix of personal goals very different from an earlier one.

A Republican member of my group, having finally achieved national prominence, decided to retire nonetheless, because he found it impossible as a member of the minority party in Congress to make "substantive contributions to public policy." If he could not achieve his goal of helping to make good public policy, he did not want reelection. In Chapter 5, we noted the members' desire to use their home support to secure voting leeway as well as reelection. Many, no doubt, would not seek reelection if it meant the loss of all such leeway. Recall, also, Congressman L (Chapter Six) who decided to retire rather than undertake a strenuous reelection campaign. Having given greater weight to his Washington career goals, he was unwilling to cycle back to a situation in which reelection was paramount. "What's the use of having high seniority with the opportunity of being influential in Congress if you have to spend all your time in your district?" He did not want reelection at the price of reduced influence in the House.

It is probably fair to say that at some point most members ask themselves how badly they want to be reelected. Doubtless, the question is posed, seriously, at a variety of junctures in their two careers. Like the three members just discussed, however, most members probably ask it when they are in the protectionist stage of their constituency careers and well established in their Washington careers. This, at any rate, is the status of most House members who retire. As for the reasons why members begin to question their devotion to reelection, political scientists cannot say. Doubtless, like any other personal decision, the decision to retire is complicated. But many observers have noted the recent marked increase in retirements from the House of Representatives. So we may be witnessing a secular decline in the devotion to reelection. If we are, the research reported in this book may provide one possible explanation for it.

The congressman's home activities are more difficult and taxing than we have previously recognized. Under the best of circumstances, the tension involved in maintaining constituency contact and achieving legislative competence is considerable. Members cannot be in two places at once, and the growth of a Washington career exacerbates the problem. But, more than that, the demands in both places have grown recently. The legislative workload and the demand for legislative expertise are steadily increasing. So is the problem of maintaining meaningful contact with their several constituencies. Years ago, House members returned home for months at a time to live among their supportive constituencies, soak up the home atmosphere, absorb local problems at first hand. Today, they race home for a day, a weekend, a week at a time. Only seven of the eighteen maintain a family home in their district. The other eleven stay with relatives or friends or in barely furnished rooms when they are at home. The citizen demand for access, for communication, and for the establishment of trust is as great as ever. So members go home. But the quality of their contact has suffered. "It's like a one-night stand in a singles bar." It is harder to sustain a genuine two-way communication than it once was. House member worries about the home relationship — great under any circumstances, but greater now — contribute to the strain and frustration of the job. Some cope; but others retire. It may be those members who cannot stand the heat of the home relationship who are getting out of the House kitchen. If so, people prepared to be more attentive to home — as we suggested in Chapter Six — are likely to replace them.[1]

The interplay between home careers and Washington careers continues even as House members leave Congress. For, in retirement or in defeat, they still face a choice — to return home or to remain in Washington. The subject of postcongressional careers is too vast to be treated here. But students of home politics can find, in these choices, indications of the depth and durability of home attachments in the face of influential Washington careers. It is conventional wisdom in the nation's capital that senators and representatives "get Potomac fever" and that "they don't go back to Pocatello" when their legislative careers end. Having pursued the goals of power and policy in Washington with increasing success, they prefer, it is said, to continue their Washington career in some nonlegislative job rather than to go back home. In such a choice, perhaps, we might find the ultimate displacement of the constituency career with the Washington career.

An examination of the place of residence of 370 individuals who left the House between 1954 and 1974, and who were alive in 1974, sheds considerable doubt on this Washington wisdom.[2] It appears that most House members do, indeed, "go back to Pocatello." Of the 370 former members studied, 253 (68 percent) resided in their home states in 1974; 91 lived in the Washington, D.C., area; and 26 resided someplace else. Of those 344 who chose either Washington or home, therefore, nearly three-quarters chose home. This simple fact underscores the very great strength of the home attachments we have described in this book.

No cross section of living former members will tell us for sure how many members lingered in Washington for a while before eventually returning home. Only a careful tracing of all individual cases, therefore, will give us a full and accurate description of the Washington-home choice. Even so, among the former members most likely to be attracted to Washington — those who left Congress from 1970 to 1974 — only 37 percent have chosen to remain there. A cursory glance at all those who have chosen to prolong their Washington careers, however, tells us what we might expect —

Table 7.1

Washington Career and Home Career: After Congress

| | Place of Residence 1974 | | | |
| | Home State | | Washington, D.C. | |
Reason for Leaving	Number of Terms	Age	Number of Terms	Age
Electoral defeat (N = 193)	4.0 (N = 134)	53.2	5.2 (N = 59)	51.8
Voluntary retirement (N = 151)	6.1 (N = 118)	57.4	7.8 (N = 33)	55.3
Total (N = 344)	5.0 (N = 252)	55.2	6.1 (N = 92)	53.1

that they have already had longer congressional careers than those who returned home. Our data also tell us that these members are younger than those who choose to return home. Thus, we speculate, the success of a member's previous career in Congress and the prospect that he or she still has time to capitalize on that success in the Washington community are positive inducements to stay. And these inducements seem unaffected by the manner of his or her leaving Congress — whether by electoral defeat (for renomination or reelection) or retirement. Those who were defeated, however, had shorter congressional careers and were younger than those who had voluntarily retired. Table 7-1 describes these relationships. Table 7-1 helps confirm the existence of the Washington career while it reminds us even more forcefully of the underlying and persisting constituency career.

LINKAGE: HOME STYLE AND WASHINGTON STYLE

In probing for linkages between home and Washington, it is natural to ask if there are any connections between home style and Washington behavior. If we mean to ask whether members of Congress do certain things in Washington to shore up constituent support at home, the answer is obviously yes. And what they do is well known and straightforward. They allocate the tasks of their staffs in ways they think helpful in getting reelected. They choose committee assignments they think will bring identification with and benefit to their supportive constituencies. They vote in ways they think will be approved by their supportive constituents. Or, better, they avoid voting in ways they believe will be intensely disapproved by their supportive constituents. They will also vote in ways that help them structure their need to explain back home. There is nothing we can add here to what political scientists already know about such constituency-oriented behavior in Washington.

The question we have to ask is whether the study of home styles can tell us anything we might not otherwise know about behavior in Washington. Are home styles related in any way to Washington styles? It is not an easy question to handle. Political scientists have not produced any consensus as to precisely what might be meant by a "Washington style." [3] Also, we have produced too little Washington-related information in this study to pursue the matter constructively. Still, the question remains intriguing, if only because from time to time House members talk or act as if the behavior we observed at home is repeated in Washington.

For example, our issue-oriented Congressman O, who refuses "to play the groups" at home, also refuses to play them in Washington.

> I met a guy from the postal union [at home]. He said I gave them the brush off when they came to Washington. The trouble is they compare me to the congressman in the next district. He wines and dines every little two-bit group that comes down. He spends all his time with them. He doesn't have anything else to do. But I don't have the patience with these guys, or the time. I'm busy over on the floor doing other things.

Stylistic patterns affecting access at home can affect access similarly in Washington. Another congressman commented at home that "I love to campaign at coffee hours with ten or twelve people. I hate standup cocktail parties. . . . I'm very bad at making small talk with people I don't know. I can't do it." In Washington, he follows the same stylistic predilections — almost.

> Not long ago, I got a letter from the head of the American Legion in my state noting that I hadn't been to their Wash-

> ington cocktail party for the last two years. I don't go to any
> of those Washington parties. . . . But I make two excep-
> tions – groups in which I have personal friends and groups
> that were with me in 1968 [his first campaign]. Take the
> Machinists, for example. They were a great help to me when
> I needed help. I always go to their gatherings.

If access at home carries with it a promise of access in Washington,
this is all the more reason why it is so valued by supportive constituents. Our knowledge of home style may, furthermore, help us to
locate those constituents most likely to achieve access in Washington.

Another possible linkage might be a relationship between coalition
building at home and coalition building inside the House. For example, might not our Congressman B, the well-liked local boy who
is so suspicious of "outsiders," be handicapped as a coalition builder
in Congress by this exclusive view of politics? He was two years
on the job, he says, before he began to read *The Washington Post*.
More broadly, might not any member who writes off certain constituents as people he "never gets" be limited in his efforts to build
coalitions among House colleagues who represent such people? In
broader compass still, are some home styles more conducive to the
achievement of internal power or good policy than others? Are
members with issue-oriented home styles any more likely to provide
internal policy leadership than members with other home styles?
Such questions are intriguing. But the shortcomings of our home-
oriented perspective cannot be overcome sufficiently to answer them.

We shall offer, however, one line of speculation. It is this: Home
styles may affect Washington styles in the degree to which home
styles produce early commitments to future courses of action in
Congress. Some members will act at home, we speculate, to preserve
a maximum of maneuvering room for themselves at various points
of decision in Washington. Other members will act at home to
commit themselves to certain courses of action at various points of
decision in Washington. The former remain free to play a variety of
parts in the legislative process. The latter are more limited in their
range of legislative activity. Both stances are deliberate and, partly
at least, a function of their home styles. We are encouraged in
these speculations because House members themselves make this
distinction between an early and a late commitment to a course of
action. And we find traces of evidence in a couple of instances.

Just after his first congressional campaign victory, one individual articulated the first kind of linkage:

> I have an abhorrence of getting myself precommitted. I don't go around looking for chances to commit myself if I can avoid it. Fortunately, my opponent in the campaign didn't force me to get precommitted. He conducted a quiet hand-shaking campaign, and that's the kind I conduct. . . . I think you have an obligation to your constituents to make your vote as effective as you can. You want to keep as much bargaining power as you can. If you commit yourself to a group before you know what the situation is, you lose that bargaining power. . . . Sometimes, [in the state legislature] when I told people what they wanted to hear, I regretted it afterward. When the vote came, the situation had changed and I had to vote against my better judgment or my word.

In the middle of his third term, another House member articulated the second kind of stylistic linkage:

> I don't think the party leadership gets many votes by direct solicitation. I've been up and down the hill with the leadership on that. I tell them that I take my positions on the issues solid and early at home. "If you want my vote, have a legislative platform and stick to it. Take your position early." But they don't do that. When I can take the lead on a party position I feel comfortable with, I do. That makes them feel better toward me.

The first congressman's home style is dominantly person to person; the second congressman's home style is dominantly issue-oriented. Yet both individuals are equally policy-oriented — equally devoted to power and policy goals — in the House. And one may be as influential as the other, for strategies of commitment may be as effective as strategies of maneuver. The difference lies in the freedom to maneuver each normally has throughout the decision-making process. And therein may lie a useful classification of Washington styles.

There were two members whom I traveled with prior to their first election; I went to Washington to talk with them again four weeks into their freshman year. The differences between them provide some support for the stylistic relationships suggested.

One of them had deliberately made legislative style *the* issue against his primary opponent. "Effectiveness — who can get the most done. That's the thing I stress everywhere. . . . People have to vote on the issues. And the issue is effectiveness." When, during a debate, his opponent said, "I don't mind being called flamboyant and controversial," he countered,

> Do you want someone who does the talk and stirs the pot and then, after the pot is stirred, leaves it? Or do you want someone who gets in there to see what solution can be worked out, what legislative result can be produced?

He spelled out what he meant by an "effective" decision-making style best in another context. As we left the local AFL-CIO endorsement meeting, at which he received their endorsement ("The largest portion of my money has come from organized labor"), he said,

> The state chairman was there and asked if I would be a member of the local welcoming committee for Hubert Humphrey when he comes to the state. I don't want to commit myself. I don't have a [presidential] candidate. But labor loves Hubert Humphrey. Oh, how they love him. . . . I'm going to be at the national convention. I want to be free in making decisions there. Once you commit yourself, people put you in a slot and you're isolated. You lose your freedom to move in the party. I want to keep that freedom.

When I visited him in Washington shortly after his election, he exhibited the same reluctance to commit himself in advance that he had exhibited at home. He was pleased about obtaining a prized committee assignment as a result of some intricate, "effective" planning. Otherwise, his posture was one of avoiding unnecessary conclusions. On his career, he said, "It's all right, but it's nothing I'd want to do for the rest of my life, being a member of the United States House of Representatives." On the Democratic Study Group: "I haven't paid my dues yet. I'm going to a few more of their meetings and see whether it's the kind of group I want to be connected with. Until then, I'm withholding my dues." On the House as an institution: "I'll save my overall impressions till later. I haven't been here long enough, and we haven't gotten into the substance of things yet." These comments seemed perfectly consistent with what I had seen and heard back home — the effort to remain minimally committed to specifics and maximally free for "effective" legislative maneuver.

By the same token, I found the second newcomer much more voluble and much more engaged when I visited him in Washington that same day. Indeed, he ventured a revealing comment on the first member: "A group of us freshmen have decided to meet regularly. [He listed the names, and my other freshman congressman, Paul Kraus, was not among them.] Paul Kraus is very cautious. We've been a lot more active on reform and in the Democratic Study Group than Paul Kraus and those cats." The comment was no surprise, coming as it did from someone who during the election campaign had told his supporters that "The House of Representatives is the least representative part of the government, the one that needs the most changing, the one that changes the slowest and is the hardest to change." He had often spoken of the House reformers as "great guys" and praised "my friends in the Democratic Study Group." During his campaign he had made substantive public policy *the* issue between himself and his general election opponent. And he escalated policy issues at every opportunity. To a group of prospective supporters he had said,

> I can't think of a single issue on which he and I agree. He supports Nixon on the war; he supports Nixon's so-called family assistance plan. He opposes the land use bill. And those are the only positions he has taken so far. Oh, he does support the White House Conference on the Elderly. But I supported it before he did. So there is as complete a difference between us as you can imagine. We have completely different philosophies on what this country ought to be.

When I asked him, in Washington, if he anticipated any difficult voting decisions, he said, "No, people know my position on almost everything."

He was as free with early judgments about the House as his fellow freshman was noncommittal. "Here's a symbol of congressional impotence," he said, pointing to the telephone. "We can talk on the FTS line before 9:00 A.M. and after 5:00 P.M.; between 9:00 A.M. and 5:00 P.M. they shut it off. I'll bet the Secretary of Defense doesn't have to wait till 5:00 P.M. to make his calls. It's ridiculous, absurd." Another time, he said, "I've been reenforced in my belief that the place is unrepresentative. It is. I've heard things said here that don't represent anyone." Complaining, "They may never pass any legislation at the rate they're going," he had thrown himself enthusiastically into whatever legislative "action" he could find. He had begun, too, to think about the problem of his legislative "effectiveness" and had even made some stylistic adjustments. But it remained a different style from that of his freshman colleague.

> I wish I knew how the old guys judge you down here. I wonder if I've begun to lose my credibility by standing up in caucus to ask for a vote on every committee chairmanship. I can see where you would tear yourself apart here trying to balance representation of your district against your effectiveness. On the one hand you owe it to your constituents to voice their views; on the other hand you owe it to them to be effective within the institution. So far I've tried by everything I've done to keep from being labeled a screamer. People like Drinan and Bella are totally ineffective down here; yet they are right in expressing their constituents' views. I think it's how you say a thing more than what you say. In the briefing by Kissinger, I was the only freshman to ask a question, and I'm sure the older heads were shocked to hear a freshman ask a question. The Speaker called on me as "the Freshman Representative from _____." I hope I said what I said articulately and carefully and nicely enough so that I didn't offend anyone. But I sure as hell said what I wanted.

It is a Washington style related, we think, to his strongly issue-oriented style at home.

The suggested linkage between home styles and Washington styles depends on the distinction, in Washington, between early commitment and the retention of maneuvering room during decision making. If such a distinction can be maintained, then it seems that certain home styles will be associated with one Washington style more often than with the other. The more issue-oriented a congressman's home style, the more likely is he to commit himself early. And the more he chooses to present himself by talking about policy issues, the more the sheer density of talk will produce early commitments. They may be commitments to introduce legislation, agitate for a given decision in a given forum, vote in a particular fashion, or something else. In proportions that vary from member to member, this talk at home may be pure "position taking" — and thus, in Mayhew's terms, totally devoid of commitment.[4] All we can say, here, is that we are speaking only of that proportion of home talk that does carry some commitment to future activity. We mean to emphasize a commitment to legislative activism, publicly made, with the implied invitation for constituents to watch him in action.

On the other hand, the less issue-oriented a congressman's home style (and this includes person-to-person, constituency service, and community leadership styles) the less likely he is to commit himself to policy positions that will constrain his actions during the legislative process. He will be able to focus on targets of opportunity among policies, take an active or a passive role at one stage or another, work behind the scenes or openly, make his voting decisions early or late, and so on. It is not necessary to adopt extreme views on the distinction between commitment and maneuver. No member is so committed that he has no room for maneuver in Washington; and no member who strives to maintain maneuvering room is totally noncommitted at home.

Further, it must be said, again, that this distinction is *not* one of relative influence inside the House. The distinction may, however, be of some practical moment during the legislative process. To know whether and how strongly any given member has committed himself back home to do something in Washington may be the most important piece of political intelligence one can have about a fellow member in any given legislative struggle. As one member, a House leader, noted, "I never trade votes; I couldn't keep track of them all; I always work on someone through second or third parties in their districts." That is, he regards a commitment made by a member to his strongest supporters back home as the most durable kind of legislative commitment. The ability to classify House members with regard to their tendency to commit early at home (and to whom) or their tendency to remain flexible may represent important political intelligence. In sum, coalition builders in the House may find it helpful to know something about the home styles of House members.

All this is, admittedly, conjectural. And nothing we have said should be taken to diminish the force of our more general proposition that all House members can use their home styles to give themselves a great deal of voting leeway in Washington if they so desire. Throughout the book, we have argued that House members are not tightly constrained in their legislative votes by the necessities of constituent support. So long as members can successfully explain a vote afterward, their constituent support depends — except for one or two issues — more on what they do at home than on what they do in Washington. That is what they believe; and we have described their behavior in that light. Any constraining effect that home style may have on Washington style must be veiwed within this set of overarching propositions.

Members with issue-oriented home styles do, we think, come to Washington more constrained by prior commitments than members with other types of home style. These commitments pertain to much more than voting. But even where voting is concerned we should not think of these commitments as so specific or so binding as to force them into casting votes different from ones they would freely cast otherwise. By committing themselves early at home, they have lost some of the voting leeway they might otherwise want. But they will have lost only as much as their constituents will have forced on them. And that, as we have said repeatedly, is not very much. If their constituents have forced anything on them, it is more likely to be a home style that features issue-orientation and a commitment to visible legislative activism. It will not be overly constraining. If it is, the escape into pure position taking is always available.

The main effect we wish to suggest is simply that the distribution and strength of commitments made at home can affect the legislative process in Washington. If home commitments vary according to home styles, then students of the legislative process may find home styles of some relevance. More than this, we would not wish to claim.

REPRESENTATION: SUMMARY SPECULATION

For students of Congress, the subject of representation comes with the territory. It has not been the focus of this study because we have made no effort to examine either our members' activity in Washington or their constituents' activity at home. Nonetheless, our explorations may have turned up some implications for the family of questions, both descriptive and normative, raised by studies of representation. If our observations can shed any new light on this difficult subject, it will come from having had the vantage point of home, and from having looked at home through the eyes of the representative. What does the representative see when he or she goes home to look at the represented? How does what he

or she sees affect his or her representational activity? What can we learn, from this perspective, about the nature, the quality, and the problem of representation in this country?

The member of Congress, we have learned, has a complex, four-circled view of the people he represents. He differentiates among them in terms of their political support for him and, in some cases, their political loyalty to him. If, therefore, we start with the congressman's perception of the people he represents, there is no way that the act of representing can be separated from the act of getting elected. If the congressman cannot win and hold the votes of some people, he cannot represent any people. Further, he cannot represent any people unless he knows, or makes an effort to know, who they are, what they think, and what they want; and it is by campaigning for electoral support among them that he finds out such things. During the expansionist stage of his constituency career, particularly, he probably knows his various constituencies as well as it is possible to know them. It is, indeed, by such campaigning, by going home a great deal, that a congressman develops a complex and discriminating set of perceptions about his constituents. Conversely, only by separating the problem of running for office from the problem of representing while in office could anyone conceive of a constituency as being uncomplicated or undifferentiated or monolithic.[5] As our representatives see it, any such separation is impossible to maintain.

So long as representatives need electoral support, they can be held accountable to those they represent through the electoral process. If the represented do not get the kind of representation they want (whatever that may be), they can remove their representative from office. Whether they will thereby get the kind of representation they want is another question. But the theory of electoral accountability holds that so long as representatives want to retain their office, the knowledge that they will later be held accountable at the polls will tend to make their representative behavior more responsive to the desires of their constituents. The members of some representative bodies, as Kenneth Prewitt has pointed out, may have neither of the necessary conditions of electoral accountability — ambition for office and the sensitivity to the power of the voters.[6] But we have seen how untrue this is of House members. They work hard to get their job and they work hard to keep it. On the whole, they expend a great deal of time and effort keeping in touch with their various constituencies back home. No matter what the objective measures of political scientists may tell us about their electoral safety, members of Congress feel uncertain and vulnerable — if not today then yesterday, if not yesterday then tomorrow. A congressman who describes his or her seat as "safe," will implicitly add, "because and so long as I work actively to keep it safe." Furthermore, many a House retirement decision is made in anticipation of electoral difficulty. In all of these respects, members of Congress are not among Prewitt's "volunteerists." They possess all the electoral sensitivities that are necessary if they are to be held accountable at election time for their representative behavior.

The presence of these necessary conditions cannot tell us, however, whether and to what degree House members actually do respond to the desires of the people they represent. Nor have we done any research that might help answer that empirical question. What our congressman's-eye research angle does make clear, however, is that members feel more accountable, and doubtless are more responsive, to some of their constituents than to others. And for the reason we have emphasized. They feel more accountable to some constituents than to others because the support of some constituents is more important to them than the support of others. As persons whose very right to represent depends on getting and holding electoral support, they would be crazy not to think this way and not to take action on this basis. It is one thing, however, to generalize that House members are more accountable and more responsive to their supportive constituencies than they are to the remainder of their constituents. It is quite another thing to assume that they — and we — know precisely who it is that they respond to and, therefore, represent. Certainly they spend a lot of time trying to sort out their various constituencies, to learn who is "out there," to reach them, and to communicate with them. To watch a member going about this task, however, is to recognize how difficult it is.

The more one observes members of Congress at work in their districts, the more impressed one is by the simple fact that people are hard to find. Members (and their staffs) expend incredible amounts of time and energy just trying to locate people to present themselves to. Their ingenuity and enterprise are almost infinite. I can scarcely imagine a setting or a purpose for bringing a few human beings together that I have not been a part of during my travels. But people, it turns out, do not arrange themselves for the convenience of their member of Congress. In sparsely settled rural areas, for example, one must travel vast distances to reach a very few people. During a seven-and-a-half-hour trip of 250 miles, one congressman visited seven small communities ranging in size from 224 to 5265 — with a total population of 8500. He spent half the day riding in the car; during the other half he talked to no more than fifty people.

A member representing a fast-growing area of suburban sprawl has a different problem. It is not hard for him to "get there," but he can't get a handle on people when he does.

> It's a mystery to me. I go there and all I see are row after row of mobile homes and apartment houses. It's just a collection of shopping centers. . . . It's not a community. They have no rotary clubs or groups like that. It's just a bunch of houses. . . . I don't know how you would campaign there.

Similarly, an urban congressman, riding past a huge 25,000-person apartment complex, commented, "These people are not joiners. Not one in 300 is a member of any group or organization. They are un-reachable. . . . It's so transient, you don't know who you represent." There is hardly an event at which the congressman is to be present about which he is not anxious beforehand about the size and makeup of the people to be there. Afterward, there is usually some puzzlement — often punctuated with disappointment — as to exactly what kind of people had been in attendance.

The other side of the same coin is that although "people" are hard to find, certain people are not. Those who cluster in struc-tured, organized communities, public or private, do make themselves available for presentations by their representatives. As one congress-man explained,

> You can't create crowds. So you go where people meet. That means you spend more time talking to groups like the Cham-ber [of Commerce] than you do to people who live along the road here. . . . The great mass of people you can't reach. They are not organized. They don't have institutions you can plug into. The leadership, the elite, runs along the top of all the institutions, and you can reach them, but not the people generally.

The situation is the same among communities large and small, rich or poor, public or private. There are always community elites, organization leaders, active citizens, the politically aware. The congressman need not worry about reaching them. They will reach him. If he chooses, these people will be easy for him to represent. And to some degree, every House member does so choose. He does so because every supportive constituency must have politically aware people in it. But every supportive constituency — at least every re-election constituency — has lots of other people in it too. In view of the relative difficulty in locating and, hence, presenting himself to these other people, the congressman must be careful lest he reach, respond to, and represent only those who make it easy for him to do so.[7]

The problem is one House members are aware of — more, we would guess, in the expansionist stage of their constituency careers than in the protectionist stage. That is why they engage in such activities as open meetings, town meetings, open office hours, receptions, coffees, shopping plaza touring, mainstreeting, plant gating, door knocking, block working — all of them methods for presenting themselves directly to people. These activities supplement the congressman's ready-made organized contacts, and help him learn who is out there and who supports him. Still it is not easy. After an open meeting, Congressman D wondered, "You get a diversity of views, but whether it's *the* diversity, you can't be sure. How do you know whether it's representative?"

It might be added that the more fragmented and kinetic American society becomes, the more difficult it will be for House members to reach people. It is our observation that members of Congress thrive where some sense of community already exists. They are products of it; they identify with it; they celebrate it; they even legitimate it; but they do not create it. To travel with House members, indeed, is to observe a tremendous reservoir of community spirit throughout the country, a vibrant associational life which the members can tie into and reflect. To the degree, however, that public and private communities within congressional districts weaken, the House member will be far more adrift than he now is in his effort to find and to know the people of his district. And all of this serves to underscore something we have emphasized since Chapter 1, that the congressman views his supportive constituents with a good deal of uncertainty. It is not easy, we repeat, for anyone to say just who each congressman reaches, responds to, and represents.

One thing, however, is clear. All our observations and, hence, all our generalizations about congressman-constituent relationships involve a set of constituents far smaller than the total number in the district. No matter how a congressman allocates, presents, or explains, he reaches a relatively few people directly. Offsetting this situation, House members believe that as a result of their direct contacts with as many supportive constituents as they can reach, they will also reach a great many more people indirectly. They are strong believers in the two-step flow of communication. They have to be. But they also think it works. Their belief is that though they may not reach as many people as they would like, those they do reach — whether easy or difficult — will talk to others about them. They hope the talk will be favorable. The process can hold for the primary constituency, mostly in homogeneous districts, or for the reelection constituency, mostly in heterogeneous districts. "I have a few dedicated supporters who create an atmosphere in which others come to support me," says one member. The congressman who visited seven rural communities in a day commented on the way home, "It isn't what we did today that is important. It's what happened afterward. There will be talk in all the cafes tomorrow; 'the congressman was here.'" A congressman who holds neighborhood coffees says, "We send out seventy-five invitations. Only fifteen come, but word gets around that we've been there. There's a ripple effect in every community." The operative assumption is that if you can reach some people, they will reach others and your effort will multiply itself.

In all that we have said thus far, representation requires responsiveness to certain constituents, and responsiveness requires "reaching" those constituents. When House members speak of "reaching" certain constituents they sometimes mean finding them — learning who they are, what they think, and what they want — for the purpose of making some kind of response to them. But they sometimes use "reaching" to mean making themselves visible to certain constituents. Visibility requires nothing more than name recognition on the part of the constituent and, hence, requires no responsiveness on the part of the congressman. If he relies on a two-step flow of communication, in which people he knows talk about him to people they know, he can at least draw reasonable inferences about what the people who learn about him indirectly are like and what they might want. But when he goes one step further and seeks to reach

people only by accustoming them to his name or face, he cannot
know what they are like or what they want. He reaches them only
to get their support, not to be responsive.

Thus the congressman who sees the lonesome transients in his
25,000-person apartment complex as unreachable and unknowable
tries to reach them by handing out shopping bags with his picture
on them.

> Those shopping bags multiply themselves. You see them
> everywhere, up and down the streets. . . They are perfect
> for a district like this where people walk to the store to shop.
> They wouldn't work in Bethesda – everybody has a car. But
> in this district . . . they are a walking advertisement.

The Bethesda congressman, of course, has other ways of making
himself visible and gaining name recognition — through newspapers,
television, radio, billboards, brochures perhaps. All members advertise, to use David Mayhew's language, in some way or another.[8] In
districts of 450,000 people, some proportion of their supportive constituencies can be secured in no other way. Even at that, there will
be a large remainder within the district who still will not recognize
the member's name. Some of these unreached people, too, will be
supportive constituents.

Advertising is primarily one-way communication. The idea of
responsiveness, on the other hand, assumes the existence of *two-way
communication*. Every congressman's home style is a blend of two-
way and one-way communication, of efforts to listen to and talk to
supportive constituents and of efforts to gain visibility. In many
cases, as when the newspaper carries the story of a town meeting,
or when a question-and-answer period after a speech is televised, the
two activities can be carried on simultaneously. House members
differ as to the optimal mix of two-way and one-way communication
— not as a matter of democratic theory, but simply as a matter of
winning elections in different kinds of districts. We have examined
several different mixtures. From the standpoint of democratic theory
the greater the proportion of two-way communication, the more
likely is there to be both electoral accountability and responsiveness
on the part of the representative. Hence, the greater the proportion
of two-way communication the better. On the other hand, huge constituencies — as well as their internal makeup — place limits on the

possibilities of two-way communication, and some proportion of advertising-for-visibility is inevitable.

If we think of representation as involving some idea of responsiveness on the part of the representative, the sum of these congressman-constituent relationships is quite imperfect. It is hard to see how a congressman can be said to represent supportive constituents reached purely by advertising — much less those supporters he has not reached at all. Leaving aside the latter group, some of whom may vote their party identification and gain some kind of responsiveness though that connection, we need to acknowledge that advertising-visibility-name recognition activities can carry at least the potential for active, responsive representation. If people recognize their member's name when they see it — or, even better, if they can recall it from memory — they may at least know whom to reach if they want to and if they know how. House members do their best, of course, to transform name recognition into two-way communication of some sort — a request for action from an individual or a group, for instance. Advertising can, therefore, serve as a positive inducement to constituents. Congressman K (Chapter Six) describes the effect of his open office hours:

> We send out 9,000 or 10,000 letters in each area telling them when I'll be there. Each person who comes gets five minutes with the congressman. About forty people come, but several thousand know we have been around and *know they could see me if they wished*. Politically, that's more important than the forty.

His invitations are advertising; but they are at the same time invitations to communicate. "If you are visible to people and you take care of their problems," Congressman K sums up, "then you give them good government and you stay in office. It's one case where politics, in the crudest sense of the word, and representative government are compatible." At its best, in other words, advertising can lead to visibility and visibility can lead to two-way communication.

Responsiveness and, hence, representation require two-way communication. Although the congressman can engage in this kind of communication with only some of his supportive constituents, he can give many more the assurance that two-way communication is possible. That is exactly the kind of assurance most members try to give their supportive constituents by going home as much as they do, by presenting themselves in the great variety of contexts they do, by identifying with as many of their constituents as they can, and even, as we have said, by some of their advertising. Above all, perhaps, they stress their accessibility. Access to some carries the assurance of access to more; and the assurance of access carries with it the assurance of two-way communication. The more accessible they are, House members believe, the more will their constituents be encouraged to feel that they can communicate with the congressman when and if they wish. As we have said frequently, however, this kind of assurance is not obtained by one-shot offers. It is created over a long time and underwritten by trust. Access and the assurance of access, communication and the assurance of communication — these are irreducible underpinnings of representation. They are the elements of representation highlighted in the variety of home styles we have studied.

All this is the view from over the congressman's shoulder: nearly everything he does to win and hold support — allocating, reaching, presenting, responding, communicating, explaining, assuring — involves representation. It is a view of representation as a process. It is a view of representation as politics, with all of the uncertainties of politics. It is a view, however, that has the net effect of making representation less policy-centered than it usually is. Traditionally, representation has been treated mostly as a structural relationship in which the congruence between the policy preferences of the represented and the policy decisions of the representative is the measure of good representation. The key question we normally ask is: "How well does Representative X represent his or her district?" And we answer the question by matching and calibrating substantive policy agreements. But we need to know, as well, the answer to an intertwining question: "How does Representative X win and hold his or her district?" This is the question of political support. And to answer it we shall need to consider more than policy preferences and policy agreements.[9] We shall have to consider a broader range of House member behavior — the sorts of behavior we have summed up under the rubric of home style.

We shall have to consider the possibility that supportive constituents may want extrapolicy behavior from their representatives. They may want good access or the assurance of good access as much as they want good policy. They may want "a good man" or "a good woman," someone whose assurances they can trust, as much as they want good policy. They may want communication promises as much as they want policy promises. The point is not that policy preferences are not a crucial basis for the representational relationship. They are. The point is that we should not start our studies of representation by assuming they are the only basis for a representational relationship. They are not.

At the conclusion of Chapter Six we hazarded the guess, based on the congressman's-eye view of his various constituencies, that home style would somehow have to take its place beside party identification and issue voting as a key variable in the study of congressional elections. Indeed, the small but growing political science literature on the subject contains evidence and speculation — usually offered as explanations for the rising proincumbent vote — that voters are looking to candidate-centered reasons for tendering their support in congressional elections.[10] That is what House members believe: that though voters want to know the policy positions of their representatives, they are equally or more interested in using issue presentations as an opportunity to judge their representative as a person. The presentation of policy positions is one of several ways by which voters decide whom they should trust. It was one of the most issue-oriented members who said, "Issues are not as important as the treatment of issues." Some members of Congress choose home styles that emphasize issues; some do not. Both make their choices to gain or keep electoral support; one is no more or less concerned to provide representation than the other.

In thinking about representation here, we have stressed the basic importance of two-way communication. And communication is a stylistic matter, not a substantive policy matter. If there is to be congruence between the policy preferences of the represented and the policy decisions of the representative, however, two-way communication between them is a prerequisite. At least, in a democracy it is. Members of Congress believe, if anything, that two-way communication is more valued by their constituents than policy congruence. They believe, therefore, that in doing whatever they do to enhance two-way communication — especially between themselves and their supportive constituents — giving constituents access or the assurance of access, listening to constituent views, explaining their views to their constituents, educating their constituents, they also enhance the representative relationship.

Some readers may see in all this subordination of "policy" or "the issues" a calculated effort by House members to avoid policy congruence. But it is our view that members see the representational relationship as involving more than policy congruence. And we have tried, in view of the manifest imperfections of the representative relationship, to find, in the behavior we have observed, a set of activities that may be important to representation. We have found such activities in home style, especially as home style promotes access and two-way communication, and the trust-based assurances of same. We have subjected style to the same kinds of analyses ordinarily reserved for policy — stylistic constraints on member behavior, replacement versus conversion as the mode of stylistic change, and so forth. We have tried to encourage attention to the extrapolicy aspects of representation, not as substitutes for or alternatives to the policy aspects, but as providing a more complete view of what representation is all about. If, of course, the members of Congress are wrong about the importance of such matters as access, communication, and trust, then we are probably wrong too. For they believe that such things are not only desired by their constituents but are desirable for good representation.

Normative theorists, on the other hand, have a tendency to think of policy congruence as the only legitimate basis of representation, and to denigrate extrapolicy bases of representation as "symbolic." Their view of much of what this book describes presumably would be that it is not substantive or real. A reading of the book should alter that view, as a descriptive matter. What the congressman does at home is very real and very substantive; but theorists still might not concede their normative point. Is there, however, sufficient reason for holding that a relationship based on policy is superior to one based on home style — of which policy is, at most, only a part — as a standard for representative democracy? It may be objected that a search for support that stresses stylistic compatibilities between the representative and the represented easily degenerates into pure image selling. And, of course, it may. But the search for support that emphasizes policy compatibilities between the representative and the represented easily degenerates into pure position taking. It is, perhaps, the signal contribution of David Mayhew's elegant essay to make exactly this point.[11] Position taking is just as misleading to constituents and as manipulative of their desires as image selling. It may be just as symbolic as any form of candidate advertising.

Either representational base, we conclude, may take a corrupt form. Appearing to do something about policy without a serious intention of, or demonstrable capacity for, doing so is no less a corruption of the representative relationship, no less an impediment to accountability and responsiveness, than is the feigning of two-way communication without a serious intention of establishing it. They are equally corrupt, equally demagogic. They are substitutes for any real effort to help make a viable public policy or to establish genuine two-way communication and trust. At the least, it seems, normative theory ought to take account of both policy and extrapolicy standards of good representation, and acknowledge their respective corruptions.

The traditional focus of political scientists on the policy aspects of representation is probably related to the traditional focus on activity in the legislature. So long as concentration is on what happens in Washington, it is natural that policymaking will be thought of as the main activity of the legislature and representation will be evaluated in policy terms. To paraphrase Woodrow Wilson, it has been our view that Congress in Washington is Congress at work, while Congress at home is Congress on exhibition. The extrapolicy aspects of representational relationships have tended to be dismissed as symbolic — as somehow less substantial than the relationship embodied in a roll call vote in Washington — because what goes on at home has not been observed. For lack of observation, political scientists have tended to downgrade home activity as mere errand running or fence mending, as activity that takes the representative away from the important things — that is, making public policy in Washington. As one small example, the "Tuesday to Thursday Club" of House members who go home for long weekends — have always been criticized out of hand, on the assumption, presumably, that going home and doing things there was, ipso facto, bad. But no serious inquiry was ever undertaken into what they did there or what consequences — other than their obvious dereliction of duty — their home activity might have had. Home activity has been overlooked and denigrated and so, therefore, have those extra-policy aspects of representation which can only be studied at home.

Predictably, the home activities described in this book will be regarded by some readers as further evidence that members of Congress spend too little of their time "on the job" — that is, in Washington, making policy. However, I hope readers will take from the book a different view — a view that values both Washington and home activity. Further, I hope readers will entertain the view that Washington and home activities may even be mutually supportive. Time spent at home can be time spent in developing leeway for activity undertaken in Washington. And that leeway in Washington should be more valued than the sheer number of contact hours spent there. If that should happen, we might then ask House members not to justify their time spent at home, but rather to justify their use of the leeway they have gained therefrom — during the legislative process in Washington. It may well be that a congressman's behavior in Washington is crucially influenced by the pattern of support he has developed at home, and by the allocational, presentational, and explanatory styles he displays there. To put the point most strongly, perhaps we can never understand his Washington activity without also understanding his perception of his various constituencies and the home style he uses to cultivate their support.

Professional neglect of the home relationship has probably contributed to a more general neglect of the representational side of Congress's *institutional* capabilities. It seems that the more one focuses on the home activities of its members, the more one comes to appreciate the representative strengths and possibilities of Congress. Congress is — as James Madison, George Mason and their colleagues intended it to be — *the most representative* of our national political institutions. The Supreme Court does not even claim to be representative; and every president's predictable claim to be "president of all the people" should be viewed as just that — a claim, not a fact. To travel around in as few districts as eighteen, is to realize how great a diversity there is in the United States and how much of that diversity is mirrored in the Congress. Although Congress is in no sense that "exact transcript" of American society which some of the founders sought, nonetheless its members remain accessible to, in contact with, in communication with, and understanding of a vast variety of constituencies. Congress, not the president, best represents the diversity of the country; and members of Congress, not the president, are in closest touch with the people who live in the country.

The representational strength of Congress — in both policy and extrapolicy terms — may yet be recognized as its foremost institutional strength. It will surely be noted, against this view, that the representational strength of Congress is also a source of institutional weakness — a slowness, even an incapacity, to act. We probably should concede that Congress is, and always will be, our slow institution. (The matter of incapacity probably need not be conceded!) But an institution that is both representative and slow may have its special merits. It can work out and reflect a consensus view in the country, in circumstances where that consensus takes a considerable length of time to jell. That was one of the great accomplishments of the lengthy impeachment inquiry in 1974. People who criticized the House Judiciary Committee for its lack of speed missed the whole point of the slow but sure consensus building that went on — in the country and in the country's committee. Furthermore, news gatherers, who wanted to understand and interpret committee activity found that they had to move outside Washington to examine the home relationships of the Judiciary Committee members.[12] It was an acknowledgment that the strengths of that particular congressional performance were derived from its representational strength. On further inspection, most congressional successes may be found to be similarly grounded.

Consensus decisions are likely to be regarded as fair decisions. And what we shall be needing from our national institutions in the future — more than speed — are decisions that are felt to be fair. If we are going to try to convert a society based on assumptions of plenty to a society based on assumptions of scarcity, the government will have to call on the citizenry to sacrifice. Citizens will be willing to sacrifice only if they believe the government's communicative practices and allocative decisions are fair. An institution that is representative and slow, and also effective at consensus building, may be our best candidate for our fair institution. It will be no trivial challenge for the Congress.

However strong and however important Congress may be as a national institution, it has not fared well recently in public esteem. In May 1976, only 9 percent of the public expressed "a great deal of confidence" in the institution — an all-time low, following a decade of steady deterioration.[13] I shall offer no explanation here. But I shall offer a home-related conjecture. It is that most citizens find it hard or impossible to think about Congress as an institution. They answer questions about it; but they cannot conceptualize it as a collectivity. They think only about their own representative — whom they tend to judge quite favorably, primarily on the basis of his or her home style. When a House member becomes involved in scandal, for example, the nation in general reacts unfavorably. Congress's reputation suffers. But the member's *own* constituents usually re-elect him.[14] They do not think of what the institution would be like if every district returned a member tainted with scandal. Nor do they think about how the general public will feel about Congress with their member as a part of it. They think only about their relationship with their member. Everything we have said in this book tells us that this is exactly how each representative wants his or her constituents to think. Representatives do very little, in other words, to help their supportive constituents to conceptualize the House as an institution. And if they do not encourage their constituents to think that way, the people will be much less likely to think about, much less appreciate, the institutional strengths of the House.

If a member discusses the House as an institution in order to point out its institutional strengths, he or she runs the risk of being associated with an unpopular institution. So members tend their own constituency relations and even attack Congress from time to time to reenforce their customized political support at home. Whether or not such behavior contributes to the decline of confidence in Congress, it surely does nothing to balance the scales. It is a chicken-egg problem. It is also a problem of governance. Representative government requires more than accountability and responsiveness to constituents; it also requires the governing of constituents. From our home perspective it appears that most members of Congress have enough leeway at home, if they have the will, to educate their constituents in the strengths, as well as the weaknesses, of their institution. They have more leeway than they allow others — even themselves — to think. They can, in other words, identify themselves with their own institution even at the risk of taking some responsibility for what it does. They can, that is, if they will view the trust of their supportive constituents as working capital — not just to be hoarded for personal benefit but to be drawn on, occasionally, for the benefit of the institution. It will be a risk. But by taking that risk, they avoid a possibly greater risk: that Congress may lack public support at the very time when the public needs Congress the most. It would be a tragedy if its representational strength goes unrecognized and unused because the very representatives who make it strong are afraid to acknowledge that strength or use it to help govern the country.

NOTES

1. It is unlikely, however, that the tension between Washington and home will be resolved by an influx of home-oriented members. The home-oriented newcomers presently in the House have been at the forefront of reform efforts which have decentralized power in the House, thus multiplying their own Washington responsibilities. By acting so as to "spread the action" internally, they have acted to speed up and to enlarge the demands of the Washington career upon them. Thus they have heightened rather than relieved the tension between the two careers. We can look forward, probably, to more heat in both kitchens.

2. The 370 names were taken from the list of living former members and their residences maintained by Former Members of Congress, an organization located in Washington, D.C. Their 1975 lists included 674 former members. We have eliminated from our calculations all those who left Congress before 1954, all those who ran for the Senate, and all those who represented Virginia or Maryland — states we have classified as Washington, D.C., for purposes of residency.

3. The most admirable effort to connect home events (i.e., recruitment) with Washington behavior is Leo Snowiss, "Congressional Recruitment and Representation," *American Political Science Review* 60 (September 1966), pp. 627–39. But his study failed to yield a coherent or reliable classification of performance patterns in Washington. Other attempted classifications of legislative styles (i.e., insider-outsider, trustee-delegate) have not been convincingly related to behavior.

4. David Mayhew, *The Electoral Connection* (New Haven: Yale University Press, 1974). But as Mayhew also notes, when a member "register(s) an elaborate set of pleasing positions, (it is) a course that reduces the chances of vote trading." *Ibid.*, 121.

5. It is the only weakness of Hanna Pitkin's study of representation that she employs a monolithic view of "the constituency" in her analysis. Had she not separated the problem of running for office from the problem of representation, she would have been pulled toward a more differentiated, complex view of the constituency. She understands the complexity but does not incorporate it into her study. Hanna Pitkin, *The Concept of Representation* (Berkeley: University of California Press, 1972).

6. Kenneth Prewitt, "Political Ambitions, Volunteerism and Electoral Accountability," *American Political Science Review* 54 (March 1970): 15–17. Evidence on the seriousness with which House members take the representational aspects of their job is found in Roger Davidson, *The Role of the Congressman* (New York: Pegasus, 1969), pp. 84–86.

7. For citizens, of course, the lesson is clear: organize, ask, and your congressman will come running.

8. Mayhew, *The Electoral Connection*.

9. A strong argument for paying attention to the political support question will be found in John C. Wahlke, "Policy Demands and System Support: The

Role of the Represented" *British Journal of Political Science* 1 (July 1971): 271–290.

10. Alan Abramowitz, "Name Familiarity, Reputation and the Incumbency Effect in a Congressional Election," *The Western Political Science Quarterly* 28 (December 1975): 668–84; Albert Cover, "One Good Term Deserves Another: The Advantage of Incumbency in Congressional Elections," paper delivered at American Political Science Association Convention, Chicago, September 1976; John Ferejohn, "On the Decline of Competition in Congressional Elections," *American Political Science Review* 71 (March 1977): 166–76; Morris Fiorina, "The Case of the Vanishing Marginals: The Bureaucracy Did It," *American Political Science Review* 71 (March 1977): 177–81; Robert Arseneau and Raymond Wolfinger, "Voting Behavior in Congressional Elections," paper delivered at the American Political Science Convention, New Orleans, 1973. See also Edward N. Muller, "The Representation of Citizens by Political Authorities: Consequences for Regime Support," *American Political Science Review* 64 (December 1970): 1149–66, esp. p. 1157; Glenn R. Parker and Roger H. Davidson, "Bases of Public Assessments of Governmental Performance: The Content of Congressional Evaluations," unpublished paper, University of California, Santa Barbara.

11. Mayhew, *The Electoral Connection.*

12. An elaboration will be found in Richard F. Fenno Jr., "Strengthening a Congressional Strength," paper presented at a conference on "The Role of Congress" sponsored by *Time*, Inc., Washington, D.C., 1975, and reprinted in *Congress Reconsidered*, ed. Lawrence Dodd and Bruce Oppenheimer (New York: Praeger, 1977), pp. 261–268.

13. Harris Survey, Rochester *Democrat and Chronicle*, May 20, 1976.

14. Another discussion will be found in Richard F. Fenno Jr., "If, As Ralph Nader Says, Congress Is the 'Broken Branch,' How Come We Love Our Congressmen So Much?" paper presented at *Time* Inc. Symposium, December 1972, and reprinted in *Congress in Change*, ed. Norman Ornstein (New York: Praeger, 1974), pp. 277–287.

Notes on Method:
Participant Observation

METHOD AND PROJECT

In a book that urges more scholarly attention to congressional activity outside of Washington, D.C., it might be helpful to say something about how this kind of research is done. This is a kind of research — the study of people in their natural setting — that is not much written about by political scientists. Described in the Introduction as "soaking and poking — or just hanging around," it is more formally known as field research, or qualitative research, or — our preference — participant observation.[1] This Appendix elaborates our earlier description. It is a largely autobiographical case study of participant observation, written less about how this kind of research is done than about how one particular research project was done. However, because of the current dearth of understanding of these research methods — in this case a blend of observation, interviewing, and participation — even a case study can have broad benefits.

In the first place, students of Congress may find some instructive comparisons with Washington-based research. There, the typical researcher starts with a set of questions, obtains appointments with some set of legislators, goes to each legislator's office for a forty-five-minute interview, leaves, and moves on to the next interview. That is what my own experience had been. Many of the problems of research in the district are the same as those encountered on Capitol Hill because, after all, both take place in the milieu of the legislator. But in home district research, one typically watches, listens to, and talks to one congressman morning, noon, and night for several days. This degree of immersion in the natural setting is so great that it is a qualitatively different experience from that on Capitol Hill — a research difference to match the behavioral differences reported in the book. Or so, at least, it seemed to me; and it is the primary reason for writing this Appendix.[2]

In the second place, political scientists with a general interest in method may find the following comments helpful in bringing participant observation more comfortably under the tent of political science methodology. As long as political scientists continue to study politicians, some of us certainly will want to collect data through repeated interaction with these politicians in their natural habitats. If that is so, we should be as self-conscious as we can be about this kind of political science activity and about the relationship between political scientists and politicians that it entails. And not just because people doing this kind of research can benefit; but also because, through their lack of understanding, political scientists who do not do this kind of research can unintentionally impede the work of those who do.

Furthermore, participant observation does have some method to it. It is difficult to standardize in canonical form — a difficulty which will become exasperatingly obvious in a moment. One can hardly be very pretentious about it. Still, a research project like this one does not just happen; it does not proceed without a degree of planning and care and methodological worry. It is these "worries," perhaps, that are most revealing about any research project. I hope the particular worries of this one will be instructive to those political scientists who like to generalize about methodological worries.

Research based on participant observation is likely to have an exploratory emphasis. Someone doing this kind of research is quite likely to have no crystallized idea of what he or she is looking for or what questions to ask when he or she starts. Researchers typically become interested in some observable set of activities and decide to go have a firsthand look at them. They fully expect that an open-minded exposure to events in the milieu and to the perspectives of those with whom they interact will produce ideas that might never have occurred to them otherwise. Only after prolonged, unstructured soaking is the problem formulated. Indeed, the reformulation of a problem or a question may be the end product of the research. The idea of home style had never occurred to me until I had taken quite a few trips around the country. I had been interested in a very different set of questions when I began my travels — questions of perception and questions relating these perceptions to behavior on Capitol Hill, especially roll call voting. I was not at all interested in the effect of perceptions on behavior in the district. In other words, participant observation seems less likely to be used to test an existing hypothesis than to formulate hypotheses for testing by others or to uncover some relationship that strikes others as worth hypothesizing about and testing. It may be an appropriate method, however, at *any* stage of a research endeavor where there is a felt need for a fresh line of thought.

This particular project was undertaken for several reasons. Like any other political scientist interested in representative-constituent relations, I had been teaching the received wisdom on the subject. Part of that wisdom tells us that the representative's *perception* of his or her constituency is an important variable. But, in the absence of much empirical exposition of such perceptions and in the presence of politicians who seemed less than cognizant of all segments of their "constituency," I had been telling students that the subject — like dozens of others every term — deserved "further research." Someone, I kept saying, should address the perceptual question: What does a member of Congress see when he or she sees a constituency? The decision to be that someone was made, however, partly because the perceptual question seemed researchable by a method I had used before and with which I felt especially secure — the personal interview. The method was not the only method available; but it was appropriate to the question I wanted to answer. Had it not been for the appropriateness of a familiar method, the perceptual question would undoubtedly have been left for someone else.

I had no idea what kinds of answers I would get. I had no idea what questions to ask. I knew only that I wanted to get some number of House members to talk about their constituency perceptions — up and down and all around the subject. I knew that I had had some practice talking to legislators and that if I had developed any professional skills as a political scientist it was as an interviewer of, and a listener to, politicians. My hope was that I might be able to piece together their perceptions, categorize them in some way, and generalize about them. The decision to interview, to watch, and to listen *in the districts* was made simultaneously with the decision to do the research. I thought that if I could see what they saw in the district at the same time they saw it, I could better understand their perceptual statements. I could not only listen, but I could listen in context. I could check what I heard *from* them with what I observed *with* them — something I could not do in a Capitol Hill office interview.

There were other reasons for doing this research in this particular way. First, all my previous research had been conducted in Washington, from a Washington perspective. I knew intellectually that activity in Washington reflects to some uncertain degree what people are saying, thinking, and doing out in the country; but I felt I did not know what went on "out there." I wanted to acquire, at first hand, this extra-Washington perspective. Indeed, in the early months of the research, I spoke of myself primarily as a traveler, as a John Steinbeck without a camper or a "Charlie." Thus, the research question appealed to me partly because the research site — the country — appealed to me.

As a sometime Congress-watcher, I also felt that interviews were becoming increasingly difficult to get in Washington, as more and more researchers descended on the Capitol and as senators and representatives felt beset by ever more burdensome job demands. I had then (and I have now) no doubt whatever that good interviews can be obtained on Capitol Hill. But a personal reaction I had had to the increasing difficulty was to wonder whether a better quality interview might not be had — irrespective of subject matter — if the legislator could be approached in some setting other than the Capitol Hill office. Because of my interest in perceptions, a constituency interview seemed particularly appealing. The member's view of a constituency, I guessed, would take shape mainly *in the constituency* rather than in Washington. Furthermore, it would probably take shape within many different contexts within each constituency. So, the more contexts I could place the member in, the richer would be the perspectives he or she would communicate to me. The standard Capitol Hill interview captures the legislator at one point in time, in one mood, in one response set, in one interaction; a few days in the district, however, might yield a variety of such contextual factors. Besides, it seemed, the House member might just have more time to talk and be more relaxed in the home environment. All this seemed plausible — that interview *quality* might be better in the home setting. The opportunity to test this hunch gave the project added appeal.

Finally, once the idea seemed appealing enough to undertake

"sometime," it was clear that the time had to be soon. Not to start immediately might mean I would never do it. That is because I think field research on Congress is a young person's game. It requires a degree of physical stamina and psychological adaptability that, taken together, are optimized in people of their twenties and thirties more than in their forties and fifties (even though people in their forties do have the advantage of being closer to the average age of House members). So I figured that I had better get going before I became too weary or too inflexible to tolerate the discomforts endemic to this type of data-grubbing operation.

THE "SAMPLE"

Once the decision was made to do the research, the question became: Whom should I observe? This is, somewhat elegantly, the sample problem. My answer at the beginning was I don't know; my answer today is I'm not sure. Nothing better characterizes the open-ended, slowly emerging, participant observation research than this admission. If I had been certain about what types of representatives and what types of districts to sample, I would already have had answers to a lot of the questions raised in this book. My procedure was slowly to build up the size of the group being observed and constantly to monitor its composition to see what commonly recognized types of members or districts I might be neglecting. Then I would move to remedy any imagined deficiencies. I spent a lot of time trying to figure out a priori what types of members or districts might pose serious tests for, or exceptions to, whatever generalizations seemed to be emerging — with the intent of bringing such members or districts into the group. At one point, I noticed there were too many lawyers; the next two people I chose were nonlawyers. At another point, I had been traveling with a string of younger members; the next one I chose was a House veteran. My *Almanac of American Politics* is dog-eared from constant thumbing; and my note folders are still thick with tentative, revised, and re-revised lists of prospective traveling companions. Articles about congressional politics and congressional elections, census statistics, the *Congressional Record* were read with an eye to the adequacy of the current "sample." Do I have one of these? Should I? What is the marginal value of one of these as opposed to one of those? In 1974 I pursued a target of opportunity, by loading up on Republicans whom I could watch explain their impeachment vote. By the time I reached their districts, however, the need to explain had evaporated; and I had to use two House members not in my group as examples in Chapter 5. As a result, the group remains unrepresentatively Republican (ten Democrats, eight Republicans).

Of course, in no technical sense do I have a sample. But I did not make a decision to travel with any member without first assessing or reassessing the characteristics he or she might add to the group and without comparing each addition with several other possibilities. Each person added to the list represented a heavy commitment of my time, energy, and money, so no decision was made lightly. And no decision was made quickly. In 1970, the group numbered four; in 1972 it jumped to twelve; in 1974 it went to sixteen; and in 1976 it stopped at eighteen. Decisions were made deliberately, but on the basis of limited information, by incremental, successive comparison. The decision to stop at eighteen was arbitrary, occasioned not by the thought that the "sample" was complete, but by the thought that it was about time to stop running around and to begin to communicate what I was finding.

I have tried to assemble what I thought would be a variety of House members and districts. I shall not add to the discussion of demographics in the Introduction — partly because I wish to help preserve anonymity, partly because I do not believe that any eighteen members could ever be definitely established as representative, and partly because the text provides a basis for some judgments as to what types have been included or excluded. I have tried to make it clear, however, that no claims are being made for the representativeness of the group — only for its adequacy in opening up the subject for scholarly inquiry.

One nonobvious criterion worth mentioning is "receptivity to academics." During my previous research on Congress, I formulated a heuristic proposition: there are only two classes of legislators in the world — "good interviews" and "bad interviews." There is a great temptation to apply this proposition to district research by saying, "I'll only travel with people I already know are articulate, responsive, and comfortable with academics." But if I do that, if I limit my group to "good interviews," won't that produce bias? The easy way out would be to avoid the pain of dealing with people who are suspicious of academics, difficult to reach, and difficult to interview. But at what price? Once, I wrote to a political science friend asking him to recommend which of two House members from his state I should select. He recommended one on the grounds that he was well regarded by the local political scientists. He called the other "a clunk . . . who has made no impression here." I decided to go with the "clunk," precisely because he had a style that seemed unappealing to academics. By recognizing a variation on the receptivity problem, I was able to offset it. And I was able to formulate a second heuristic proposition: Beware of political scientists bearing gifts of access. In the end, seven of the eighteen members were people who were used to and comfortable with academics, six were neither accustomed to nor comfortable with academics, and five were somewhere in between on this version of the at-homeness index.

It is an obvious characteristic of this project, and of participant observation research generally, that it deals with a small number of cases. It is the "small N" that makes this type of research unamenable to statistical analysis. At the point in the project when I had traveled with twelve members, I gave much thought to collaborating with another political scientist and interviewing a much larger, more reliable sample of House members, one that would give us the chance to do some statistical analysis. I finally decided that I did not yet feel confident that I knew what to ask in such a survey-type questionnaire and that I preferred, for the time being, to proceed with the study of a few cases. It was a deliberate decision to sacrifice analytical range for analytical depth. It was also a decision that placed severe limits on the number of members who could be studied — twenty, no more than twenty-five. The problem is one of span of control, the control of one mind. Each case must be known in depth. Regular contact with each member must be maintained. As a matter of fact, I never did keep in as close contact as I wished. But the desire not to fall too far out of touch set limits to the size of the group. So, too, did financial and professional constraints. This kind of research is both costly and hard to finance. And I could not get away from the classroom as often as would be necessary to travel personally with very many members.

Table A charts the thirty-six trips made to the various districts between 1970 and 1977. It also charts the spacing between visits to each of the eighteen members. As noted in the Introduction, the vast majority of the trips were made in election years; mostly in the fall. That was the easiest time to catch members at home, to parlay consecutive visits, and to observe in the greatest number of contexts.

Table A Timing and Spacing of District Visits

	Jan.	Feb.	March	April	May	June	July	August	Sept.	Oct.	Nov.	Dec.	Totals	
													Trips	Days
1970						A[a]-3[b]				B-3[c] A-2 C-3	D-4		5	15
1971					A-2 C-3								2	5
1972				E-3	F-2		G-2 H-3 I-3		D-4	J-5 K-4 L-3			9	29
1973													0	0
1974						F-3	G-2		M-4 I-4	N-3 O-3 J-2 H-4 B-3 A-4		P-2	11	34
1975													0	0
1976		N-3		P-3	Q-4				C-3	M-3 R-3 D-3			7	22
1977					Q-3 O-2								2	5
Totals Trips	0	1	0	2	6	2	4	0	4	15	1	1	36	
Days	0	3	0	6	16	6	10	0	15	48	4	2		110

[a] Representatives are given identifying letters (A, B, etc.) in the order in which I visited their districts. These letters bear no relation to the letters given to representatives in the text.

[b] The number opposite the representative's identifying letter is the number of working days I spent in the district on that particular trip. It does not include traveling time except when I accompanied the member on an active schedule on the same day I traveled.

[c] Within any given month, I have preserved the order in which I took the trips.

It may have distorted my view of home activity by giving it an intensity it might not have had during another part of the electoral cycle. In some cases, that was surely true. But the out-of-season visits displayed the same variations in intensity as the in-season ones, leading me to guess that generalization about seasonal effects would be hazardous. The chart clearly shows, however, that one watches certain people at certain times of their lives and their careers. If I had come earlier or returned later, each individual might have shown a different face, a different home style. If I had come at some period other than 1970 to 1977, member attacks on their institution might not have been so strong; or, the members might not have placed so much emphasis on access. I cannot know. The book's conclusions about individuals and the group are time-bound and cannot be cast in brass. They are only a best estimate — at the time.

ACCESS

I made contact with my prospects in two ways — a personal contact of some sort or "cold turkey." The first four members I took on as an experiment in 1970 were all people with whom I had had some contact — two from my previous research, one whose administrative assistant I knew and one for whom an undergraduate student of mine was working as an intern. In ten of the next fourteen cases, I wrote a "cold turkey" letter. Here is that standard letter:

> Dear Representative _____,
> I am writing to ask if you might be willing to let me travel around with you when you are in your district for a three- or four-day period sometime this spring. I am a professor of political science at the University of Rochester and am writing a book on the relations between congressmen and their constituencies. I'm trying to learn about the subject by accompanying a dozen or so House members as they work in their districts.
> About myself: I am forty-five years old and have been writing in the field of American politics for a number of years. Books I have written include *The President's Cabinet*, 1959, *National Politics and Federal Aid to Education*, 1962, *The Power of the Purse: Appropriations Politics in Congress*, 1966, and *Congressmen in Committees*, to be published in 1973.
> Needless to say, I'd be tremendously pleased if you could see your way clear to letting me accompany you in _____.

> Of course, all of this would be entirely at my own expense. I
> could even come to Washington should you wish to talk with
> me about it in person. I look forward to hearing from you and
> thank you in advance for your consideration of this request.
>   Sincerely,

To this letter, I sometimes added, as a personal reference, the name
of one or two members I had already traveled with — members with
whom the new prospect might have ties. Thus, I pyramided later
trips on the foundation of earlier ones. I know of one case in which
that personal reference was essential. But I have no idea of how
many people took me purely on the face value of the request.

I had two outright refusals. One was from a powerful senior member whom I had met and who had reportedly lost touch with his
district — a type I do not have in my group. He said he wasn't going
to do any campaigning — that he had no opponent and that his wife
was very ill. The second refusal came from a member who wrote,

> I think you would find my kind of activity dull, boring, and
> completely unworthy of your time. I am sure you have a
> limited amount of time and I feel you ought to devote it to
> those areas wherein some of our more dramatic members do
> their work. Accordingly, while I deeply appreciate your in-
> terest, I must respectfully decline the opportunity to work
> with you on your project.

My best guess is that he is suspicious of academics. There is the possibility that my letter, in which I present myself as an academic, will
trigger a strongly negative reaction in some cases.

Arranging a visit to the district is not always easy — mostly because
the plans of House members are subject to sudden changes. I preferred to plan for and schedule certain blocks of time or specific dates
well in advance. The members' tendency was to say "keep in touch
and we'll work something out — maybe around the middle of September." So I would have to place an entire two- or three-week
period "on hold" to accommodate a member. Rather than send out
many letters at once — as one would do before heading for a two-
week stay in Washington — I had to dribble them out in ones or
twos. If distances and expenses were great, it was desirable to co-
ordinate a couple of trips; then, the representatives' vagueness made
planning doubly difficult. In California, I chose the Republican

member partly by asking the administrative assistant of my California Democrat which Republican assistants he got along with, so that *they* could negotiate across offices for a time for a single California visit.

In nearly half of the cases, I had some scheduling choice; someone on the member's staff would read me the itinerary for two or three trips home and ask me to choose. When that happened, I opted for the dates that promised to let me observe the greatest number of events, settings, and locales; and I avoided dates where events — like conventions or lengthy meetings or totally unscheduled days — promised to keep me separated from the congressman. Logistically, the research was always subject to uncertainty. One morning, I had my bag packed at home and was planning to leave for the airport in twenty minutes when the congressman's secretary called to say the deal was off; it was the congressman's birthday, and his wife did not want any outsider around during the festivities. On one occasion, when I had arranged to fly back to Washington with the congressman and had saved up some questions, I overslept and missed the plane entirely — an example of what experimentalists would call "instrument decay."

In this kind of research, which brings you into face-to-face working relationships with influential political people, there needs to be some mutual understanding about the relationships — its boundaries, its proprieties, its exchanges. Because you approach each other as strangers, this mutual understanding is worked out very gradually. It is useful to think of this relationship as a *bargain* between two professionals.

For my part, I began by presenting myself as a serious scholar, with a long-term professional interest in studying Congress. I came seeking information with which to write a book, information that I could not get anywhere else but from them. I presented as little as possible about the details of my project — only the few words necessary to justify a trip to the district, nothing more. My initial commitments were professional, and were unrelated to research content. If, in the letter, I gave the name of another member as a reference, the only quality I suggested they might wish to check on was my "personal integrity." Implicitly I agreed, as a professional scholar, not to write an exposé, not to kiss and tell, not to cause a member personal or political damage, not to quote a member when he or she wished not to be quoted. It was my hope that if I presented myself as a professional, they would realize that I have high standards to uphold and that my career, *just as much as theirs*, would be placed in great jeopardy if I did not keep my end of the bargain.

As for what the projected book was all about, each member formed his own idea of that. Each wanted only to be able to explain to his constituents why I was accompanying him. "He's come to see how we do it here in Southern Illinois." "He's writing a book about how members of Congress campaign back home and has chosen this district to study. If we behave ourselves, we may become a footnote." "He's writing a book about how members of Congress deal with their constituents, and he's using me as a guinea pig. As I understand it, he'll write a book of 500 to 600 pages whose only buyer will be the Library of Congress — and his students. That's what professors do, you know, when they aren't grading papers." "He's collecting a lot of information. I don't know what he'll do with it. But he likes to watch these things. He doesn't bother the women and he doesn't talk too much." A detailed outline of what I was doing was not essential to our bargain. It was almost beside the point. Even when I answered their subsequent (but infrequent) probes by telling them that I was interested in the perceptual question, they continued to internalize and to describe my subject in behavioral terms (i.e., "campaigning," "how we do it," "dealing with constituents," etc.) rather than perceptual terms. This reaction encourages me to think that the perceptual question is, indeed, a political science question. It is not one politicians naturally think about or generalize about.

For their part, why would they enter into this bargain at all? Why would they agree to subject themselves to a presence and a scrutiny that was at best a nuisance and brought no very striking benefits? I was, after all, one of a horde of supplicants — people who wanted something from them. Probably their reasons were varied. For some, the visit may have been a welcome change in the routine, something different. They spend their lives reaching out to include different people within their orbit; and, if they do not normally associate with academics or writers, the opportunity for closer contact with such a person may interest them. For some, acceptance may have been a conditioned reflex. They are used to having journalists ask to interview them, and they view such requests as something that goes with the job. Some may have seen it as part of their civic duty to educate teachers of politics. Some may enjoy attention from whatever quarter — the more so because, compared to senators, they attract so little outside interest. They live by publicity; and any chance to get some, however remote, may be deemed worth an inconvenience. For some, scholarly attention may be flattering, the more so when the scholar comes as a student who wants to learn from them rather than as a professor who wants to instruct them. For some, even, the prospect of an academic amanuensis may have stirred acceptance. Some House members would like to be immortalized between book covers; and political scientists are among the gatekeepers to book covers. For one or more, or none, of these reasons perhaps, they agreed to take me on.

Whatever their reasons, they were all completely confident of their ability to protect themselves. It was, of course, a part of the bargain — which I sometimes mentioned explicitly — that they could exclude me from any event they wished to. House members are, moreover, well practiced in talking for the record. They are, in short, professionals just as I am a professional. My confidence in my ability to get them to talk was matched by their confidence in their ability to say nothing they did not wish to say. If we were equally good at our businesses, then the result would not be a disaster for either of us. Thus, from their point of view, although there might be no big gain from my visit, there would be no big loss either.

When you talk with members of Congress and when you write up your research you are especially aware of acting as a representative of the scholarly community to a relatively small but very important group of people — people whose continued good will is a vital scholarly resource. There is only one United States Congress; and its members stay around for a long time. If you blunder in any way with any of these people, you do irreparable damage to every future congressional scholar and, hence, to the scholarly dialogue. It is not like finding another city in which to study community power or another classroom in which to study political socialization.

When I first went to Washington to study the Appropriations Committee in 1959, only one out of the fifty members refused to speak with me. Less than a month before I arrived, another political scientist had walked into that member's unguarded office late in the day and tried to pressure him into giving an interview. The congressman vowed he would never give an interview to a political scientist; to my knowledge, he never has; and he is now a senior member of the Appropriations Committee. Whether or not there was a cause and effect relationship here, I never forgot the incident. It has underscored a kind of Burkean view of my responsibility to other political scientists. If I leave every relationship I have with a member of Congress in as good or better repair than when I started, then I will leave Congress more, rather than less, accessible to later generations of scholars. In the interview situation, this means: Always act in an interview as if another interview with that same person were to follow soon. Psychologically, if there is no such thing as "the last interview" with a legislator, the impulse to kiss and tell is reduced. This is one way interviewers and participant observers demonstrate a commitment to science. So long as legislators are there and will grant access to political scientists, our fellow scholars can go to them and test any propositions or generalizations we present. I do, therefore, everything I can to help others continue the scientific enterprise by doing all I can to enhance the prospects of future interviewers.

If, in the long run, I think of myself as maintaining access for all congressional scholars, in the shorter run, of course, what I am doing is maintaining access for myself. But that turns out, too, to be a long-term endeavor. When I present my scholarly credentials to a member of Congress, I want them to reflect as good a past record as possible — in the eyes of all types of members. A lot of my personal decisions in life have been made with access problems uppermost in mind. I have not registered in a party; I have not engaged in partisan activity; I sign no political petitions; I join no political organizations or interest groups; I engage in no radio, TV, or newspaper commentary. I do not allow my name to be used for political purposes. Only once have I agreed to testify before Congress, reluctantly, on the subject of committee reorganization, a situation in which I felt I would lose future access unless I paid back members I had interviewed on that very subject. In short, I deliberately keep a low public profile — in the face of countless opportunities to do otherwise.

I do this to maximize the likelihood that *all* senators and *all* representatives and *all* their staffs will accept my professionalism, and to minimize the likelihood that any of them will have heard anything at all of a non-professional nature about me. It is altogether a very conservative approach. The point is that maintaining across-the-board access is a sine qua non of this kind of research, and it is both a long-time and a full-time effort. I keep in touch with a number of staff people as well as House members, by telephone or occasional trips to Washington. A lot of time that my fellow political scientists have to spend keeping up their statistical skills — to keep themselves in research readiness — I have to spend maintaining my access to Congress, likewise, to stay in research readiness. It is a large, yet hidden part of the research iceberg — a capital investment, an overhead cost. All this accumulated effort, for whatever it is worth, went into each travel request I made. Of course, I do not know how much, or whether, it mattered to the recipients. But it matters a lot to me: I worry about it all the time; and I consider it a necessary condition for everything else I do as a political scientist.

The preceding paragraphs have been overloaded with first-person pronouns. The purpose was to accent, for political scientists unfamiliar with the research methods reported here, the indispensability of across-the-board access. There was no intention to speak for, or preach to, other political scientists engaged in field research on Congress. On the main proposition, all will agree. Problems of access are constant topics of conversation, comparison, and debate among congressional scholars. But the solutions we have arrived at are personal ones, and they vary from the deepest involvement in congressional activity to the deepest disdain for it. The personal stance I have reported here is only one variant — not better, not worse than others, just more comfortable for me. It was reported only to illustrate the pervasiveness, the continuousness, and the seriousness of the access problem for people doing participant observation research. It is especially desirable that political scientists who have never encountered the access problem understand its fundamental importance, so that they will not act mindlessly to undermine the research of those colleagues who live by it.

RAPPORT

If access bespeaks a willingness to have me around, then *rapport* bespeaks an added willingness to be forthcoming and frank during our travels. Rapport refers to the state of the personal relationship — of compatibility, of understanding, of trust — between researcher and researched. It cannot be prescribed or taught. Sometimes it is a matter of luck. Always, it is a challenge and a preoccupation. Because you must constantly evaluate the quality of the data you are getting, you must, perforce, constantly evaluate the quality of your relationship with the person who is giving it to you. Much of what you do out in the district is done to enhance your rapport with the people you find there. Mostly, of course, the way you establish good rapport is by being nice to people and trying to see the world as they see it. You need to be patient, come on slow, and feel your way along. Two handy hints: Go where you are driven; take what you are given; and, when in doubt, be quiet. Rapport is less a special talent than a special willingess to work hard — a special commitment. And one reason it is hard work is because of the many contexts and types of people you find yourself confronted with.

I arrived in each district with only the knowledge I had obtained from the *Almanac of American Politics* and *Congressional Quarterly*. I did not do preliminary research, because I wished to come to the scene without preconceptions — to see it as exclusively as possible through the eyes of the member. It was a useful caution. In a district that I had selected because of its exploding population and because I wanted to see how the congressman coped with such instability, I found that he did not see it as I had assumed he would. "There's been a great deal of population change here," he volunteered.

> But beneath that surface change is a fairly stable layer of people who moved to the city between 1945 and 1955. These people have a very parochial feeling about the city. And they resented my opponent who had just moved from [a town twenty-five miles away]. He hadn't lived here before, and I think the old guard kind of resented it. . . . I came to the city, started my law practice and joined the Lion's Club and the Methodist Church. I think those groups were more important to my winning my city council race than the party . . . for volunteer workers and in getting endorsements. Endorsements are very important here if you are a newcomer in politics.

I had the same experience in a border area district, described by political demographers as Copperhead country. The congressman talked constantly about the prevailing weather patterns from the South, but not once during my two visits did he so much as hint at any southern influence on district politics.

Early in my travels, I flew with a congressman to his district. When we got off the plane, we were met by a man who had just picked up several new suits and was delivering them to the congressman. They walked along together; and I immediately concluded that the man must be a district staffer, a person of importance with whom I would be spending a good deal of time. Somewhat later, I learned that he was only a local cheerleader of some sort; and I never saw or heard of him again. But I also later learned that the new wardrobe, which seemed insignificant at the time, provided an important clue to the congressman's home style. One month later, I flew with a second congressman to his district, whereupon we were again met at planeside by a man carrying several suits fresh from the cleaners. Recalling my earlier experience, I made a mental note that here was a typical local flunky, another spear carrier of no consequence to me. It turned out that the man was the congressman's oldest, closest, most trusted, most skilled, most knowledgeable friend.

> I trust Frank more than anyone else in the world. He's the guts of my operation. He knows how I want to say things as well as I know myself. He has insight into political situations that I wouldn't have. . . . He knows one hundred times more about the district than I do.

The freshly cleaned suits carried no clues to the congressman's home style. These twin experiences early in the game helped me learn to feel my way, without preconceptions, into each set of personal relationships and each new context.

When you reach the district, everything is unfamiliar. You confront a strange House member, surrounded by a totally unknown collection of people, in a new political culture, at some unknown point in an unstoppable stream of political events. One member drove fifty miles to the airport to meet me, and took me to stay in his home — thus plunking me into the middle of an unfamiliar family situation. Another arranged to meet me at his campaign headquarters, came and chatted with a group of us for fifteen minutes, and announced, "I'm going to go play golf with my son." Then, as an afterthought to me, "You wanna play golf?" A third had his staff tell me he would meet me at an evening meeting, then canceled the meeting — leaving me riding around a strange city at night running up a huge taxi bill. The next day he kept me waiting in his district office most of the day; and when at last he met me he said, "You should have been with us at my talk this morning. Sorry we didn't tell you about it."

Of these three situations, the most difficult is the last. In this research, getting to your respondent is the name of the game. The entire object of the trip to the district is to accompany and talk with the member — in as many contexts as possible. Yet it may not be easy. Interviewers on Capitol Hill are familiar with the secretary-gatekeeper who guards the member's office door and considers it a duty to protect the member from academic questioners. And we are familiar with the tactics — blandishment, persistence, outside intervention — for circumventing the office gatekeeper. In the district also there are gatekeepers, but they come in more complicated varieties; they may be members of the family, district staffers, campaign staffers, local politicos, and long-time personal friends. In fifteen years of interviewing on Capitol Hill, I never walked into a congressman's office and found his wife there. Yet in eight district visits, I spent a great deal of my time in the company of wives — most of whom were suspicious of my motives and the effect of my activities on their husbands' careers. Several district operations were strictly "mom and pop" enterprises. Wives, like other gatekeepers, can facilitate rapport or retard it. Gaining rapport with them and with the other people around the member can be nearly as important and just as challenging as achieving it with the member.

Almost always, you are thrown into a close and necessary interaction with district gatekeepers in a way that never happens in Washington. In Washington, you may choose to spend time with a staff member; in the district, it is not a matter of choice. I was able to ride around the district alone with only five of the eighteen members. And on only six of the thirty-six visits did I do so consistently. Nearly always, therefore, someone other than the congressman drives. Sometimes there is an entourage. The researcher rarely gets the undivided attention he gets in the congressman's Washington office. I once spent my entire three-day trip riding around attending events with a congressman, his wife, and a freshly hired district representative. The insecure district aide spent every spare minute trying to impress the congressman and ingratiate himself with the wife. He never stopped talking. I could hardly squeeze a question in edgewise. Obviously, his need for rapport was as great as mine and his claim on the congressman's time greater. I had no choice but to wait him out.

Waiting, I should note, usually paid off. The members came to feel that, as part of the bargain, they owed me something for my time and trouble. And I could count on a pang of conscience to give me what I came for. In this case, the congressman, his wife, and I went to dinner — minus the staffer — my last night in town. On the other hand, a secure and sympathetic staff member is the best insurance you can carry while in the district. In half the districts, staffers were of major importance to me, as informants, interpreters, intercessors and friends. In two cases, the wives were extremely helpful. This is not lone ranger research. Relations with the district gatekeepers are inevitable, important, and hard to predict.

Obviously, one key to effective participant observation is to blend into each situation as unobtrusively as possible. Oftentimes, the easiest way to do this is to become an active participant. When the opportunity to participate presented itself, I snapped it up. It is an easy way to increase rapport with everyone concerned — gatekeepers as well as members. Once, for example, I arrived in a district in time to make a Friday night event, only to find the congressman had been unable to leave Washington. I called his campaign headquarters; a staffer came to pick me up and took me to headquarters to meet a collection of campaign managers and workers. They answered a few questions ("How's it going?" etc.) and then went back to their work. I sat down beside someone and started stamping and sealing a huge stack of envelopes. An hour or two later, someone asked me to help with a telephone poll, which I did. Most of the people there had no idea who I was; those who did didn't know what to do with me; and no one came to speak to me. I didn't know who they were or what each person's relationship to the congressman might be. That set of circumstances is very common. But I busied myself; and late in the evening I was shown the results of the confidential telephone poll. When I met the congressman in the morning, he greeted me with "Herr Professor, I dub thee Knight of the Telephone Poll. I hear you did yeoman service. We're going to have a campaign strategy meeting. Come on." During my ostensibly unproductive evening, I accumulated enough extra capital to be taken in as one of the group.

I have had the same results from handing out leaflets, pens, recipe books, pot holders, and shopping bags, from putting stickers on car bumpers and campaign cards under windshield wipers, and from riding around in a sound truck. Less political activities, too, proved helpful — bouncing around with the congressman on a storefront water bed, winning $19.00 from the congressman at bridge, fixing the congressman's flat tire on a mountain road, thumbing a ride when the congressman and I ran out of gas at midnight. Members can identify with you easier if you engage in some activity — any activity — with them than they can through just answering your questions. The shared experience provides a special bond for a long time thereafter. "We missed you on election night," they often said months later, not because they really missed me but because they had come to include me in a special category — a category I had not been in when I first arrived on the scene.

The more immersed one becomes in the member's district activities, the more the terms of the original bargain change and are fleshed out. Time almost always produces better rapport. Over time there are opportunities such as the participant activities just recounted, to demonstrate personal adaptability. My hope was that whereas, at the time of the initial bargain, I might have been viewed prospectively as a professorial pain in the ass, I would come to be recognized as someone who adjusts easily to the unpredictability of events, shows sensitivity to the moods of others, and needs no periodic psychological feedings. I hoped they might learn that college professors are not aloof or overbearing or self-important, that the political scientist in their midst could be ignored, patronized, laughed at, forgotten, and ordered about without being offended. In time, then, they might come to respect, if not like, a professional who would put up with all the incivilities of a political campaign to get what he wanted — one who took notes, not umbrage. Whenever working politicians can be convinced that they have found someone who wants to and does understand them and their life, they will, I believe, open up more than they would otherwise.

Rapport is increased, too, by the demonstration of loyalty. I took every opportunity, verbal or behavioral, to reassure them that I would not use my experience or my information to hurt them, that I was a person who could be trusted. My participation — materially trivial — was a symbolic tender of loyalty to them. I never asked people I met in the district what they thought of the member. Thus I eliminated the possibility of anyone telling the member or his associates that I was soliciting unfavorable opinions. When unfavorable evaluations of the member were offered to me, I would exit as quickly as possible. When members asked me who else I had traveled with, I willingly told them. A few names — of members they would be likely to know — invariably satisfied their curiosity. When they asked what I had learned from the others, my standard reply was "All districts are different and each member has different problems." By not saying more, I hoped to signal them that I could be trusted with *their* information, too. I let them know that I was not interested in their opponent's campaign. I also told them that (except in California and New York) I was only interested in one member per state, so that local political or personal conflicts would not intrude. I told them, in other words, that within the scope of their political world, I recognized a single loyalty — to them.

I did not openly evaluate their performance — offering either praise or criticism — because my posture was one of learning not judging. Requests for evaluation that might be interpretable as tests of my political intelligence were answered — as vaguely as would suffice. After his television debate with his opponent, one member asked me directly, "How did I do? A little too namby-pamby?" Answer: "If you think you are ahead, you were right not to get into charge and countercharge with him. It would only give him the publicity he needs." It was a less common kind of exchange than one might imagine.

If members found it beneficial to display me before their constituents, I allowed myself to be exploited. One member introduced me at public functions as evidence that people in other parts of the country were interested in their locality. He even introduced me in church, whereupon the minister said, as I stood amid the congregation, "Now you write good things about our congressman." Another member asked me to stay an extra day to accompany him to a college speaking engagement where he wished, I assumed, to show that group that he was at home in academic company. I agreed — as a tender of loyalty, as an extension of the bargain, and as a guarantor of our future relationships.

Only one of my group was defeated. After my postelection interview with him, I decided to get in touch with the person who defeated him, my idea being that two perspectives on the same district would be instructive. But I faced a test of my devotion to a single loyalty. Should I tell the new member that I had already traveled in the district with his defeated opponent, during the bitter election campaign? If I told him, would it contaminate all his answers? If

I didn't, would I be uncomfortable acting deceitfully? I played out both possibilities at length in my mind, and finally decided that my end of the bargain required that I reveal my previous incarnation. The opportunity came before his press aide and I had left the airport. "Have you ever been here before?" "Yes, with your opponent two months ago." So far as I can tell, it did not matter. My flirtation with covert research ended.

Success in developing rapport varied. Half of them took me along when they were with their closest friends or advisors, their personal constituency. And there is not one whom I could not embarrass politically if I were to repeat remarks they made in confidence. Consider this running commentary by a member contemplating his annual appearance at a Veteran's Day observance — a member whose status as a veteran had once been essential in maintaining his reelection constituency:

> One of the things I least like to do is to sit upon the platform with my veteran buddies. [But] I'll go and put on my long face. . . . Next year my wife will have to come to this instead of me. She doesn't believe in veterans, doesn't believe in cemeteries, and doesn't even believe in the Good Lord. . . . Maybe if I win by 65 percent, I won't come back here next year.

Or consider these thoughts by a member on his way to a Catholic church carnival in a district he sees as 30 percent Catholic:

> You can get more votes for fetuses in Congress right now than you can for the pork barrel. Maybe I should change my campaign button from a star to a fetus. I'm up there tightroping along the high wire, defusing the issue whenever I can. . . . My secret here will be to keep moving through the crowd — to make an elusive target. It won't be a leisurely stay. The odds are prohibitive against someone asking me about abortion. I just hope it isn't the man with the loudest voice in the parish.

Or consider this appraisal by one member of his respected opponent in a very close race. "He's paranoid. He is a right wing crazy; and he attracts crazy opposition like shit draws flies. People come out just to boo him." Such comments, if attributed, would not be helpful politically.

Such comments remind us, too, that the research topic of this book is no ordinary one. It involves the most sensitive of political subjects for the House member — private opinions about public issues and public people, electoral problems and electoral strategies, career ambition and career survival. I am not so naive as to believe that House members would disclose their innermost thoughts on these subjects. But their willingness to discuss them and to put themselves in some jeopardy in so doing indicates that a measure of mutual trust had been established. In answer to the question, "Compared to what?" I cannot say. More trust, probably, than is required for an ordinary Capitol Hill interview; and enough trust, probably, to justify the expenditure of time and effort put into the enterprise.

Still, rapport varied. One member, for example, remained suspicious and uncomfortable with me even after two visits to his district and a couple to his office in Washington. On my second trip to the district he and his district aide dropped me off at the hotel on a Saturday afternoon and said they'd see me "sometime Monday." I thought the treatment excessively cavalier, and my notes on the episode reflect heat and frustration:

When they let me out at the hotel and said they'd see me Monday I was hopping mad. What the hell they thought I was going to do sitting in a hotel room from 4:00 Saturday till noon or so on Monday (don't you call us, we'll call you), I do not know. Fred is personally quite inconsiderate. . . . He never suggested I come over [to his place] or anything. In fact, I asked if I could go to his Sunday evening campaign meeting and he said, "They wouldn't want anyone from the outside." He also said he was going to some party on Sunday and said, "It will only be for friends." And when I got out of the car, he said "Don't get into trouble. But if you do, make sure you make it worthwhile. . . ." To say this to me as if I had anything else to do but wait for him to call next Monday was the height of insensitivity. He was treating me like some casual acquaintance he'd just met on the street someplace — not someone who had taken four days and spent several hundred dollars to come here and be with him as much as is humanly possible. Of course, he doesn't owe me one thing. But it was not what I would call friendly. I guess what really frustrates me is that I have not been able to get him to trust me. That may or may not be my fault, of course.

With regard to such an instance, however, it needs to be said that observation does not stop just because participation stops. His treatment of me provided a vantage point from which I could reflect on his behavior toward others. Does he present himself to others the way he presents himself to me? Why should he be less trusting toward me than other House members are? All behavior, in other words, is grist for the observer's mill. Even when he is denied the opportunity to observe, he observes.

If insufficient rapport is one problem, then too much rapport is another. Sometimes, that is, a professional relationship threatens to slide into a personal friendship. After all, when two people spend several days in constant personal contact — two people who share one major interest in common, politics — it is natural that a personal friendship could develop. I worried about it and tried to guard against it. I did not want them as friends — only respondents. It is impossible to be objective about one's friends. In some cases, however, it could not be stopped; if I had not acknowledged a friendship, I would have lost a respondent. If members insisted on inviting me to their homes, for example, I could not refuse. This led to occasions when I was told not too little but too much. On such occasions I deliberately pulled in my research antennae. I took no notes and tried to forget what I had heard and seen. I assumed the member was not turned on for research purposes when he or she told me about or allowed me to watch certain things — family relationships, for example. I felt it would be taking advantage of members to turn their personal revelations into data. Indeed, I felt that my refusal to get involved on such occasions was part of the bargain. I may have lost information; but I helped to keep, in my mind, some personal distance between us.

On one occasion, too much rapport became a nearly total impediment to research. A representative I had visited before was near the end of a difficult, bitter campaign when I arrived. And, from the moment his wife met me at the airport, I was treated as a trusted friend in a time of trouble, not as a political scientist who had come to learn about the member in his district. The member either could not or did not want to act as my teacher, as he had previously done. Again, a few excerpts from my nightly notes will indicate the frustrations — and the acceptance — of too much rapport:

I'm so inside this campaign, I'm out. I find myself saying to people that I'm a friend of Carl's and I'm out here to help him out — instead of saying that I'm writing a book. I can't ask Carl questions I'd like to because it's a little like standing around someone who may be dying and asking him where it hurts the most and how bad he feels. My questions have to be carefully phrased so that they are, at the least, sympathetic, and, at the most, innocent. I can't ask anything with a bite to it, anything hard, anything critical, etc. I'm treated as one of the family and I'm expected [by Carl] to act that way. As I say, I'm so far "in" that I can't be sufficiently "out" to probe. Maybe half in, half out is the best description.

I have got myself into a situation where almost no communication passes between us during the day — in contrast to my other visit when we rode all over and talked. But he is fighting for his life and he has drawn his family around him, and I'm just "there" as a kind of friend in the background. It's even out of place to ask a question. I tried one this morning as we got to Beaver Rapids. "What kind of town is Beaver Rapids, Carl?" "Well, here it is," was his only answer.

This trip has been strange. I have been accepted and welcomed this time as a friend and not an analyst. I have been placed in a role from which I cannot extricate myself — as emotional supporter and friend. I'm introduced everywhere as "our friend Dick Fenno, from Rochester, New York" — not as a political scientist, not as an author. . . . I have almost been anointed an *intimate* for this trip. When I asked Joanne [his daughter] on the way back to the house today if I shouldn't go back to the motel and leave Carl alone, she said, "No, you are good for him. He likes you and you strike just the right note with him. You are quiet when he doesn't want to talk, and you talk when he wants to. He wants people around now, and he needs people. You do it so well, you should be in public relations." She was telling me that I was needed — and I was. . . . [The family was busy and] he was alone, vulnerable, apprehensive, exhausted, and needed a friend. I was it. Not a political scientist. A friend.

The initial terms of our bargain were no longer recognizable. But I tried to keep my end of it as best I could, not only by acquiescing in an intensified loyalty but by keeping a blocked ear, a closed eye, and a forgetful mind to much that I observed at the time.

THE OBSERVER AND THE OBSERVED

The problem of over-rapport is part of the larger problem of the relationship between the observer and the observed. It is particularly acute in participant observation research. At one level, the presence of the observer may contaminate the situation, causing the people being observed to behave differently than they otherwise might. When, for example, I allow myself to be introduced as someone writing a book about a member, those listening may view the member in a changed light. Or, if I am introduced at a strategy meeting with the comment that "He's writing a book," the participants may pull their punches so as not to place the member in an unfavorable light. My guess is that contamination effects in these cases are pretty minor.

I have wondered, too, whether my anticipated presence in the district might cause any alterations in the scheduling. On one occasion, a member insisted on taking me to a part of the district where he had never been (during which trip he had to stop and ask some schoolchildren where we were: "I'm the congressman from Wayne and I'm looking for my district"); this unscheduled trip caused him to be late for another engagement and left him extremely irritable for the rest of the day. Because they could, and did, exclude me from events if they wished, I concluded that their schedules were probably not altered much on my account. I have also questioned whether my observation of explanatory consistency (Chapter Five) might not have been an artifact of my presence. If, that is, members were conscious of my note taking, wouldn't they have been abnormally careful not to behave like explanatory chameleons? I have no way of knowing, although I believe that I would have picked up some inconsistency somewhere along the line if such were a major behavior pattern.

Finally, the possibility of observer intrusion inheres in the very way the interviewing is done — as part of a running conversation more than as a question-and-answer session. On Capitol Hill it may be possible to nod sympathetically while listening to an interview answer, but in the district you must talk, because you are often part of a group carrying on a conversation. It is possible to have a one-sided Capitol Hill interview. It is not possible to have a one-sided three-day visit with someone. You must give as well as take; and in giving you may alter the situation you have come to observe. This is the subtlest kind of contamination. And I cannot think of a way to avoid it, except to be aware of it. Awareness will lead, usually, to saying less rather than more. It is not the object of this kind of research to gratify yourself or advance yourself personally by "making an impression" on the people you have come to observe.

On occasion, efforts to blend into the local landscape brought noteworthy success. One occurred when a very conservative member spent ten minutes of his twenty-five-minute press conference — before me and about eight newsmen — attacking the tax exempt status of foundations "who hire eastern egghead college professors to do social experimentation for left-wing causes." After that, the two of us went out to lunch where he talked openly about himself and his political life — to a Director of the Social Science Research Council, holding a Ford Foundation Fellowship. On another occasion, I was in a rural southern town with a congressman and the family of the local tax collector in their home. I sat quietly for an hour or so while the others gossiped. Eighty-year-old Uncle Aubrey also sat quietly, in the chair next to me. At the end of the evening Sue Ann Thorp, the tax collector, asked me if I had any children and how old they were. When I said one was in his mid-twenties, everyone expressed surprise, said I wasn't old enough, feigned disbelief, and asked how come I looked so young. After a short silence, Uncle Aubrey offered his sole comment of the evening. "He takes care of hisself. He shoots and goes fishin'." His explanation settled the matter for everyone present. For a tennis player and a skier, it was the highlight of seven years of research.

The larger danger in the relationship of observer and observed is what anthropologists call "going native" — becoming so close to your respondents, so immersed in their world and so dependent on this close relationship that you lose all intellectual distance and scholarly objectivity. Thus does the observer of Congress, having lost any critical capacity, become an apologist for the members and the institution. This is a problem to which there is no completely satisfactory solution. I recognize it, I worry about it, and I have tried to cope with it — again, mainly by keeping relationships professional. The effort has had only partial success.

The primary bulwark of one's professionalism in these matters is a natural one. Political scientists live within a scholarly community; and so long as they identify with that community, they will remain outsiders in the world they go to observe. After my earliest set of four district visits, university colleagues asked me how things had gone. And I can recall telling them that things had gone well, but it was "good to be home" — that only by going out of the intellectual community could one realize how much more at home he was there than in any of the districts. Everywhere I went I had been an outsider; and I had felt like an outsider. The four districts visited definitely ranked differently on my personal at-homeness index; but compared to the university, all ranked far behind. However comfortable I may have felt, I was uncomfortable compared to the way I felt within the scholarly community. It was a contrast that continued to the last. That contrast in feeling is, perhaps, the academic's surest barrier against going native.

I had gone to the district thinking, perhaps, that Robert Merton's classification of "local" and "cosmopolitan" (among others, of course) might help me differentiate among House members. I left the districts thinking that the distinction was useful, not for differentiating among members, but for differentiating between members as a group and the political scientists who study them, between the observed and the observer. Compared to academics, nearly all House members are locals. Compared to a university, most congressional districts are less cosmopolitan. Members tend to be rooted in the values and the institutional life of local communities. They belong; they know where they belong; and it is the very strength of our representative institution that they do. The academic, on the other hand, is likely to be less locally rooted, more mobile, more attached to free-floating intellectual communities, an outsider in any context beyond the scholarly one. And most so, perhaps, in a local space-and-place bounded context like a congressional district. In terms of going native, the marginality of the academic to almost all native contexts is a natural asset. In terms of understanding the working politician with local ties, however, it complicates the task of participant observation.

As a complement to this natural professional marginality, I have found it personally helpful to remain marginal to the congressman's world in Washington. I have never lived there. I have never spent more than three weeks at a stretch there. Between 1968 and 1977, with the exception of a single two-week stay, I never spent more than three days in Washington at any time. When I am there I do not socialize with members or their families; nor do I become entangled in the alliances of the Washington community. It has been my habit to go there, collect data, and return to Rochester to puzzle over what I have found and to work out my conceptual and analytical structures within the scholarly community. Because other academics find it equally beneficial to spend much time — or live — in Washington, I suspect my hit-and-run relationship with Capitol Hill is a personal idiosyncrasy. (It is also a matter of what one has chosen to study in Washington.) I am sure, however, that the practice has raised the odds against going native in my particular case. And I mention it only in that respect.

Out in the districts, as noted earlier, some members became friends. But they remained business friends rather than personal friends, social friends, or family friends. It is the best measure of our personal relationship that not more than two of the eighteen know anything but the most superficial things about me personally. I never volunteered; most of them never asked; and that is the way I like it. (It was always reassuring to return to a district after two years and be introduced by a member with whom I had developed fairly good rapport as a professor from "Syracuse University" or from "Fordham.") A clear failure in my efforts to preserve a business relationship, however, is the fact that I could not bring myself to be indifferent to their electoral success. *I wanted them all to win.* Nothing I did, however, had the slightest effect on whether or not they did. In one bizarre set of circumstances, however, I became emotionally involved in the campaign of my oldest and closest congressional friend; I had no effect on the electoral outcome, but I became an intimate for the duration of the campaign; and in the process I abandoned all social science activity. Luckily, I had nearly completed my research in that district.

A final, less soluble part of the observer-observed, going native problem is that in doing the things that must be done to maintain desirable levels of access and rapport, the participant observer can slowly lose the ability and the willingness to criticize. Some loss of objectivity comes inevitably, as increased contact brings sympathy, and sympathy in its turn dulls the edge of criticism. Some blurring of intellectual distance is produced, too, by the pleasures of participant observation research. The problem is that across-the-board access and continued rapport require a sympathetic understanding on the part of the observer. By the same token, they probably also require that highly opinionated and unflattering commentary be avoided. I have felt, for example, that my access might be adversely affected if I jumped heavily into the debates on congressional reform — which are, after all, debates among partisans within Congress. (If they are not, they are trivial and meaningless exercises, and it doesn't matter to anyone which side a political scientist might be on.) This conservative posture, taken in the interests of access, provokes scholarly criticism for being insufficiently sensitive to congressional change, too wedded to the status quo — in short, "a Congress lover." I think the thrust of such criticism is correct. Political scientists who are less encumbered than I by a felt need to protect across-the-board access and rapport will have to produce the most thoroughgoing critical work on Congress.

I also think that the kind of work done in this book is necessary if others are to produce informed, relevant criticism. The book has not been uncritical. When all members engage in the same behavior — running against Congress, for example — serious criticism has been levied. But, of course, blanket criticism is not as likely to affect access as the criticism of individuals would. In that respect, the book is less biting and critical than it might have been. Still, I know that some of my judgments — however mild — will bother individual members, because their view of themselves is bound to be more flattering than mine. (This is largely, I think, because my judgments — that they are issue-oriented, or hard working, or personable, or creative, or whatever — are inevitably comparative and, hence, relative to their colleagues. Their self-estimates, on the other hand, cannot be made relative to what their colleagues do at home, since they have no opportunity to observe. Hence, they judge themselves more in comparison to other politicians in their home context — most of whom are less successful than they.) By protecting their anonymity, I have tried to shield them from any criticism from their colleagues and from people at home who might use attributed material against them.

If there were any way that I could have "named names" in the book, without destroying my access and without jeopardizing the access of future political scientists, I would have done so. It would have given the book's ideas a much wider national audience than they will ever get, attached as they now are, antiseptically, to Representatives A, B, C. But it could not be done. Political science friends of mine know the names of some of the House members with whom I have traveled. Doubtless, some will play games matching names to letters. But they cannot expect any helpful signals from this quarter.

DATA

When I am with each House member, I do a lot of what I call in the Introduction "hanging around." That is, a lot of watching, listening, and talking, a lot of sitting, standing, and riding, some participation, and a lot of questioning — all for the purpose of collecting data. A three-day trip would produce twenty-five to thirty-five pages of notes, typed and double-spaced. How good, then, are the results? How reliable and valid are the data collected in this manner? In the end, each reader will have to make some judgments. I can only describe how it was done, what the problems were, and how I tried to hedge against them.

The data I use in the book are my notes; note taking is central to the work. I do not use a tape recorder. In the unresolved dispute among elite interviewers, I continue to stand with those who prefer not to use it. I am most comfortable interviewing politicians in a relaxing, conversational manner, without intrusion of mechanical devices that have to be started, reloaded, and stopped. To some degree, doubtless, this reflects the defense of an established style against the unknown — against the fear that whatever effect it might have on the interviewee, a tape recorder would cramp my style as an interviewer. To some degree, it reflects an unwillingness to risk the costs involved in a test that might confirm my fears and result in as much as a single bungled interview.

But, more than just taste or conservatism, my reservations about a tape recorder relate to its possible adverse effect on the interview — in light of the purpose and uses to which I put the interviews. In exploratory research, the emphasis is on discovering relationships and on generating ideas about them. And the interviews are most useful when the conversation is most frank and most spontaneous. I would gladly trade many a whole interview for one personal reflection that provides me with a new way of looking at things, for one insightful formulation that is rooted in personal experience, or for one particularly apt and pungent commentary. If insight and nuance and example and free association are to be encouraged, it is my belief that one's chances of getting a "better" interview are increased when no tape recorder is used and person-to-person rapport is the only reliance.

To be sure, most House members will talk with a tape recorder present. And the fact that they will talk for the record is good enough for some research purposes. Where data collection is to be followed by quantification, where content analysis and coding will be necessary, the need for reportorial accuracy is probably the paramount consideration. In such cases, a tape recorder may be mandatory. Such is also the case where journalists seek comment for attribution. But where you want to maximize the likelihood of qualitatively interesting comments, the tape recorder can only be inhibitory.

Every congressman has a fairly stylized set of comments that he is willing to make for the record. Some will do so more willingly and volubly than others. But all of them — or so I believe, and this is probably the crucial assumption — have a second, qualitatively different level of off-the-record commentary they *could* engage in. That is the level I want to reach: the level of commentary for private consumption that lies between a level for public consumption and a level for no consumption. If there are members who give all they have to give on tape, they will do so without tape. For the others — and a key assumption is that there *are* many "others" — my belief is that the only chance to get a nonroutine, nonreflexive interview is to converse casually, pursuing targets of opportunity without the presence of a recording instrument other than myself. If worst comes to worst, they can always deny what they have said in person; on tape they leave themselves no room for escape. I believe they are not unaware of the difference.

Contrasting viewpoints on recording methods will be resolved only by the different tastes and assumptions of researchers and by the different purposes of their research. It is impossible to prove that an interview obtained in one way was not as "good" as the interview that would have resulted from the use of a different technique. I have simply made an educated guess for my kind of research. I would only add that whatever the interview technique, the proper attitude toward the results should be skepticism, leading to reevaluation and, wherever possible, cross-checking. We should not be beguiled by the mere fact that politicians will talk to us. They are professional talkers — professional "presenters" as we have said.

They have a big personal investment to protect, and they have learned how to protect it against all outsiders, whether we come carrying our tape recorders or not.

For home district research, the tape recorder issue is largely moot. Most of the time it would be impossible to use, because so much of the interviewing is conducted on the run, because it is utterly impossible to predict when or under what conditions the member will be responsive to questioning, and because the best results often come in isolated moments of informality and spontaneity. There is no one "best time" for this kind of interview; there are many such times, most of them brief and unexpected. The closest thing to a generalization might be that morning proved the least promising; the member was usually preoccupied with organizing and rehearsing the day's activities.

My technique was to carry a pocket-sized notebook and to record, as nearly as my powers of recall would permit, verbatim quotations. I recorded whenever I had a chance during the day. Sometimes I made brief jottings — of key phrases, for example — to remind me of things I did not want to forget; sometimes I recorded a few of the most salient comments completely and immediately. Just how much I could get into the notebook during the day was in the lap of the gods. During the first day or two when I was working hard at rapport, I often sacrificed data to rapport by not taking notes unless I was totally alone. I wanted to appear relaxed, to blend into the picture, and to encourage the members to relax by not giving them the feeling that I was recording everything they said. When I felt I had achieved decent rapport, I would very conspicuously take notes, to remind them of our professional relationship and to reassure them that I was really working on a book. I began to do this routinely because, once we got to know each other, some members would ask, "Aren't you going to take any notes? How do you remember all this?"

The answer to the "how do you remember" question is simply that you train yourself to do so. You learn to switch on and off as subjects of interest come and go and to spend the time when you are switched off rehearsing and imprinting the items you wish to remember. The most revealing comments are unforgettable. In any event, my technique was to take mental notes, transcribe them briefly when I got the chance during the day, and then to spend two, three, or four hours in the evening recording everything I could remember about the day's activities and about the member's comments. I did this in the same notebook. Besides writing the data, I wrote down my reactions to what I had seen and heard, all the additional questions that had come to mind, all the analytical ideas that had occurred to me, illuminating comparisons between this member and other members — a running commentary on the data. I reread my notes whenever I got the chance to jog my memory and add items I had forgotten.

The major organizing principle of the notes was chronological. It aided me both in my recall and in my reflections if I recreated the day chronologically when debriefing myself at night. I found, too, that I could remember the context in which statements were made or actions taken if I thought about the day's activities in sequence. The minor organizing principle of the notes was a running speculation on "what makes this particular member tick." This involved an effort to find some consistency in his or her actions and comments. I would describe for myself a tentative pattern, then worry over behaviors that did not seem to fit the pattern and entertain tentative revisions that would accommodate the unexplained patterns. Much of this theorizing has been excluded from the book — for instance, my private speculations about "personality" characteristics. But I tried to understand "the whole member" in some depth as a precondition for any attempt to offer generalizations about all members. The more I satisfied myself that I understood one member's perceptual and behavioral patterns, the more confidently I could add one more case to my generalizing base. In some cases (see Chapter Four) the effort produced no consistent pattern and, hence, uncertainty on my part. But the effort always helped me to remember and organize what I had observed.

In trying to make sense out of each member's activity, I found it particularly helpful to compare him or her with other members. Practically, this meant comparing two members — occasionally three — with whom I traveled consecutively. While one experience was still very fresh, I would think about a given member's home style by comparing it in detail with that of the last member and vice versa. Table A illustrates the frequency with which such stimulative bunchings occurred. These "constant comparisons" helped to highlight what was special about each member while also building a tentative set of generalizations about their similarities. These comparisons were an additional aid to memory and to reflection. But in my notes they always had a limited, two- or three-member scope and never of a comprehensive, eighteen-member scope.

This discussion of note taking illuminates a basic characteristic of participant observation research. Data collection and data analysis do not proceed in linear progression. They proceed simultaneously. Participant observation is not like survey research, in which you make up a permanent set of questions, put your questionnaire "into the field," wait for the data to come in, and then proceed to do "data analysis." In participant observation research, data analysis accompanies data collection, and the questionnaire that goes into the field may change in the course of the research. The differences should not be exaggerated; but the ones that exist stem from the different strengths of the two kinds of research — the one more confirmatory, the other more exploratory.

This bare-bones description of my data collection methods is sufficient to indicate numerous problems. But whatever problems inhere in the technique are compounded by the conditions under which this kind of research is done. First, it is physically tiring. When people ask me what I have learned, my first answer is that politicians have incredible stamina and that, surely, when we think of recruitment we should take this basic factor of sheer human energy into account. At its worst, it means getting up at 5:30 for the factory gates and going to bed after the last evening meeting at night. For them, there may be sleep; for the observer, there are two or three hours of note taking left — to bed at 2:00 A.M. and up again at 6:30. There is no time to leave the scene to pull yourself together; you just keep going. After three or four or five days of this, I was worn out — but they kept right on.

Worse than the physical fatigue, however, is the mental weariness that results from this kind of research. For the member, there is a lot of routine to what he or she does at home. Besides, there is a lot at stake. Even more, it is, for members, an ego trip and they are buoyed up by being on center stage. Standing in line for a drink at a realtor's open house, I said to a bone-weary member (who had to be dragged to the party), "A drink will pick you up." He smiled, "No, the people will. As soon as I get on stage, I'll begin to dance a little." All this makes it easier for him to keep up the mental as well as the physical pace. For the observer, however, nothing is routine or ego-gratifying. Everything is strange, yet everything must be accommodated to — new people, new culture, new challenges. The sheer overload of information — faces, places, events, statistics, history, all different from those of the last district — is overwhelming. Yet they must be quickly assimilated, retained, and fed back to the people around you in familiar usages, at appropriate times.

Moreover, the benefits of all this are not so certain for the observer as they are for the member. How do I know whether I'll get anything useful? I am 2000 miles from home and $600 poorer, and how do I know I'll have any decent rapport with these people? If I know the member is going someplace but no one has suggested that I go along, should I speak up and run the risk of seeming too pushy or sit back and run the risk of not being asked to go? Should I ask my question now or should I wait? I carried around a shotgun loaded with questions, but had to feel my way into a situation where it seemed propitious to squeeze the trigger. Once, when I held back on my questions for two days, the member got a cold and a sore throat on the third. Once, flying in a small Cessna, I had just begun to ask some questions when the pilot suddenly turned the controls over to the congressman. Sometimes, with a staffer driving the car, a trip across the district can be an ideal time for asking questions. But what do you do when you find that one member likes to sleep on such trips, another likes to listen to tapes, and another likes to play the harmonica? Do you try to get a conversation going or do you wait? I waited, realizing that they might be trying to defend themselves against my questions — to find a private, quiet time for themselves before plunging in again. But I couldn't relax. If the member awakened, turned off the tapes, or put down the harmonica, I had to have my questions lined up in order of priority and ready to fire.

The uncertainty and the anxiety associated with this kind of adventure are great. In a forty-five-minute interview on Capitol Hill you typically have the undivided attention of the congressman, and you keep firing questions until he (or you) terminates the interview. It is not a matter of discretion whether or not to ask a question. It is part of the bargain that, for the duration of the interview, you will ask and he will answer. But in the district, the bargain is that you are allowed to tag along and observe whatever they do and ask appropriate questions at appropriate times. Each time you ask a question, however, it is a matter of tact, of judgment. Frequently, you are asking the member to change the focus of his attention from something else to your questions. (I always carried a detailed map of the district with me, and found that taking it out and asking "Where are we now?" was one fairly easy way to shift focus.) You must constantly assess the situation for its appropriateness, its ripeness. On Capitol Hill, you do not care about the congressman's state of readiness, how fatigued he is, where he has been, where he is going, what is worrying him, whether now will be "better" than later. You walk in at the appointed time, sit down, and ask your questions. In the district, you must worry both about whether to ask questions and, if so, which ones — hoping to fit questions most naturally into the flow of conversation and events.

These matters of discretion are anxiety producing. If I blow one interview on Capitol Hill, it's no big loss — on to the next office! Anyway, it probably wasn't my fault. But if I blow one in the district, it costs a lot and it probably *was* my fault. In sum, *my* behavior is a good deal more consequential in the less routinized, more complicated, and totally unpredictable district setting than it is on Capitol Hill.

There is a lot of time, too, to brood about such matters. Despite the frenzy of activity all around, the role of the observer is very solitary. You are marginal — deliberately so — to every group you are with. Rarely will anyone come up to make you feel at home — at a dinner, a cocktail party, a celebration, a meeting. They are playing their games. The House member is playing with them. The more the member is interacting person to person with others, the less can the participant observer either participate or observe. You must move away from the member as he goes about the business of handshaking, greeting, and talking with his constituents. Although no one in this gathering of total strangers is paying the slightest attention to you, you can give no indication of being anything less than completely comfortable, of not thoroughly enjoying yourself. It's a little bit like the basketball player's ability to "move without the ball." It is lonesome duty; and anyone who tends toward paranoia should not volunteer. This is not a complaint. Like the House members running for reelection, my first comment is "I must be crazy to do this," and my second comment is "I can't think of anything I'd rather do." But — given the physical and mental fatigue — I found I could not visit more than two districts in succession or last more than seven or eight days on the road, however much more economical and intellectually stimulating longer trips might have been.

These working conditions only exacerbate the problems of data collection. What are these problems? One is that because so much of my note taking is done after the event, a subtle reconstruction of the event or comment can take place in the interim. Another is that I will have selectively perceived and simply have missed a lot that was said or happened. This danger is made worse by the oceans of talk that wash over the observer in such a visit, only a tiny fraction of which can conceivably be remembered. It is, at best, only a partial solution to try to record, as I did, as much as I could, whether or not it interested me or made sense to me at the time. Such words and events tend always to be "second thoughts," recorded after the apparent highlights. Another problem is that I will have failed to record the context in which a comment was made, thus endowing it with greater generality than it was intended to have. Finally, because I was not the same person when I began in 1970 as I was when I finished in 1977, changes in my own interests and abilities may have made generalizing across time hazardous. These defects in the human recording instrument are made more serious by physical and mental weariness. And I would never claim that my notes do not suffer from all these limitations.

Data so collected produce any number of worries. One is the matter of accuracy. Did I get what he said — the right words, the right order, the complete thought? Did I observe what he did correctly or fully? One is the matter of validity. Am I using each example of words or of actions to illustrate something appropriate to the meaning the member gave it? Another is the matter of reliability. Have I arrived at a fair, durable representation of each member's thoughts and acts in making my generalizations about his or her perceptions or behavior?

I have tried to cope with these problems and worries. Mainly, I have done so by making two trips to as many districts as possible (fourteen) and by supplementing these trips with an interview (eleven times) in Washington. My hope is that, by repeated as well as prolonged soakings in the district and by the kind of cross-checking that a Washington interview will provide, I will increase my chances of getting it right, using it right and portraying it right. I know that my own confidence in the data and in my use of it increases exponentially when I can add a second set of observations to the first.

The more you observe, the more practice you get in matters such as note taking and recall; and the more practice you get, the more accurate you become. Oftentimes, the same thing will be said twice during a visit; and the second account is more nearly verbatim because you need only fill in the blanks. Sometimes, the same perception is articulated on both trips and cross-checking increases accuracy. During the Washington interviews, I took close to verbatim notes and tape recorded immediately thereafter, thus giving me another check. The hiatus between visits — usually at least a year — allowed me to accumulate a fresh list of questions, some repeats and some new ones. I could reformulate my earlier hunches, and puzzlements, as to home style patterns or as to "what makes this member tick." When you see or hear the same thing repeated more than once after a period of years, you feel more certain how to interpret what you see. If, for example, you visit a district and see the member do nothing except give speeches (or never give a speech) you wonder whether this represents stylistic preference or a contextual coincidence. When you return for a later stay and see the identical pattern, you feel more secure about making a stylistic generalization based on observation. Or, if you make very different observations on successive occasions, you may be able to interpret this in terms of a consistent developmental pattern or as some idiosyncratic activity related to a very specific context.

Generalizations made by working politicians tend to be based on recent events and are, on that account, always suspect. It is not a matter of deceit. It is just that politicians live pragmatically from immediate problem to immediate problem and have neither the time nor the incentive to generalize beyond what happened yesterday or last week or, maybe, last month. The observer needs methods, therefore, for determining whether a given comment — seemingly important — is to be interpreted as a considered generalization or as an artifact of a specific context. When you hear the same thing repeated on more than one occasion — especially on occasions widely separated in time — you can have more confidence that it is a usable generalization.

Conversely, if a comparison of the notes from two visits shows a marked change in emphasis, you may be able to see the relevance of context. For example, when I asked a congressman in a heavily Jewish district, in 1970, whether any single vote cast in Congress could defeat him, he answered with unusual confidence, "I can't think of any vote that would defeat me. Not a single one. Even if I voted against arms for Israel, I could prepare a defense and say that

there weren't *enough* arms for Israel." In 1976, when I returned to
the district, he spontaneously volunteered the comment, "If I voted
against aid to Israel . . . that would be it! If I did something absurd like that and voted counter to a massive opinion in my district,
I would lose." The generalizations he made in the two cases were
important. But they have to be seen as contextually produced — by
the upbeat confidence resulting from the Six-Day War which prevailed during my first visit, and by the shaky uncertainty following
the Yom Kippur War which prevailed during my second visit.

In short, two sets of observations are better than one — much
better. It is not just that you can compare notes taken across time
and contexts. It is also that rapport invariably is better during the
second visit than the first and, hence, you learn more and learn
better. Here, for example, is a congressman discussing his reelection
and career goals. On the first trip, his only comment on the subject was:

> Eighty or ninety percent of all members of Congress are
> always looking ahead to the next election. They pick each
> other's brains on the subject all the time. I don't care what
> they say, that's on their minds. Just like a business with a
> profit and loss statement, the politician looks at the next elec-
> tion as his test. There are some independent cusses down
> there. They know what's right for the world and they go
> ahead and do it. But most of them aren't like that.

On the second trip, we had not been together an hour before he
launched into a soliloquy, part of which went:

> I don't know what I'm doing in this business or why I ever
> got into it. The family situation is terrible. I just spent ten
> days in the district. Dottie and the kids were here for the first
> three days and then they drove back to Maryland to start
> school. I went back Wednesday, went to the office and then
> had to go to a dinner for the life underwriters group. A con-
> gressman from our state has to go. If you don't, they won't
> speak to you again. Then I got home late that night. The next
> day I had to go to a breakfast and another cocktail party to
> see some people from the district who were in town. So I got
> home late again. That was yesterday and here I am back in
> the district again for five days. I'm a yo-yo. . . . You work so
> hard to get it and when you get it you wonder what you did

it for. It's like joining a fraternity – I worried so much about it, but when I got to be president of the House, it didn't matter anymore. It's so competitive. I like that. And I like the excitement. But you spend so much time and effort – for what? I'll tell you – to get reelected. I'll be more frank with you than I would be with most people. We spend all our time running for reelection. . . . I guess I told you before, I'm not going to grow old in Washington. I may run for the Senate if things work out. If I win, OK; if I don't win, OK. I'll be happy to go back home. If I do win, I'll make a solemn promise to myself that it won't be for long. But I would love to have six years and not have to run all the time. I'd say, "I don't care what happens, I'm not going to spend all my time running for reelection."

During my first trip, this same member had kept me waiting in a parking lot while he went inside to talk strategy with some intimates. On the second trip, he took me to his strategy meeting.

One characteristic of the interview data is that it is nonstandardized and, hence, not quantifiable. Questions are tailored to particular individuals and are posed in dissimilar contexts – not to mention in scrambled orderings. Nonstandardization is, indeed, essential to getting and keeping rapport. And the result is that the material is not easily coded or described in terms of frequencies. It was never my intention to quantify this material; it was not collected with quantification in mind; and I do not think it would be methodologically sound to quantify it retrospectively. But I have, of course, supplemented my field work with two kinds of quantifiable data: first, data on numbers of trips home and allocation of staff resources, and, second, data taken from the appointment books of members. The first body of data, anyone can collect. But data from private appointment books could not be had by anyone lacking good rapport with the member. In addition, several members gave me precise rankings of the importance and the comfortableness of their various activities at the end of my visit. That, too, is not something that would be done for the casual observer. Thus, maybe this type of research, although not in itself quantitative, can open up avenues of research that are.

The book's data are, however, mostly nonquantifiable. That is the reason so much of it has been presented in the form of quotations. Some are lengthy and complicated. Altogether they may become tedious. But they need to be struggled with, like any other kind of data. Data analysis, of course, will have to be done by making non-numerical assessments of meaning, appropriateness, consistency, context, and importance. Readers should not think of the quotations and anecdotes herein as any less worthy of serious examination than other kinds of data. They are, of course, primarily discovery data and should be viewed in this light. Because "data analysis" is often assumed to mean only the statistical manipulation of numerical data, it should be noted that participant observation is likely to produce data of a different sort and require different modes of data analysis. In the final accounting, we ought to ask the same serious question we would ask of any set of data: Have they served the purpose for which they were gathered?

One way to rephrase this question about the adequacy of the data is: Are your data any better than, or any different from, what you would have gotten by interviewing on Capitol Hill? The answer is, I think: For the particular purposes of the book "better," and in a more general sense "different." The data are better because there are some questions I would not have known enough to ask had I not put myself in the district — all the questions about home style, for example. Had I simply taken some perceptual questions to Capitol Hill, this book would have ended with Chapter One. Even then, it would not have been as informed a chapter. Questions about perceptions (of each group or area as we visited them, for instance) can be formulated and answered more knowledgeably at the point where the member is actually engaged in perceiving.

Passing a number of pickup trucks on the road, one congressman in a heterogeneous district commented, "This is Wallace country. You can tell a Wallacite because he has a pickup truck, a hound dog, and a gun. He'll give you his dog and his pickup truck, but he won't give up his gun." The next day, spotting several pickup trucks as we entered the parking lot of a VFW hall, he said, "I'd love to get the pickup truck vote, but I never do." A congressman trying to win support from lower-middle-class voters despite his strong civil rights record revealed a relevant view of these constituents as we drove along a city street: "We're a very artsy community here. A few years ago, they built a theatre in the round across the park there. And do you know what it turned into after two years? A wrestling hall. I guess that tells you something about the state of culture in the district." During the evening's rehash of another member's days activities, someone mentioned the morning hour of handshaking, howdying, and hijinks with twenty people in a small country store. The congressman turned to me and said simply, "Dick, those are the people who elect me." In each case, the circumstances elicited spontaneous perceptual statements; and, because I had observed what the congressman was talking about, I understood better what he meant.

Through repeated and prolonged observation in the districts I also discovered patterns of behavior that I would not have known about otherwise — the lawlike tendency of House members to run for Congress by running against Congress, for example. In these several respects, I think the data are "better" than they might otherwise have been.

Equally, however, the data are simply different. I did not learn many things I did not know before. But I came to know through experience things I had known only intellectually; I got "a feel" for things. It is one thing to know that a district is "agricultural" and that "the farmers are worried about the drought"; it is another thing to find yourself unable to place campaign cards under car windshield wipers that have been glued to the windshield by inches of caked dust. It is one thing to know that a district is "inner city" and that "the people there feel powerless"; but it is another thing to scrape your car axle on cratered, unpaved streets in the heart of one of America's largest cities. It is one thing to consult a map and note that one of the two districts you are about to visit is "small" and that the other is "large"; it is another thing to sit in a strategy meeting in the first district where it is concluded that three billboards will capture all the traffic in the district, and then go to the second district to spend one whole day driving to a town of 2500 people.

When these things happen, you begin to *weight* factors differently in your thinking, giving more weight to things experienced than they otherwise might have. Because these experiences are selective, it may be dangerous to pay special attention to them. On the other hand, it may be possible to better understand the congressman's own weighting when you have experienced his concerns at first hand. And, no matter what else it accomplishes, a better "feel" for a district helps offset the natural disadvantages — discussed earlier — that university-oriented academics face in understanding locally oriented politicians.

Just as you gather different data about the districts, so do you come to form a different picture of politicians. Again, the point is that you do not learn anything new so much as you place different emphasis on old knowledge. Intellectually, I knew that politicians required physical stamina; having flogged myself around eighteen districts with them, I now think physical attributes are more important to political success than I had previously believed. The second attribute of politicians that has been highlighted by these visits is their sheer competitiveness. It is not, at this stage, so much a matter of a driving ambition to be a congressman. They have achieved that ambition; and there are other things they can do to make a living. But they do not want to lose. They may have learned how to lose gracefully; but they *hate* to lose. We know they want to win; but they seem now to me more driven by a determination not to lose. They are, above all, tough competitors.

A third attribute that looms somewhat larger to me now is the politician's ability to keep from taking himself too seriously. It is something an outsider has less opportunity to observe on Capitol Hill, where each House member seems, at least, to be a king or queen in his or her empire — isolated from everyday life, fawned over by staff, pampered by Capitol Hill employees, sought after by all manner of supplicants. House members may, of course, be able to take a wry view of this existence. But it may be easier to do so in the district, where they are more likely to be reminded of their ordinariness. In any case, they display a marked ability to break the tension of competition at home by indulging in humor or whimsy, to keep some private perspective on their public selves.

> *Congressman:* I dreamt last night that I was defeated. No fooling, I really did. And do you know what bothered me most? The House gym! My wife said to me, "You're a distinguished person; you'll get a job, don't worry." I said, "Yes, I know; but where will I find a gym like that?"
>
> *Wife:* A man called and asked you to call him back no matter how late you get home tonight.
> *Daughter:* Your opponent says you're only interested in big business, and not the little folks.
> *Congressman:* Well, I'll find out who he is first. If he's big business, I'll talk to him. If he's little folk, I won't.
>
> *Staffer:* What are you going to say at the next meeting?
> *Congressman:* I'm going to ask somebody to give me a haircut. Or, I could walk in and hang from the chandelier. No, I guess I'll walk in, undress, and say, "Any questions?"

There may be no generalizations possible about politicians. But when people ask me what they are like, I now stress stamina, competitiveness, and a stabilizing perspective on themselves. I would not have stressed the same things after my Capitol Hill experience.

Because my research was undertaken partly to acquire the vantage point of "the country," one might wonder whether I developed any "feel for the country." Only this, that any claim by anybody to have a feel for the whole country would be preposterous. For ill or good, no one can comprehend the United States. Watching eighteen people will tell anyone that much. Perhaps, of course, looking at "the country" through the eyes of members of Congress is not the best way to comprehend it. But if House members, whose business it is to know only a small segment, express so much uncertain knowledge of their segment, it is not immediately clear who is better equipped to comprehend the whole. Only *institutionally*, not individually, can it be done. To travel outside Washington is to experience and, hence, to weight more heavily the diversity of the country. That weighting, in turn, emphasizes the enormity of the institutional task. One returns to Capitol Hill asking of our representative institution not, "How come you accomplish so little?" but, "How come you accomplish anything at all?"

EVALUATION

Despite what seems to be a monumentally uneconomical method of collecting data, I think the results *are* different from what I would have gotten in Washington. Whether the data are "different enough" or "better" depends on what you want them for. And so we return to the most serious question about data: Are they adequate for our purpose?

It is a final characteristic of participant observation research that this judgment must be made by two groups — political scientists *and* the people being observed. It matters little to the machinist's wife in Dayton what Scammon and Wattenberg's book says. It matters even less to Scammon and Wattenberg what she thinks about their book. But it matters enormously to me what House members (and the people around them) will think of my study. If they say, "That's how it is; that's the way we think," then I have captured something of their world. And I will have passed what I consider the first test. For if they cannot recognize their world in what I have written, I will have failed in the most elementary way.

I will have soaked and poked in their world and not been able to see what they see there. Not that they would or could *generalize* about it the way I have. That is my job. But I want them to recognize their perspectives and their perceptions in my observations.

Members of Congress do not normally "rush to judgment" on academic work — not in my experience. Many of them will not even acknowledge receipt of academic works, let alone read or comment on them. A few members, however, and more staff people do read what political scientists write and do pass judgment. Some journalists, too, perform a similar function. I have had no experience with the reactions of political people in the district — whose judgment will be important in this case. On Capitol Hill, although most people remain oblivious to what we do, nonetheless, the judgment of the few percolates around and provides an ultimate check on our scholarship. On the whole, the Capitol Hill community — again, I have no experience with people in the districts — is predisposed, if not eager, to demolish political science scholarship for its lack of contact with real world politics. Favorable judgments are all the more important, therefore, because they are hard to come by.

Among political scientists, community controls will operate to produce judgments on this research. For them, several questions will be raised. Does the description ring true, in accordance with whatever experience political scientists have had with the people and the activities covered in the book? Vast numbers of political scientists have had firsthand experience in the world about which I have written; their sense of my descriptive accuracy and relevance, therefore, will also be necessary to any favorable evaluation of the research. Political scientists will ask, further, whether the description sheds any light on problems they have been worrying about. Does the study say anything that other political scientists — whether or not they use participant observation — might think worth incorporating into their thinking? Will political scientists find questions posed here interesting enough to pick up and pursue — by participant observation or any other method?

In sum, political scientists will ask whether the work seems accurate and, if so, whether it is worth remembering. They will not answer yes to these questions unless they think the research has been conducted with some care and unless they think the data are adequate to the project's exploratory purpose. If the data are judged sufficiently "different" or "better" to produce some yes answers, then the data are — for all their obvious problems — good enough for me. In the end, whatever research methods we use, we keep each other honest.

NOTES

1. Three political scientists who have written helpfully about the subject are: Lewis Anthony Dexter, *Elite and Specialized Interviewing* (Evanston, Ill.: Northwestern University Press, 1970); Alexander Heard, "Interviewing Southern Politicians," *American Political Science Review* 44 (December 1950): 886–896; and James A. Robinson, "Participant Observation, Political Internships and Research" in *Political Science Annual, Volume 2*, ed. James Robinson (Indianapolis: Bobbs Merrill, 1970), pp. 71–110. The other works I have found most useful are: *Issues in Participant Observation: A Text and a Reader*, eds. George McCall and J. L. Simmons (Reading, Mass.: Addison-Wesley, 1969); Leonard Schatzman and Anselm Strauss, *Field Research: Strategies for a Natural Sociology* (Englewood Cliffs: Prentice-Hall, 1973); Barney Glaser and Anselm Strauss, *The Discovery of Grounded Theory: Strategies for Qualitative Research* (Chicago: Aldine, 1967); William Foote Whyte, *Street Corner Society*, 2d ed. (Chicago: University of Chicago Press, 1955), appendix.
2. The experience of political scientists doing research while working as interns (for instance, as American Political Science Association Congressional Fellows) would fall somewhere between that of people who go to Capitol Hill for research purposes only and the experience reported here. An illuminating assessment of the APSA program is found in Ronald D. Hedlund, *Participant Observation in Studying Congress: The Congressional Fellowship Program* (Washington, D.C.: American Political Science Association, 1971).

Index